The Azar Grammar Series

TEST BANK for
FUNDAMENTALS OF
ENGLISH
GRAMMAR

Third Edition

Stacy A. Hagen

Longman

longman.com

Test Bank for Fundamentals of English Grammar
Third Edition

Azar Associates
Shelley Hartle, Editor
Susan Van Etten, Manager

Pearson Education, 10 Bank Street, White Plains, NY 10606

Editorial manager: Pam Fishman
Project manager: Margo Grant
Development editor: Janet Johnston
Vice president, director of design and production: Rhea Banker
Director of electronic production: Aliza Greenblatt
Executive managing editor: Linda Moser
Production manager: Ray Keating
Senior production editor: Robert Ruvo
Director of manufacturing: Patrice Fraccio
Senior manufacturing buyer: Edie Pullman
Cover design: Pat Wosczyk
Text composition: Carlisle Communications, Ltd.
Text font: 10.5/12 Plantin

ISBN: 0-13-096714-9

Printed in the United States of America
1 2 3 4 5 6 7 8 9 10–BAH–07 06 05 04 03

LONGMAN ON THE **WEB**

Longman.com offers online resources for
teachers and students. Access our Companion
Websites, our online catalog, and our local
offices around the world.

Visit us at **longman.com.**

CONTENTS

INTRODUCTION x

Chapter 1   PRESENT TIME

Quiz 1   Simple present tense 1
Quiz 2   Simple present tense and present progressive 1
Quiz 3   Present verbs: questions 2
Quiz 4   Frequency adverbs 2
Quiz 5   Simple present tense vs. present progressive 3
Quiz 6   Pronunciation: final *-s*/*-es* 3
Quiz 7   Spelling: final *-s*/*-ing* 4
Quiz 8   Simple present tense and present progressive 4
Quiz 9   Non-action verbs 5
Quiz 10 Review 5
Quiz 11 Review 6
Quiz 12 Present verbs: questions and short answers 6
Practice Test 7
Final Test 9

Chapter 2   PAST TIME

Quiz 1   Simple past 11
Quiz 2   Simple past forms 11
Quiz 3   Simple past forms 12
Quiz 4   Past negatives 12
Quiz 5   Simple past: questions 13
Quiz 6   Regular verbs: pronunciation of *-ed* endings 13
Quiz 7   Spelling of *-ing* and past tense 14
Quiz 8   Simple past: irregular verbs 14
Quiz 9   Simple past tense 15
Quiz 10 Simple past tense 15
Quiz 11 Simple past: regular and irregular verbs 16
Quiz 12 Simple past tense 16
Quiz 13 Simple past 17
Quiz 14 Simple past 17
Quiz 15 Simple past and past progressive 18
Quiz 16 Simple past and past progressive 18
Quiz 17 Simple past and past progressive 19
Quiz 18 Present and past verbs 19
Quiz 19 Present and past verbs 20

Quiz 20   Present and past verbs 20
Quiz 21   Time clauses 21
Quiz 22   *Used to* 21
Quiz 23   *Used to* 22
Quiz 24   Error analysis 22
Practice Test 23
Final Test 25

Chapter 3   FUTURE TIME

Quiz 1   Present, past, and future 27
Quiz 2   *Will* and *be going to* 27
Quiz 3   *Will* and *be going to* 28
Quiz 4   *Will* 28
Quiz 5   Questions with *will* and *be going to* 29
Quiz 6   Sureness about the future 30
Quiz 7   Sureness about the future 30
Quiz 8   *Be going to* vs. *will* 30
Quiz 9   *If*-clauses 31
Quiz 10   *If*-clauses 31
Quiz 11   Using *be going to* and the present progressive to express future time 32
Quiz 12   Using *be going to* and the present progressive to express future time 32
Quiz 13   Expressing future time 33
Quiz 14   Error analysis 33
Quiz 15   Error analysis 34
Quiz 16   Past, present, and future 34
Practice Test 35
Final Test 37

Chapter 4   THE PRESENT PERFECT AND THE PAST PERFECT

Quiz 1   Simple past and past participle forms 39
Quiz 2   Present perfect negatives 39
Quiz 3   Present perfect questions 40
Quiz 4   Simple past vs. present perfect 40
Quiz 5   Time expressions with the present perfect and the simple past 41
Quiz 6   *Since* vs. *for* 41
Quiz 7   Time clauses with *since* 42
Quiz 8   *Since* vs. *for* 42
Quiz 9   Present perfect vs. present perfect progressive 43
Quiz 10   Present perfect progressive 43
Quiz 11   Present perfect progressive 44
Quiz 12   Present perfect vs. present perfect progressive 44
Quiz 13   *Already, yet, still, anymore* 45
Quiz 14   *Already, yet, still, anymore* 45
Quiz 15   Past perfect 46
Quiz 16   Present perfect vs. past perfect 46
Quiz 17   Past progressive vs. past perfect 47
Quiz 18   Present perfect, past progressive, and past perfect 47
Quiz 19   Present perfect, past progressive, and past perfect 48
Practice Test 49
Final Test 52

Chapter 5   ASKING QUESTIONS

Quiz 1	Short answers to yes/no questions	55
Quiz 2	Questions with *do, does, is,* and *are*	55
Quiz 3	*Where, why, when,* and *what time*	56
Quiz 4	Questions with *who, whom,* and *what*	56
Quiz 5	*What* + a form of *do*	57
Quiz 6	*Which* vs. *what*	57
Quiz 7	*Who* vs. *whose*	58
Quiz 8	*Who's* vs. *whose*	58
Quiz 9	Questions with *how*	59
Quiz 10	Questions with *how*	59
Quiz 11	Questions with *how: how often, how far, how long*	60
Quiz 12	Questions with *how*	60
Quiz 13	Review of *how*	61
Quiz 14	Review	62
Quiz 15	Tag questions	62
Quiz 16	Tag questions	63
Quiz 17	Error analysis	63
Practice Test		64
Final Test		66

Chapter 6   NOUNS AND PRONOUNS

Quiz 1	Pronunciation	69
Quiz 2	Plural nouns	69
Quiz 3	Subjects, verbs, and objects	70
Quiz 4	Objects of prepositions	70
Quiz 5	Prepositions of time	71
Quiz 6	Word order	71
Quiz 7	Subject–verb agreement	72
Quiz 8	Subject–verb agreement	72
Quiz 9	Adjectives	73
Quiz 10	Adjectives and nouns	73
Quiz 11	Using nouns as adjectives	74
Quiz 12	Personal pronouns: subjects and objects	74
Quiz 13	Possessive nouns	75
Quiz 14	Review: nouns and possessives	75
Quiz 15	Possessive pronouns and adjectives	76
Quiz 16	Reflexive pronouns	76
Quiz 17	Singular forms of *other*	77
Quiz 18	Plural forms of *other*	77
Quiz 19	Forms of *other*	78
Quiz 20	Error analysis	78
Practice Test		79
Final Test		81

Chapter 7   MODAL AUXILIARIES

Quiz 1	The form of modal auxiliaries	83
Quiz 2	Expressing ability	83
Quiz 3	Permission vs. possibility	84
Quiz 4	Expressing possibility	84

Quiz 5   Meanings of *could* 85
Quiz 6   *Could* and *might* 85
Quiz 7   Polite questions 86
Quiz 8   *Should* and *ought to* 87
Quiz 9   *Had better* 87
Quiz 10   *Should, had better, ought to* 88
Quiz 11   *Have to, have got to, must* 88
Quiz 12   Necessity: *must, have to, have got to* 89
Quiz 13   Expressing lack of necessity and prohibition 89
Quiz 14   Logical conclusion or necessity 90
Quiz 15   Logical conclusions 90
Quiz 16   Imperative sentences 91
Quiz 17   Stating preferences 91
Quiz 18   Review 92
Practice Test 93
Final Test 95

Chapter 8   CONNECTING IDEAS
Quiz 1   Punctuation with commas and periods 98
Quiz 2   Connecting ideas with *but, and,* or *or* 98
Quiz 3   *So* vs. *but* 99
Quiz 4   Using auxiliary verbs after *but* 99
Quiz 5   Using auxiliary verbs after *and* and *but* 100
Quiz 6   *And* + *too, so, either, neither* 100
Quiz 7   *So* and *neither* 101
Quiz 8   Connecting ideas with *because* 101
Quiz 9   Connecting ideas with *because* and *so* 102
Quiz 10   *Even though/although* and *because* 102
Quiz 11   *Even though/although* and *because* 103
Quiz 12   Punctuating adverb clauses 103
Quiz 13   Error analysis 103
Practice Test 104
Final Test 106

Chapter 9   COMPARISONS
Quiz 1   Comparisons with *as . . . as* 108
Quiz 2   Comparisons with *as . . . as* 108
Quiz 3   Comparative and superlative 109
Quiz 4   Comparatives 109
Quiz 5   Comparatives 110
Quiz 6   *Farther* and *further* 110
Quiz 7   Completing a comparative 111
Quiz 8   *Very* vs. *a lot/much/far* 111
Quiz 9   *Less . . . than* and *not as . . . as* 112
Quiz 10   Unclear comparisons 112
Quiz 11   Using *more* with nouns, adjectives, and adverbs 113
Quiz 12   Repeating a comparative 113
Quiz 13   Using double comparatives 114
Quiz 14   Superlatives 114
Quiz 15   *The same, similar, different, like, alike* 115

Quiz 16   *The same, similar, different, like, alike* 115
Quiz 17   *The same, similar, different, like, alike* 116
Quiz 18   Error analysis 116
Practice Test 117
Final Test 119

Chapter 10   THE PASSIVE

Quiz 1   Active vs. passive 122
Quiz 2   Active vs. passive 122
Quiz 3   Review of past participles 123
Quiz 4   Forms of the passive 123
Quiz 5   Active vs. passive 124
Quiz 6   Active vs. passive: question forms 124
Quiz 7   Passive vs. active meaning 125
Quiz 8   Passive to active 125
Quiz 9   Transitive vs. intransitive 126
Quiz 10   Active and passive 126
Quiz 11   Using the *by*-phrase 127
Quiz 12   Progressive tenses in passive 127
Quiz 13   Passive modals 128
Quiz 14   Passive modals 128
Quiz 15   Passive vs. active 129
Quiz 16   Review 129
Quiz 17   Stative passive 130
Quiz 18   Stative passive 130
Quiz 19   Participial adjectives: *-ed* vs. *-ing* 131
Quiz 20   Participial adjectives: *-ed* vs. *-ing* 131
Quiz 21   *Get* + adjective and past participle 132
Quiz 22   *Get* + adjective and past participle 132
Quiz 23   *Be used to / accustomed to / used to* 133
Quiz 24   *Used to / be used to* 133
Quiz 25   *Be supposed to* 134
Quiz 26   *Be supposed to* 134
Quiz 27   Review 135
Quiz 28   Error analysis 136
Practice Test 137
Final Test 139

Chapter 11   COUNT/NONCOUNT NOUNS AND ARTICLES

Quiz 1   *A* vs. *an* 142
Quiz 2   *A* vs. *some* 142
Quiz 3   Count and noncount nouns 143
Quiz 4   Count and noncount nouns 143
Quiz 5   *Much/many* 144
Quiz 6   *A few/a little* 144
Quiz 7   *Several, a lot of, some, many/much, a few/a little* 145
Quiz 8   Nouns that can be count or noncount 145
Quiz 9   Units of measure with noncount nouns 146
Quiz 10   Units of measure with noncount nouns 146
Quiz 11   *The* vs. *a/an* 147

Quiz 12   Making general statements 147
Quiz 13   Using *the* for specific statements 148
Quiz 14   Using *the* for second mention 148
Quiz 15   Summary: *a* vs. *Ø* vs. *the* 149
Quiz 16   Summary 149
Quiz 17   Using *the* or *Ø* with names 150
Quiz 18   Capitalization 150
Practice Test 151
Final Test 153

Chapter 12   ADJECTIVE CLAUSES

Quiz 1   Adjective clauses with *who* 156
Quiz 2   Adjective clauses with *who* and *whom* 156
Quiz 3   Adjective clauses with *who, who(m),* and *that* 157
Quiz 4   Adjective clauses with *which, that,* or *Ø* 157
Quiz 5   Review of adjective clauses 158
Quiz 6   Review of adjective clauses 158
Quiz 7   Subject–verb agreement in adjective clauses 159
Quiz 8   Prepositions 159
Quiz 9   Prepositions 160
Quiz 10   Adjective clauses with *whose* 160
Quiz 11   Error analysis 161
Practice Test 162
Final Test 164

Chapter 13   GERUNDS AND INFINITIVES

Quiz 1   Verb + gerund 166
Quiz 2   Verb + *go* + *-ing* 166
Quiz 3   Verb + gerund or infinitive 167
Quiz 4   Verb + gerund or infinitive 167
Quiz 5   Verb + gerund or infinitive 168
Quiz 6   Preposition + gerund 168
Quiz 7   Preposition + gerund 169
Quiz 8   *By* vs. *with* 169
Quiz 9   *By* + gerund 170
Quiz 10   Gerunds as subjects 170
Quiz 11   *It* + infinitive 171
Quiz 12   Using *in order to* 171
Quiz 13   Expressing purpose with *to* vs. *for* 172
Quiz 14   Using *in order to* 172
Quiz 15   *Too* and *enough* + infinitive 173
Quiz 16   *Too* and *enough* + infinitive 173
Quiz 17   Review: gerunds vs. infinitives 174
Practice Test 175
Final Test 177

Chapter 14 NOUN CLAUSES

Quiz 1   Information questions and noun clauses 179
Quiz 2   Noun clauses that begin with a question word 179
Quiz 3   Noun clauses with *who, what, whose* + *be* 180
Quiz 4   Noun clauses and yes/no questions 180
Quiz 5   *That*-clauses 181
Quiz 6   *That*-clauses 181
Quiz 7   Substituting *so* or *not* for a *that*-clause 182
Quiz 8   Quoted speech 182
Quiz 9   Quoted speech 183
Quiz 10   Quoted speech vs. reported speech 183
Quiz 11   Reported speech: changing verbs 184
Quiz 12   Reported speech 184
Quiz 13   *Say* vs. *tell* vs. *ask* 185
Quiz 14   Error analysis 185
Practice Test 186
Final Test 188

Appendix 1 PHRASAL VERBS

Quiz 1   Group A 191
Quiz 2   Group B 191
Quiz 3   Group C 192
Quiz 4   Group D 192
Quiz 5   Group E 193
Quiz 6   Review (Groups A → E) 194
Quiz 7   Group F 195
Quiz 8   Group G 196
Quiz 9   Group H 196
Final Test 197

Appendix 2 PREPOSITION COMBINATIONS

Quiz 1   Group A 199
Quiz 2   Group B 199
Quiz 3   Group C 200
Quiz 4   Group D 201
Quiz 5   Group E 201
Quiz 6   Group F 202
Quiz 7   Group G 202
Final Test 203

ANSWER KEY 205

INTRODUCTION

This test bank accompanies *Fundamentals of English Grammar, Third Edition.* Instructors can choose from nearly three hundred quizzes and tests to use for evaluation. Teachers familiar with the second edition of the test bank will find that all new material has been created for this third edition.

Quizzes

Each chapter contains a series of quizzes keyed to individual charts in the student book, followed by a practice test and a final test. The quizzes are intended as quick checks for both teacher and student. Mastery of a quiz is a strong indicator that students are ready to progress to the next section.

Practice Test and Final Test

The practice test and the final test at the end of each chapter are comprehensive, covering as many points as possible in the chapter. The practice test is identical to the final test in format, only shorter. It is recommended that teachers administer the practice test first so that students will be familiar with the format of the final test.

Format

Because students bring a variety of learning styles to the classroom, there is a wide selection of test formats, including sentence completion, sentence connection, multiple-choice, and error analysis, as well as more-open completion. To maximize use of the answer key, open-ended writing practice has been kept to a minimum. Teachers wishing to incorporate more writing into the tests are encouraged to add their own material at the end of the practice and final tests.

Answer Key

An answer key for all quizzes and tests can be found in the back of the text.

Duplication

The material has been formatted so teachers can easily make copies for their students. Permission is granted to duplicate as many copies as needed for classroom use only.

CHAPTER 1   PRESENT TIME

QUIZ 1   Simple present tense   *(Chart 1-1)*

Directions: *Complete the sentences with the words in parentheses. Use the simple present.*

1. Ben (**eat**) _____ breakfast at 6:00 A.M. every morning.

2. Suzie (**eat, not**) _____ any breakfast.

3. Her neighbor, Mrs. Jones, (**enjoy**) _____ her breakfast on her front porch.

4. Many children in our neighborhood (**walk**) _____ to school every day.

5. Some parents (**take**) _____ their younger children to school.

6. A few teenagers (**drive**) _____ themselves.

7. The teacher (**begin**) _____ class at 9:00 A.M. every day.

8. The bell (**ring**) _____ at 8:55.

9. Several students often (**come**) _____ late.

10. They (**have, not**) _____ a good reason.

QUIZ 2   Simple present tense and present progressive   *(Charts 1-1 and 1-2)*

Directions: *Complete the chart with the correct form of the verbs.*

He works	He _____is working_____
I study	I _____
They drive	They _____
We _____	We are building
The teacher _____	The teacher is explaining
Mr. and Mrs. Miller live	Mr. and Mrs. Miller _____
She _____	She is buying

Present verbs: questions *(Charts 1-1 and 1-2)*

Directions: Complete the questions with **Does she** *or* **Is she**.

1. _____ a tourist?

2. _____ have a tourist visa or a student visa?

3. _____ travel often?

4. _____ speak English?

5. _____ enjoying her time here?

6. _____ have any plans for staying here?

7. _____ happy here?

8. _____ planning to return?

QUIZ 4 **Frequency adverbs** *(Chart 1-3)*

Directions: Complete each sentence, using an appropriate frequency adverb from the list.

always	often OR usually	sometimes
never	seldom OR rarely	

Example: Samantha eats out three times a week.

Samantha ___*often eats out.*___

1. Ari is late for work about once a month.

   Ari _____ late for work.

2. Every time I buy something, I use a credit card.

   When I buy something, I _____ a credit card.

3. Every once in a while, my computer printer stops printing in the middle of a page.

   My computer printer _____ printing in the middle of a page.

4. I go running at 5:00 every morning, rain or shine.

   I _____ running every morning.

5. I see the dentist about once every five years.

   I _____ the dentist.

Directions: Circle the correct verb.

1. Right now, Janice *relax / relaxes / is relaxing* on her sofa.

2. She *read / reads / is reading* a good book.

3. The newspaper usually *come / comes / is coming* by 7:00.

4. Frequently it *get / gets / is getting* wet because the newspaper carrier
   throw / throws / is throwing the paper on the grass.

5. A: The phone *ring / rings / is ringing.*

   B: I'll get it.

   A: Who *call / calls / is calling?*

6. My phone is loud! Every time it *ring / rings / is ringing,* I *jump / jumps / am jumping.*

7. The Wilsons *work / works / are working* in their garden right now. Sometimes they
   garden / gardens / are gardening for several hours on weekends.

Directions: Circle the correct pronunciation for the verb ending.

1. tries	/s/	/z/	/əz/
2. belongs	/s/	/z/	/əz/
3. helps	/s/	/z/	/əz/
4. plays	/s/	/z/	/əz/
5. kisses	/s/	/z/	/əz/
6. rents	/s/	/z/	/əz/
7. realizes	/s/	/z/	/əz/
8. enjoys	/s/	/z/	/əz/
9. picks	/s/	/z/	/əz/
10. stops	/s/	/z/	/əz/
11. answers	/s/	/z/	/əz/
12. sells	/s/	/z/	/əz/

Spelling: final -S/-ING   *(Charts 1-4 and 1-5)*

Directions: *Write the simple present and the present progressive.* **He** *or* **She** *is the subject of the verbs.*

1. visit   _____   _____
2. stay   _____   _____
3. rent   _____   _____
4. see   _____   _____
5. go   _____   _____
6. finish   _____   _____
7. pay   _____   _____
8. touch   _____   _____
9. try   _____   _____
10. do   _____   _____
11. polish   _____   _____
12. run   _____   _____
13. cry   _____   _____
14. mix   _____   _____
15. put   _____   _____

QUIZ 8   Simple present tense and present progressive   *(Charts 1-1 → 1-6)*

Directions: *Complete the sentences with the words in parentheses. Use the simple present or the present progressive.*

1. Right now, the Professor Kim (**help**) _____ his students individually. He

   usually (**help**) _____ them the last ten minutes of each class.

2. In addition to Japanese, Tomo (**speak**) _____ four other languages. Right now

   he (**speak**) _____ to his friends in English. They (**need**)

   _____ more oral practice.

3. Look. An eagle (**fly**) _____ overhead with a snake in his
   mouth!

4. Vivian usually (**exercise**) _____ at a fitness center after work.

   Tonight she (**work**) _____ late. She (**exercise, not**)

   _____ .

5. (**you, like**) _____ to exercise?

6. Shhh. Grandma (**sleep**) _____ on the couch. She

   (**need**) _____ some rest.

QUIZ 9 **Non-action verbs** *(Chart 1-6)*

Directions: Circle the correct verb.

1. The teachers *need / are needing* a break. They *are / are being* tired.

2. Mrs. Brown *understands / is understanding* her students well.

3. I'm sorry. I *don't remember / am not remembering* your name.

4. This package *belongs / is belonging* to Mr. Johnson.

5. I *think / am thinking* about my family now.

6. I *think / am thinking* that my parents are wonderful.

7. *Do you have / Are you having* a good time?

8. What *do you know / are you knowing* about your work schedule for next week?

QUIZ 10 **Review** *(Charts 1-1 → 1-6)*

Directions: Choose the correct answer.

1. A: _____ you need anything at the store? I _____ now.

   a. Do   c. leave

   b. Are   d. am leaving

   B: No, thanks.

2. A: Your homework assignment _____ long. _____ it hard?

   a. looks   c. Is

   b. is looking   d. Does

   B: Shhh. I _____ to study.

   a. try   b. am trying

3. This party is a great idea. We _____ a wonderful time.

   a. have   b. are having

4. A large car _____ more gasoline than a small car.

   a. uses   b. is using

5. My parents _____ in hard work. They _____ two restaurants. They _____ seven days a week.

   a. believe   c. own   e. work

   b. are believing   d. are owning   f. are working

6. Every time it _____, our water pipes _____ .

   a. snows   c. freeze

   b. is snowing   d. are freezing

7. A: What _____ right now?

   a. do you do   b. are you doing

   B: I _____ an e-mail to my teacher.

   a. send   b. am sending

   A: _____ e-mails often?

   a. Do you send   b. Are you sending

   B: Only when I _____ to hand my homework in late.

   a. have   b. am having

Directions: *Complete the sentences with any appropriate verb. Use the simple present or the present progressive.*

1. My job _____ at 8:00 A.M. and _____ at 5:00 P.M.

2. Listen. The birds in the trees _____.

3. A: The baby _____.

   B: I know. He _____ hungry.

4. A: Why _____ the stove on?

   B: I _____.

5. Ellen _____ the bus every evening at 6:00. Then, she _____

   from the bus stop to her house.

6. The children _____ circles and squares right now. They are using

   blue, yellow, and red paint.

QUIZ 12 Present verbs: questions and short answers *(Chart 1-7)*

Directions: *Complete the questions with* **do, does, am, is,** *or* **are.** *Then complete the short answers, using the negative as needed.*

1. A: _____ you watching this show?

   B: Yes, _____.

2. A: _____ the TV loud enough?

   B: Yes, _____.

3. A: _____ you and Sam want to watch a video later?

   B: No, _____.

4. A: _____ your roommate, Mary, have a cat?

   B: Yes, _____.

5. A: _____ your neighbors have a dog?

   B: Yes, _____.

6. A: _____ he bark a lot?

   B: No, _____.

7. A: _____ he friendly?

   B: Yes, _____.

8. A: _____ your parents planning to get a dog?

   B: No, _____.

CHAPTER 1 PRACTICE TEST

Simple present vs. present progressive

Directions: *Complete the sentences with the simple present or the present progressive.*

1. Joseph, come inside. It (**begin**) _____ to rain.

2. Beth (**work**) _____ at a golf course two days a week. She

   (**teach**) _____ golf classes to young children. The children

   (**like**) _____ her because she (**be**) _____

   very patient.

Part II Simple present vs. present progressive

Directions: *Complete the sentences with the correct form of the verb in parentheses.*

Thomas (**have**) _____ two summer jobs. He (**pick**) _____

apples in the morning. It (**be, not**) _____ easy work, but he (**like**)

_____ to be outdoors. In the afternoons, he and his friends (**repair**)

_____ cars. Today, they (**work**) _____ on a 1940 classic

car. It (**need**) _____ many repairs.

Part III Simple present vs. present progressive

Directions: *Complete the sentences with any appropriate verb. Use the simple present or the present progressive.*

1. The classroom _____ very quiet right now. Some students _____

   _____ at their desks. Others _____

   on the blackboard. Their teacher _____ some papers.

2. John _____ to the park every day. He _____ soccer with his

   friends. Right now, two soccer players _____ on the field. They _____

   _____ the ball.

Directions: Choose the correct verb.

1. Hurry! The bus _____.
   a. comes
   b. is coming

2. I _____ Mrs. Brown. She never _____ her children play outside.
   a. don't understand   c. lets
   b. am not understanding   d. is letting

3. A: Where are the children?
   B: Upstairs. They _____ a video.
   a. watch
   b. are watching

4. A: Excuse me. Is this purse yours?
   B: No, it _____ to me.
   a. doesn't belong
   b. isn't belonging

5. A: Let's stop at a bank. I _____ some money.
   a. need
   b. am needing
   B: O.K.

Part V Error analysis

Directions: Correct the errors.

1. The teacher is yelling never at her students. She is very patient.

2. What time are you leave school every day?

3. The Smiths no have a car. They take the bus everywhere.

4. Is Jonathan own an apartment or a house?

5. Wait. The sandwiches is ready, but not the pizza.

PAST TIME

Simple past *(Charts 2-1, 2-2, and 2-7)*

Directions: *Change the sentences to past time. Use the simple past and* **yesterday** *or* **last**.

1. Andrew studies for two hours every day.

Andrew _____ .

2. Mark and Jan go to bed at 10:00 every night.

Mark and Jan _____ .

3. The alarm clock rings at 6:00 every morning.

The alarm clock _____ .

4. My grandparents visit us every month.

My grandparents _____ .

5. I take a nap every afternoon.

I _____ .

6. Dr. Hughes teaches medical students every Tuesday evening.

Dr. Hughes _____ .

7. Victoria buys coffee on her way to work every day.

Victoria _____ .

8. Mr. Wilson shops at the Farmer's Market every Saturday.

Mr. Wilson _____ .

Simple past forms *(Charts 2-1 → 2-3)*

Directions: *Write the question and negative forms for each sentence.*

1. The plane arrived on time.

Question: _____ on time?

Negative: _____ on time.

2. The restaurant was expensive.

Question: _____ expensive?

Negative: _____ expensive.

3. Julie got a promotion at work.

Question: _____ a promotion at work?

Negative: _____ a promotion at work.

4. The nurse took the patient's temperature.

Question: _____ the patient's temperature?

Negative: _____ the patient's temperature.

5. Ben worked late last night.

Question: _____ late last night?

Negative: _____ late last night.

6. Sara swam in the ocean.

Question: _____ in the ocean?

Negative: _____ in the ocean.

Directions: *Complete the questions and answers.*

1. A: **(Julia, eat)** _____ her vegetables last night?

   B: Yes, _____. She **(eat)** _____ peas and carrots.

2. A: **(you, go)** _____ to work on Saturday?

   B: No, _____. I **(be)** _____ on vacation.

3. A: **(Beethoven, write)** _____ symphonies?

   B: Yes, _____. He **(write)** _____ nine symphonies.

4. A: **(the Warrens, build)** _____ a new home last summer?

   B: Yes, _____. They **(build)** _____ a vacation home.

5. A: **(you, sleep)** _____ well last night?

   B: No, _____. I **(hear)** _____ noises outside and **(stay)**

   _____ awake for a long time.

6. A: **(a fish, jump)** _____ out of the water a few moments ago?

   B: Yes, _____. It **(jump)** _____ very high.

7. A: **(the monster movie, scare)** _____ the children?

   B: No, _____. It **(scare, not)** _____ them. It

   (make) _____ them laugh.

8. A: **(you, attend)** _____ the symphony last night?

   B: No, _____. We **(miss)** _____ the bus and **(decide)**

   _____ to see a movie in our neighborhood instead.

Directions: *The statements are not correct. Correct them, using the negative.*

Example: Dinosaurs lived in the ocean.

Dinosaurs ___*didn't live*___ in the ocean. They lived on land.

1. It was 100 degrees Celsius yesterday. It snowed.

   It was 100 degrees yesterday. It _____. It was sunny.

2. Marco Polo was one of the first Europeans to travel in South America.

   Marco Polo _____ in South America. He traveled in Asia.

3. Louis Pasteur developed the chicken pox vaccine.

   Louis Pasteur _____ the chicken pox vaccine. He developed the rabies vaccine.

4. A tornado damaged San Francisco in 1906.

   A tornado _____ San Francisco in 1906. An earthquake did.

5. People drove cars in the 15th century.

   People _____ cars in the 15th century. They rode horses.

6. Mozart wrote famous literature.

   Mozart _____ famous literature. He composed music.

Part I   Simple present vs. present progressive

Directions: Complete the sentences with the simple present or the present progressive.

1. Look outside. The sky (**get**) _____ dark. A storm (**come**)

   _____ .

2. My plants look dry. They (**need**) _____ water.

3. Julie is very talented. She (**play**) _____ several musical instruments well.

   Every afternoon after school, she (**practice**) _____ for several

   hours.

4. Please quiet down! The movie (**start**) _____ .

5. A: (**you, exercise**) _____ every day?

   B: Not every day. I (**run**) _____ and (**lift**) _____ weights

   three times a week.

Part II   Simple present vs. present progressive

Directions: Complete the sentences with the correct form of the verbs in parentheses.

My aunt and uncle (**own**) _____ a small farm. Every morning they (**wake**)

_____ up before sunrise. My aunt (**feed**) _____ the animals. My

uncle (**take**) _____ care of the vegetable garden. They also (**have**)

_____ day jobs in town. My uncle (**leave**) _____ for work at 8:00.

My aunt (**catch**) _____ the bus at 9:00. Today is a holiday, so they (**stay**)

_____ home and (**enjoy**) _____ a quiet day off.

Part III   Simple present vs. present progressive

Directions: Complete the sentences with any appropriate verb. Use the simple present or the present progressive.

1. Jack _____ an antique car. He loves it.

2. The window washers _____ the windows right now. They

   _____ to our house once a month.

3. Right now the chicken _____ in the oven. It _____

   delicious.

4. Joe _____ coffee with his breakfast every morning.

5. It is 2:00 P.M. Helen _____ on her bed. She _____

   a headache.

Directions: *Choose the correct verb.*

1. Mary _____ her children's hair once a month. She _____ a good job.

   a. cuts   c. does

   b. is cutting   d. is doing

2. A: _____ classical music?

   a. Do you like

   b. Are you liking

   B: I _____ jazz.

   a. prefer

   b. am preferring

3. Slow down! I _____ a siren. An ambulance _____.

   a. hear   c. comes

   b. am hearing   d. is coming

4. Martha _____ the newspaper on the Internet every morning. She _____ a lot of newspapers in her house.

   a. reads   c. doesn't want

   b. is reading   d. isn't wanting

Part V Error analysis

Directions: *Correct the errors.*

1. Are you go to school always by bus?

2. I no like movies with sad endings.

3. Oh no, look! A rat plays in the garbage can.

4. Is Maria go to work on Saturdays?

5. The books is on sale, but not the magazines.

6. Michelle have a beautiful engagement ring from her boyfriend.

7. Mr. Green is elderly, but he isn't want to live with his children.

*Directions: Complete the sentences with **did**, **was**, or **were**.*

1. _____ you go to work yesterday?

2. _____ John take his mother to the airport yesterday?

3. _____ she nervous about her trip?

4. _____ you happy to stay home last weekend?

5. _____ the Johnsons leave for their vacation last Thursday or last Friday?

6. _____ you see the movie at the theater or on video last weekend?

7. _____ you and your friends enjoy it?

8. _____ Mary and Elizabeth on time for class this morning?

9. _____ I already give you directions to my house?

10. _____ they make sense?

Directions: Circle the correct pronunciation.

1. ordered /t/ /d/ /əd/

2. clapped /t/ /d/ /əd/

3. questioned /t/ /d/ /əd/

4. asked /t/ /d/ /əd/

5. helped /t/ /d/ /əd/

6. needed /t/ /d/ /əd/

7. buzzed /t/ /d/ /əd/

8. washed /t/ /d/ /əd/

9. tried /t/ /d/ /əd/

10. wanted /t/ /d/ /əd/

Directions: *Write the* **- ing** *and past tense forms of the verbs.*

	-ing	past tense
1. study	_____	_____
2. live	_____	_____
3. work	_____	_____
4. stay	_____	_____
5. try	_____	_____
6. sleep	_____	_____
7. help	_____	_____
8. swim	_____	_____
9. think	_____	_____
10. know	_____	_____
11. stop	_____	_____
12. buy	_____	_____
13. type	_____	_____
14. play	_____	_____
15. drive	_____	_____
16. cut	_____	_____

Directions: *Write the past tense for the verbs.*

1. eat	_____	9. put	_____
2. win	_____	10. say	_____
3. choose	_____	11. see	_____
4. leave	_____	12. read	_____
5. speak	_____	13. drink	_____
6. become	_____	14. forget	_____
7. pay	_____	15. keep	_____
8. upset	_____		

Directions: Complete the sentences with the simple past tense of the verbs.

1. A: What (**you, wear**) _____ to the party last night?

   B: It (**be**) _____ casual, so I (**wear**) _____ jeans and a T-shirt.

2. A: Something smells delicious!

   B: I just (**bake**) _____ some bread.

3. A: How (**you, lose**) _____ your purse?

   B: I (**leave**) _____ it on the subway.

4. A: (**you, have**) _____ a doctor's appointment yesterday?

   B: Yes, I _____ .

   A: What (**she, say**) _____ ?

   B: She (**tell**) _____ me to exercise more and eat less.

5. A: When (**you, graduate**) _____ from college?

   B: In 2001. I (**finish**) _____ one year early.

Directions: Write the simple past tense of the verbs.

1. I **run** at night.   _____

2. They **don't have** time.   _____

3. He **is** a chef.   _____

4. It **works** well.   _____

5. They **aren't** ready.   _____

6. You **understand**.   _____

7. My hand **shakes** a little.   _____

8. Julia **has** many friends.   _____

9. The baby **cries** in her crib.   _____

10. Shelley **doesn't yell** at anyone.   _____

11. Your book **isn't** here.   _____

12. It **hurts**.   _____

13. You **know** them.   _____

14. My brother **snores** loudly.   _____

15. Ron and Nancy **clean** together.   _____

Directions: Complete the sentences, using the simple past.

1. Mari (**work**) _____ six days in a row last week.

2. Jennifer (**send**) _____ her parents three e-mails yesterday.

3. Our taxi driver (**take**) _____ a wrong turn on the way to the airport this morning.

4. A bear (**get**) _____ into our garbage when we (**go**) _____ camping last week.

5. The ground (**shake**) _____ several times during the night after the earthquake.

6. Before the fire stopped, it (**burn**) _____ the surrounding forest, but it (**touch, not**) _____ any houses.

7. A: You brought home lots of packages. What (**you, buy**) _____ at the store?

   B: I (**pick up**) _____ lots of clothes on sale.

8. Jeff (**ask**) _____ his question several times before the teacher (**hear**) _____ him.

9. A: How (**the glass, break**) _____ ?

   B: I (**drop**) _____ it on the floor.

10. A: What (**you, order**) _____ at the restaurant last night?

    B: I (**order**) _____ wild salmon and crab legs. They (**be**) _____ delicious.

Directions: Make sentences using the simple past. Punctuate them.

Example:
open / the computer store / three weeks ago
The computer store opened three weeks ago.

1. start / a software company / last month / Ben

2. two pizzas / eat / Jose / last night

3. he / not / feel / later / well

4. fall / out of a tree / Betsy / last week

5. to the doctor / go / not / she

6. last year / borrow / the Bakers / money / from their parents

Directions: *Complete the sentences with the words in parentheses. Use the simple past or the past progressive.*

Last Friday (**be**) _____ my 30th birthday. I (**want, not**) _____

a party, so I (**tell, not**) _____ my friends. I (**take**) _____ the

day off from work and (**decide**) _____ to go shopping. I (**ride**)

_____ the bus downtown and (**get**) _____ off at Center Mall. It (**be, not**)

_____ crowded because it (**be**) _____ the middle of a work day. I (**shop**)

_____ for clothes and (**buy**) _____ some dresses and several pairs

of shoes. I (**find**) _____ a restaurant with a view of the city and (**order**)

_____ a delicious lunch. Finally I (**walk**) _____ to a nearby pastry

shop and (**buy**) _____ dessert and coffee. I (**sit**) _____ outside in a

small park and (**enjoy**) _____ my dessert and the beautiful weather. It (**be**)

_____ one of my best birthdays ever.

Directions: *Complete the sentences with any appropriate verb.*

1. The students are unhappy because they ___failed___ their test. No one passed.

2. Ken _____ dinner at 11:00 last night. Then he _____ to bed and

   _____ for ten hours.

3. Nicole _____ chemistry for thirty years. She was a skilled teacher.

4. Samir _____ in his office until 5:00 P.M. Then he _____ home.

5. The policeman _____ a white car on the freeway for 10 minutes. Finally, the

   car _____ on a hill.

Directions: *Complete the sentences with the words in parentheses. Use the simple past or the past progressive.*

1. Last week the Whites (**decide**) _____ to sell their home and move into a condominium.

2. I'm sorry I'm late. I (**hear, not**) _____ the alarm clock.

3. The O'Briens (**spend**) _____ last winter in Mexico. While they (**live**) _____ there, they (**study**) _____ Spanish.

4. George (**plan**) _____ a retirement party for his office manager, and more than 100 people showed up.

5. Our soccer team (**make**) _____ a goal in the last few seconds, and we (**win**) _____ the championship.

6. Melissa's dog (**run**) _____ away from home while she (**travel**) _____ in South America last month. She (**try**) _____ to find him when she (**return**) _____, but she (**have, not**) _____ any luck.

Directions: *Complete the sentences. Use the simple past or the past progressive.*

Yesterday, while Sara (**walk**) _____ home from work, she (**see**) _____ an old friend from high school. While they (**talk**) _____, another friend of Sara's (**join**) _____ them. They all (**chat**) _____ for a while and then (**decide**) _____ to have dinner at a new restaurant nearby. At the restaurant, they (**know, not**) _____ what to order because the menu (**be**) _____ in another language. They (**ask**) _____ the waiter for suggestions, but he (**be, not**) _____ very friendly and (**help, not**) _____ them much. They finally (**point**) _____ to some food on the menu and (**hope**) _____ for a tasty meal.

QUIZ 17 Simple past and past progressive *(Charts 2-1 → 2-9)*

Directions: *Complete the sentences with the words in parentheses. Use the simple past or the past progressive.*

Last weekend, my grandparents (**go**) _____ to a summer arts festival in the harbor.

It (**be**) _____ a hot day, so they (**sit**) _____ down on a bench and (**watch**)

_____ all the activity. There (**be**) _____ lots of things to see and do. All

afternoon, clowns (**walk**) _____ around and (**entertain**)

_____ the children. An artist (**sell**) _____

scenes of the waterfront. My grandparents (**buy**) _____ a picture. Lots of

restaurants (**serve**) _____ delicious food, so my grandparents (**have**)

_____ lunch there. They (**want, not**) _____ to leave, but

finally did when the festival (**close**) _____ at 6:00.

QUIZ 18 Present and past verbs *(Chapter 1 and Charts 2-1 → 2-9)*

Directions: *Choose the correct verb.*

Example:

Paul usually _____ a few minutes late for work, but yesterday he _____ an hour early.

    (a.) arrives   d. arrives

    b. arrived   (e.) arrived

    c. was arriving   f. was arriving

1. A: Where _____ you last night?
       a. were   b. was   c. did

   B: I _____ home.
       a. stay   b. stayed   c. was staying

2. A: What _____ you have for breakfast this morning?
       a. did   b. were   c. are

   B: I _____ eggs and toast.
       a. eat   b. ate   c. was eating

3. A: When _____ you get your job promotion?
       a. did   b. were   c. was

   B: Last week.

   A: _____ you like your new job?
       a. Are   b. Do   c. Did

   B: Yes, I _____. I _____ 10-hour days a week and _____ three days off.
       a. am   d. am working   g. have
       b. do   e. work   h. am having
       c. did   f. worked   i. had

Directions: Complete the sentences with the words in parentheses. Use a present or past form.

1. Jack usually (**pay**) _____ his telephone bill with a credit card, but last month he

   (**pay**) _____ by check.

2. Paul (**drive**) _____ to work in his sports car every day, but yesterday he

   (**drove**) _____ his father's car. While he (**drive**) _____ ,

   he (**pass**) _____ the time by listening to CDs.

3. Sam usually (**wake up**) _____ at 7:00 in the morning, but yesterday

   he (**wake up**) _____ at 5:00. While he (**get**) _____ ready for

   work, he (**listen**) _____ to a financial report about the stock market.

4. At least once a week, the cat (**catch**) _____ a mouse, but last week she

   (**catch**) _____ three mice. While she (**chase**) _____

   one of them, she (**knock**) _____ over the dog's water bowl.

5. Every year, the Smiths travel to Africa, but last year they (**travel**) _____

   to Southeast Asia. While they (**travel**) _____ , they (**visit**)

   _____ several small villages. They (**stay, not**) _____

   in any big cities.

6. The Bentons usually (**watch**) _____ videos on Saturday night, but last

   weekend they (**watch**) _____ their neighbor's children instead.

Directions: Complete the sentences, using the words in parentheses. Use simple present, present progressive, simple past, or past progressive.

1. A: What time (**you, get up**) _____ every day?

   B: I usually (**wake up**) _____ before the sun (**rise**) _____ , but

      yesterday I (**sleep**) _____ until 9:00. It (**feel**) _____ wonderful!

2. A: Arnie, why are you on the floor? What (**you, do**) _____ ?

   B: I (**clean**) _____ the kitchen floor. Your dog (**get**) _____

      into the garbage last night while we (**sleep**) _____ . He

      (**make**) _____ a mess!

3. A: You (**look**) _____ calm and relaxed.

   B: I (**be**) _____ . While I (**work**) _____ at my desk earlier

      today, I (**take**) _____ a short nap.

4. A: (**you, see**) _____ the newspaper this morning?

   B: No, I _____ . Why?

   A: There was an article about your former boss. He (**go**) _____ to jail for theft.

Directions: *Check the sentence with the time clause that makes the most sense. In some cases, both sentences are correct.*

1. _____ After Donna got a ticket for speeding, she drove home very slowly.

   _____ Donna got a ticket for speeding after she drove home very slowly.

2. _____ While Mary and Greg watched an exercise video, their children watched cartoons on another TV.

   _____ Mary and Greg watched an exercise video while their children watched cartoons on another TV.

3. _____ Until Joy got her driver's license, her parents drove her to school.

   _____ Joy got her driver's license until her parents drove her to school.

4. _____ Eric took a shower after he got home.

   _____ After Eric took a shower, he got home.

5. _____ While Rachel cooked dinner, Rick gave the children a bath.

   _____ Rachel cooked dinner while Rick gave the children a bath.

6. _____ As soon as I got home, I went to bed.

   _____ I got home as soon as I went to bed.

Directions: *Using the given information, complete the sentences. Use **used to**.*

1. When I was a teenager, I sat in the sun. Now I stay out of the sun.

   I _____ in the sun, but now I don't.

2. When I lived in Italy, I ate lots of pasta. Now I live in Japan and eat rice instead.

   I _____ lots of pasta, but now I don't.

3. When I was younger, I stayed out late. Now I'm in bed by 9:00 P.M.

   I _____ out late, but now I don't.

4. When my parents lived in a house, they had two large dogs. They live in an apartment now and have two small cats.

   They _____ dogs, but now they have cats.

5. When my brother was a child, he thought that people on TV could see him.

   My brother _____ that people on TV could see him.

6. Did your wife at some time in the past walk to work?

   _____ walk to work?

7. What kind of books did you read when you were a child?

   What kind of books _____ when you were a child?

Directions: Complete the sentences with **used to** and a verb from the list.

be	drink	have	wake up
chase	eat	swim	work

1. I _____ peanuts for a snack, but now I'm allergic to peanuts.

2. I _____ in the ocean when I was a child, but now the water is

   too cold for me.

3. My hair _____ long, but now I cut it every month.

4. I _____ carrot juice, but then my skin began to turn orange.

5. My father _____ on weekends until he had a heart attack.

6. We _____ a lot of sand on our beach, but a storm washed it

   away.

7. Our dog _____ cars, but now she just watches them.

8. The baby _____ several times during the night, but now she

   sleeps through the night.

QUIZ 24 Error analysis *(Charts 2-1 → 2-11)*

Directions: Correct the errors.

1. Joe no walk to work yesterday. He take the bus.

2. Mary was go to the emergency room at midnight last night.

3. While Dr. Hughes listen to his patient, his cell phone rang. He wasn't answer it.

4. Marco no use to swim, but now he does because he was taking swimming lessons.

5. Po got a new job after he celebrated his success with his friends.

6. When the phone was ringing at 11:00 last night, I was in a deep sleep. I almost not hear it.

CHAPTER 2 PRACTICE TEST

Part I   Past verbs

Directions: *Complete the sentences with the simple past or past progressive of the words in parentheses.*

Last weekend, we (**take**) _____ a day trip in our sailboat. We (**see**)

_____ a small island in the middle of a lake. We (**want**) _____ to

explore it, so we (**leave**) _____ our boat on the beach on the island. We

(**find**) _____ a trail and (**hike**) _____ around the island. While we

(**hike**) _____, we (**hear**) _____ noises in the bushes. We

(**stand**) _____ on the trail and (**wait**) _____ . While we

(**wait**) _____, a small bear (**come**) _____ out of the

woods. He (**eat**) _____ blackberries. We slowly (**walk**) _____

backwards. Fortunately, the bear (**follow, not**) _____ us, and we

(**get**) _____ back to our boat safely.

Part II   Present and past verbs

Directions: *Complete the dialogue with the correct form of the words in parentheses.*

1. A: How old were you when you (**learn**) _____ to swim?

   B: I (**be, not**) _____ very old, probably three or four. My father first

   (**teach**) _____ me to blow bubbles under water. Then he

   (**show**) _____ me how to kick properly.

2. A: (**you, like**) _____ to swim now?

   B: I (**love**) _____ it!

Part III   Present and past verbs

Directions: *Choose the correct answer.*

1. A: _____ you remember to call the dentist?
      a. Do   b. Did   c. Were
   B: Yes. I _____ an appointment for Tuesday.
      a. make   b. made   c. was making
2. A: What time _____ Jason leave last night?
      a. does   b. was   c. did
   B: I don't know. I _____ him.
      a. don't hear   b. didn't hear   c. wasn't hearing

3. A: How are you doing? You _____ tired.

      a. look   b. looked   c. were looking

    B: I _____. I _____ well last week, and I'm still tired.

      a. am   d. am not sleeping

      b. was   e. wasn't sleeping

      c. did   f. didn't sleep

Part IV   Error analysis

Directions: *Correct the errors.*

1. Bees use to making honey in a tree next to our house until lightning split the tree in half.

2. Carol no was go to work yesterday because her son sick.

3. Doug and Peter were having a party last weekend. Everyone from our class come.

4. Did you upset with your test results yesterday?

5. After Bill got up, he woke up.

CHAPTER 2 FINAL TEST

Part I Simple past and past progressive

Directions: *Complete the sentences with the simple past or past progressive of the words in parentheses.*

Traffic was very slow yesterday. There (**be**) _____ an accident on the freeway. I
(**sit**) _____ in my car for 15 minutes and (**go, not**) _____
anywhere. While I (**sit**) _____ in the car, I (**watch**)
_____ the other drivers. One woman (**talk**) _____
on her cell phone the entire time. Another driver (**try**) _____ to
entertain her baby. He (**cry**) _____ . An elderly man (**eat**)
_____ an ice-cream cone. He (**look**) _____ like the only
happy driver. Finally, traffic (**begin**) _____ to move again. We all (**feel**)
_____ relieved.

Part II Present and past verbs

Directions: *Complete the dialogue with the correct form of the words in parentheses.*

A: Hi, Bill. What (**you, do**) _____ ?

B: I (**look**) _____ at pictures of my vacation. I (**spend**)
_____ it at my cousins' house.

A: Where (**they, live**) _____ ?

B: They live on a lake in the country.

A: What (**you, do**) _____ there?

B: One day we (**rent**) _____ a canoe. We (**spend**) _____ all
afternoon fishing and swimming. We also (**take**) _____ long walks in the
woods. Once, while we (**walk**) _____ , we (**see**) _____
some raccoons and a family of foxes.

A: How long (**you, stay**) _____ there?

B: For a week. I (**want**) _____ to go back there next summer too.

Part III Present and past verbs

Directions: *Choose the correct answer.*

1. Tina _____ her young daughter carefully right now. A few hours ago, while

   a. watching   b. is watching   c. watched

   she _____ on the phone, her daughter quietly _____ a sack of flour.

   d. talks   g. is opening

   e. was talking   h. was opening

   f. talked   i. opened

First, she _____ it all over the floor. Then, she _____ water to it.

          j. is pouring   m. adds

          k. was pouring   n. was adding

          l. poured   o. added

What a mess it made! Tina _____ it up, and now the floor _____ fine.

          p. cleans   s. looks

          q. was   t. is looking

          r. cleaned   u. looked

2. A: Where _____ you have lunch yesterday?

      a. are   b. were   c. did

   B: I _____ at Ellen's new restaurant. I _____ chicken and rice.

      a. am eating   d. am having

      b. was eating   e. was having

      c. ate   f. had

   A: _____ your meal good?

      a. Is   b. Was   c. Did

   B: Yes, delicious.

Part IV   Error analysis

Directions: *Correct the errors.*

1. Dr. Martin used to working in a hospital, but now she has a private practice.

2. I was home alone last night. First, I was cooking dinner. Then, I was washing the dishes.

3. Matt busy yesterday. He wasn't go to the party.

4. The Millers buy a restaurant last month. They open for business last week.

5. The baby tryed to crawl a few times, but her legs aren't strong enough yet.

6. Liz and Ron planed to get married last summer, but just before the wedding, Ron is losing his

   job. Now they are waiting until next summer.

7. Professor Scott no have time to help us with our lab experiment yesterday. Maybe she can

   today.

8. Ernesto was building a model train set by himself in his basement. He finished it last month.

FUTURE TIME

Present, past, and future *(Chapters 1, 2, and 3)*

Directions: Circle the correct time word.

1.	Mike is going to clean his apartment.	yesterday	tomorrow
2.	Bill will celebrate his birthday.	yesterday	tomorrow
3.	Do you work in the city?	every day	yesterday
4.	Susan woke up early.	every day	yesterday
5.	Does Rick take the bus to school?	every day	yesterday
6.	Jan broke her leg.	every day	yesterday
7.	Will you be here?	yesterday	tomorrow
8.	The mail comes at 1:00 P.M.	every day	yesterday
9.	Is Alex going to visit us?	yesterday	tomorrow
10.	Dr. Smith saw two patients at the hospital.	every day	yesterday

QUIZ 2 **WILL and BE GOING TO** *(Charts 3-1 → 3-3)*

Directions: Complete the sentences with **will** and **be going to** and the verbs in parentheses.

1. (**rain**) It _____ tomorrow.

 It _____ tomorrow.

2. (**depart**) The plane _____ soon.

 The plane _____ soon.

3. (**return**) I _____ the library books tomorrow morning.

 I _____ the library books tomorrow morning.

4. (**meet**) Our book club _____ tomorrow night.

 Our book club _____ tomorrow night.

5. (**be**) Your car _____ ready next week.

 Your car _____ ready next week.

6. (**leave**) The Wilsons _____ for their trip next Saturday.

 The Wilsons _____ for their trip next Saturday.

Directions: Complete the sentences with **will**.

1. Ted _____ understand.

2. Susie _____ understand.

3. I _____ understand.

4. My parents _____ understand.

5. Professor Davis _____ understand.

6. You _____ understand.

7. Your brother _____ understand.

8. We _____ understand.

Complete the sentences with **be going to**.

9. Ted _____ know soon.

10. Susie _____ know soon.

11. I _____ know soon.

12. My parents _____ know soon.

13. Professor Davis _____ know soon.

14. You _____ know soon.

15. Your brother _____ know soon.

16. We _____ know soon.

QUIZ 4 WILL *(Chart 3-3)*

Directions: Complete the dialogues with **will**.

1. A: (**I, hear**) _____ about my application soon?

   B: Yes, _____ in two weeks.

2. A: (**Jerry, get**) _____ here on time?

   B: No, _____ . Traffic is very heavy.

3. A: (**your family, be**) _____ at the wedding?

   B: Yes, _____ .

4. A: (**you, do**) _____ my homework for me?

   B: No, _____ .

5. A: (**your bank**) _____ accept an out-of-state check?

   B: Yes, _____ .

*Directions: Write questions with **will** and **be going to**.*

1. you/study

    _____ tomorrow?

    _____ tomorrow?

2. Dr. Brown/retire

    _____ next month?

    _____ next month?

3. the cat/catch

    _____ the mouse?

    _____ the mouse?

4. our team/win

    _____ the game?

    _____ the game?

5. Mr. and Mrs. Bell/find

    _____ their lost puppy?

    _____ their lost puppy?

QUIZ 6 Sureness about the future *(Chart 3-4)*

Directions: Make complete sentences about the future with the given words.

Example: the airplane / take off / very late / probably
→ The airplane will probably take off very late.

1. the passengers / be / happy / probably / not

2. the flight attendants / serve / extra snacks / may

3. the children / get restless / maybe

4. their parents / get restless / probably

5. they / travel / again soon / may / not

Directions: *Decide if the speaker is 100% sure, 90% sure, or 50% sure.*

	100%	90%	50%
Example: Your package may arrive as early as tomorrow.			✔
1. The new hotel is not going to open next month.			
2. The owners will refund travelers their money.			
3. Some people will probably be upset.			
4. The hotel may give them discounts for future stays.			
5. Amanda isn't going to pass her classes.			
6. She won't be surprised.			
7. She'll probably be a little upset.			
8. Her parents will be very upset.			

QUIZ 8 BE GOING TO vs. WILL *(Chart 3-5)*

Directions: *Complete the sentences with* **be going to** *or* **will**.

1. A: I just spilled some milk.

   B: Don't worry. I _____ clean it up.

2. A: Why did Greg rent a truck?

   B: He _____ pick up a new refrigerator and stove.

3. A: What are your plans for the weekend?

   B: We _____ to paint our living room.

4. A: How does this dress look?

   B: I think it's a little too short.

   A: O.K. I guess I _____ get the other one.

5. A: Does Joan have a new phone number yet?

   B: Yes. It's in my purse. I _____ get it.

6. A: There's a potluck dinner at Scott's this weekend.

   B: I know. Tony and I _____ make a spicy chicken dish.

*Directions: Complete each sentence with an **if**-clause. Use a comma if necessary.*

    Example: Maybe I'll get an "A" on my biology exam.

          <u>If I get an "A" on my biology exam,</u>   I'm going to celebrate.

1. Maybe my friends will give me a surprise birthday party.

    _____ I will act surprised.

2. Maybe Luis won't be available.

    Jake will go camping with another friend _____.

3. Maybe the snow will melt.

    We won't go skiing _____.

4. Maybe Fred will cook dinner.

    Jane will wash the dishes _____.

5. Maybe the phone will ring.

    _____ tell people I'm sleeping.

6. Maybe there will be a sunset tonight.

    _____ I'll take a picture.

*Directions: Decide which phrase is part of the adverb clause. Then complete the sentences, using the given words and **will**.*

    Example: buy a new car / earn enough money

          As soon as Matt <u>earns enough money</u>, he <u>will buy a new car</u>.

1. pick up their airplane tickets / fly to Thailand

    Before the Smiths _____, they _____.

2. get dressed / go to work

    As soon as Sonya _____, she _____.

3. feel better / stay home

    Chris _____ until he _____.

4. wash her hands / make lunch

    Before Ellen _____, _____.

5. go to the pharmacy / get a prescription

    After Mr. Hill _____, he _____.

6. get a new phone / call us

    When the Thompsons _____, they _____.

Directions: Correct the errors.

to

Next week, I plan ∧ take a vacation in the mountains. I am hiking and and going to climb for several days. At night, when I will get tired, I will find a place to set up my tent. I will building a campfire and cooking my food. Then I am looking at the stars through my small telescope. I will probably tired, so I go to bed early. I will sleeping very hard because my muscles are going be very tired. When I will wake up in the morning, I will going to feel much better.

QUIZ 16 Past, present, and future *(Chapters 1, 2, and 3)*

Directions: Complete the sentences with the words in parentheses.

1. As soon as the weather (**clear**) _____ , the plane (**take off**)
   _____ . I (**hope**) _____ we (**have**) _____ a
   smooth flight.

2. When the pizza (**come**) _____ , let's eat. I (**get**) _____
   hungry.

3. I have a busy day tomorrow. First, I (**take**) _____ the children shopping
   for back-to-school clothes. Then we (**meet**) _____ friends for a quick
   lunch. As soon as we (**finish**) _____ lunch, we (**pick up**)
   _____ the dog at the vet and (**take**) _____ her
   home. Once we (**be**) _____ home, we (**get**) _____ ready for
   the next day when school (**start**) _____ .

4. A: Who's at the door?
   B: I (**check**) _____ .... It's your newspaper carrier. She has a bill.
   A: O.K. I (**come**) _____ right now.

5. A: (**you, watch**) _____ the soccer match with us later?
   B: No, thanks. I (**work**) _____ on my thesis. I (**plan**)
   _____ to turn it in next week.

6. A: Ms. Martin, can we go outside?
   B: No, Johnny. You can't leave until the bell (**ring**) _____ .
   A: When (**the bell, ring**) _____ ?
   B: In five minutes.

CHAPTER 3 PRACTICE TEST

Part I WILL and BE GOING TO

Complete the sentences with **will** *and the words in parentheses.*

1. A: I don't understand these directions.

   B: I (**help**) _____ you.

2. A: I'm frustrated. I'm not learning English quickly enough.

   B: Don't worry. You (**see, probably**) _____ a lot of

   improvement soon.

3. A: Don't forget to pick up the clothes at the cleaners.

   B: Don't worry. I (**forget, not**) _____ .

4. A: Anyone want to go to the store with me?

   B: Rachel (**go**) _____ .

Complete the sentences with **be going to** *and the words in parentheses.*

5. A: What (**you, do**) _____ on your summer break?

   B: I (**visit**) _____ some friends I grew up with. They live

   near the ocean.

   A: (**you, stay**) _____ there the entire time?

   B: No, I (**be, probably**) _____ there a few weeks. I (**look**)

   _____ also _____ for a part-time job. I want to earn

   some money for college.

Part II WILL and BE GOING TO

Directions: *Complete the sentences with* **will** *or* **be going to** *and the verbs in parentheses. If there is a plan, use* **be going to**.

1. A: I can't find my keys, and I'm in a hurry.

   B: I (**help**) _____ you look for them.

2. A: Do you plan to buy your lunch at school?

   B: No, I (**make**) _____ it. It's much less expensive.

3. A: Why are you looking at wedding rings?

   B: I (**ask**) _____ Julie to marry me.

Part III Present, past, and future

Directions: *Complete the sentences with the correct form of the words in parentheses. Use present, past or future.*

1. A: Oh no!

   B: What's the matter?

   A: My computer just (**crash**) _____ .

   B: (**you, lose**) _____ all your work?

   A: I don't know. As soon as I (**make**) _____ some repairs, I (**check**)

   _____ .

2. A: What time (**your flight, arrive**) _____ tomorrow?

   B: I'm not sure. I (**call**) _____ you as soon as I (**get**) _____ there.

Part IV Error analysis

Directions: *Check the correct sentences. Correct the incorrect sentences.*

1. _____ After we will get married, we will buy a house.

2. _____ The train leaves at 6:45 tomorrow morning.

3. _____ Julia will sing in the choir and going to play the piano at her school concert next week.

4. _____ I go downtown tomorrow with my friends.

5. _____ My husband and I are will not use our credit card so much next month.

6. _____ If Eric call, I am going tell him I am not available to work this weekend.

7. _____ School ends next week.

8. _____ Tomorrow when John is going to get home, he will help you plant your vegetable garden.

9. _____ Toshi maybe will quit his job soon.

10. _____ Yoko is crying when she hears my news.

CHAPTER 3 FINAL TEST

WILL and BE GOING TO

*Directions: Complete the sentences with **will** and the words in parentheses.*

1. A: What's the weather forecast for the rest of the week?

   B: Tomorrow it (**rain**) _____ all day, but after that it (**be**)

   _____ dry. We (**have, probably**)

   _____ sun for several days. I believe it (**rain, not**)

   _____ again until next week.

   A: Great. Let's go to the beach.

*Complete the sentences with **be going to** and the words in parentheses.*

2. A: What (**you, do**) _____ with those beautiful flowers in your garden?

   B: I (**take**) _____ some of them to work and (**put**)

   _____ them on my desk. I (**give, probably**)

   _____ the rest to my co-workers and neighbors.

   A: I'm sure they (**appreciate**) _____ that.

Part II WILL and BE GOING TO

*Directions: Complete the sentences with **will** or **be going to** and the verbs in parentheses. If there is a plan, use **be going to**.*

1. A: Do you want to wash the dishes or dry?

   B: I (**dry**) _____ .

2. A: Why are you wearing a bathing suit?

   B: I (**go**) _____ swimming.

   A: No! It's too cold out.

   B: Don't worry. I (**swim**) _____ indoors, not outdoors!

3. A: Mmmm. Those cookies sure smell good.

   B: Don't touch! We (**sell**) _____ them. There's a bake sale at school tomorrow.

4. A: That was a delicious dinner.

   B: How about some dessert?

   A. Sure. But sit down. I (**get**) _____ it.

Part III Present, past and future

Directions: *Complete the sentences with the words in parentheses. Use present, past, or future.*

1. A: Help! A bee (**chase**) _____ me.

   B: Calm down! Sit still!

   A: If I (**sit**) _____ still, it (**sting**) _____ me.

   B: Look. It just (**fly**) _____ away.

   A: Thank goodness.

2. A: Where (**you, be**) _____ last night? The study group (**wait**)

      _____ more than an hour for you.

   B: Sorry. I (**be**) _____ at the office. I (**need**) _____ to finish a project.

   A: (**you, work**) _____ late again tonight?

   B: No. I (**intend**) _____ to leave by 6:00. If I (**need**)

      _____ to work late, I (**call**) _____ you.

3. A: When (**your neighbors, return**) _____ from their trip?

   B: In about two weeks. They (**stay**) _____ in Athens right now. After

      they (**leave**) _____ there, they (**plan**) _____ to spend

      a week on a cruise ship. They (**visit**) _____ several Greek islands.

   A: It sounds like a wonderful trip.

Part IV Error analysis

Directions: *Check the correct sentences. Correct the incorrect sentences.*

1. _____ Michelle starts her vacation tomorrow afternoon.

2. _____ The business office will closing for one week next month.

3. _____ Dinner is almost ready. The oven timer about go off.

4. _____ Fortunately our teacher not gonna give us a quiz tomorrow.

5. _____ Next Saturday, Boris will stay home and cleaning out his garage.

6. _____ Are you going playing tennis during lunch today?

7. _____ The plane is going to arrive an hour late. There were delays at the airport.

8. _____ Our electric bill is going maybe to increase next month.

9. _____ Masako buy a new truck next week. She will plan to drive it to work.

10. _____ Tomorrow when Pierre will get to work, he interview several candidates for the assistant manager position.

11. _____ You're paying a large fine if you return this video late.

12. _____ I have to hurry. We leave for our trip in an hour.

THE PRESENT PERFECT AND THE PAST PERFECT

Simple past and past participle forms *(Chart 4-1)*

Directions: Complete the chart with the simple past and past participle forms.

	simple past	past participle
1. write	wrote	written
2. see	saw	_____
3. try	_____	_____
4. do	_____	_____
5. stay	_____	_____
6. be	was/were	_____
7. say	_____	_____
8. have	had	_____
9. finish	_____	_____
10. sleep	_____	_____
11. put	put	_____
12. open	_____	_____
13. fly	_____	_____
14. eat	ate	_____
15. play	_____	_____

Present perfect negatives *(Chart 4-2)*

Directions: Complete the sentences with the given verbs. Use the negative form.

Example:

(**visit**) Karen _____hasn't visited_____ yet.

1. (**pass**) You _____ yet.

2. (**come**) They _____ yet.

3. (**stop**) The rain _____ yet.

4. (**begin**) I _____ yet.

5. (**start**) We _____ yet.

6. (**call**) The Wilsons _____ yet.

7. (**met**) You and I _____ yet.

8. (**go**) Mr. Adams _____ yet.

Directions: *Write present perfect questions using the given words.*

Example:

Mike / cook / dinner / yet? ___Has Mike cooked dinner yet?___

1. they / study / for the test / already? _____

2. you / live / here / for a long time? _____

3. Ingrid / visit / ever? _____

4. I / answer / your question / yet? _____

5. we / get / a response / already? _____

Directions: *Choose the correct completion.*

1. Carol _____ a pet snake when she was a child.
   a. had   b. has had

2. Brian _____ insurance for twenty years. He still enjoys it.
   a. sold   b. has sold

3. I _____ in the rainforest twice and plan to go again next year.
   a. hiked   b. have hiked

4. Khalid _____ the keys to his car yet. He's still looking.
   a. didn't find b. hasn't found

5. I _____ a toothache since this morning.
   a. has had   b. have had

6. Anita _____ any bananas at the supermarket. They were sold out.
   a. didn't find b. hasn't found

7. Ellen _____ afraid of spiders since one fell from the ceiling into her hair.
   a. was   b. has been

8. Mr. Perez _____ golf until he had a stroke at the age of 85.
   a. played   b. has played

9. We _____ from Jack since he moved to Toronto.
   a. didn't hear b. haven't heard

10. I didn't know you lived here! How long _____ here?
    a. did you live b. have you lived

Directions: Check the correct completion. More than one answer may be correct.

1. I first met Jack . . .

   _____ for one week.

   _____ since Tuesday.

   _____ one week ago.

2. I have known Jack . . .

   _____ for one week.

   _____ since Tuesday.

   _____ one week ago.

3. Donna moved to London . . .

   _____ six years ago.

   _____ for one month.

   _____ since January.

4. Matt has lived in London . . .

   _____ since last year.

   _____ three years ago.

   _____ for a long time.

5. The test started . . .

   _____ two hours ago.

   _____ for two hours.

   _____ since 2:00.

6. Professor Miller has taught English . . .

   _____ since he got his Ph.D.

   _____ for his entire career.

   _____ several years ago.

QUIZ 6 SINCE vs. FOR *(Chart 4-5)*

Directions: Complete the sentences with **since** or **for**.

1. Mr. and Mrs. Nelson have lived in a retirement home _____ June.

2. They have been there _____ five months.

3. Carmen has been a nurse at the local hospital _____ a few weeks.

4. She has been a nurse _____ 15 years.

5. Leo hasn't worked _____ 2001.

6. He has received disability payments _____ he hurt his back.

7. Carl has felt ill _____ Sunday.

8. He has been in bed _____ three days.

9. Pam has played the violin in the school orchestra _____ two years.

10. Nathan has been a chef at a hotel _____ he graduated from cooking school.

11. He took a summer off and worked on a fishing boat _____ a few months.

12. He hasn't worked on a boat _____ then.

Directions: Circle the correct verb.

1. I have known how to read since I *was / have been* three years old.

2. Toshi has loved baseball since his father *took / has taken* him to his first game.

3. Ted and Joanne *were / have been* together since they met in high school.

4. Dr. Phillips has wanted to work abroad since she *received / has received* her medical degree.

5. The baby *had / has had* a fever since she woke up this morning.

6. Our families have been friends since they *met / have met* on a vacation in the Bahamas.

7. Luke has wanted to be a writer since he *took / has taken* a creative writing class.

8. My car hasn't run well since I *drove / have driven* it in the desert.

Directions: Complete the phrase with **since** or **for**.

Gina has had a part-time job. . .

1. _____ two months.

2. _____ April.

3. _____ a few weeks.

4. _____ last week.

5. _____ several days.

6. _____ the beginning of school.

7. _____ school started.

8. _____ she moved to the city.

9. _____ a long time.

10. _____ one year.

Directions: *Write the present perfect and present perfect progressive forms of the verbs.*

	present perfect	present perfect progressive
1. He **rides** the bus.	_____	_____
2. She **eats** alone.	_____	_____
3. I **study** by myself.	_____	_____
4. We **learn** a lot.	_____	_____
5. They **work** together.	_____	_____
6. We **sleep** late.	_____	_____
7. He **takes** a nap.	_____	_____
8. Tina **doesn't read** much.	_____	_____
9. Dr. Brown **doesn't drive**.	_____	_____
10. I **don't write** letters.	_____	_____

Directions: *Complete the dialogues with the present perfect progressive forms of the verbs.*

1. A: What's the matter?

   B: Your dog (**bark**) _____ since you left this morning. You need to do something.

2. A: Where's Linda?

   B: She's in her bedroom. She (**talk**) _____ on the phone since she woke up.

3. A: Has the bus come yet?

   B: No, and I (**stand**) _____ here in the cold for a long time.

4. A: You look out of breath!

   B: I am. I (**exercise**) _____ with weights. I'm trying to get in shape for a 10K race.

5. A: I hear a noise.

   B: It's my cell phone. It (**beep**) _____ all morning because the battery is dead.

6. A: Why is your cat scratching the wall?

   B: She (**try**) _____ to find a mouse that ran into a crack between the floor and the wall.

7. A: I'm so bored.

   B: I know. Professor Adams (**speak**) _____ on the same subject for more than an hour. Will he EVER stop?

8. A: I think we're lost.

   B: Let's ask for directions. We (**driving**) _____ around for almost an hour. That's long enough.

Directions: *Create complete sentences. Use the given words and the present perfect progressive.*

Example:

the baby / cry / for an hour ___The baby has been crying for an hour.___

1. how long / you / stand / here? _____

2. I / work / since 10:00 A.M. _____

3. it / snow / for two days _____

4. how long / they / study / for the test? _____

5. why / you / work / so long? _____

6. the taxi / wait / for ten minutes _____

7. Rachel / ride / her horse / all morning _____

Directions: *Choose the correct completion.*

1. Peter _____ to the dentist several times this month. He's having problems with his teeth.
   a. has gone   b. has been going

2. I need to use a different shampoo and rinse. I _____ my hair for fifteen minutes, and it's still tangled.
   a. have combed   b. have been combing

3. Can't you sit down and rest for a minute? You _____ nonstop.
   a. have worked   b. have been working

4. Look at all the food on the table. It looks like you _____ all day.
   a. have cooked   b. have been cooking

5. Mark is afraid of flying. He _____ on an airplane.
   a. has never flown   b. has never been flying

6. A: Are you going with us to the movie tonight?
   B: No, I _____ it already.
   a. have seen   b. have been seeing

7. A: Did you hear that Alex is quitting management?
   B: Yes. I _____ about it for a few weeks.
   a. have known   b. have been knowing

8. A: I'm sorry I'm late for work. I overslept.
   B: I _____ that excuse from you too many times. You need to be more responsible.
   a. have heard   b. have been hearing

Directions: *Choose all the correct completions.*

1. I _____ can't find my glasses. I've been looking for them all morning.
   a. already   b. yet   c. still   d. anymore

2. We don't eat red meat _____. We decided to eat just fish and chicken.
   a. already   b. yet   c. still   d. anymore

3. I haven't met all my cousins _____, but we plan to have a family reunion soon.
   a. already   b. yet   c. still   d. anymore

4. It's noon _____. This morning surely has gone by quickly!
   a. already   b. yet   c. still   d. anymore

5. Who would like seconds? There's _____ some food left.
   a. already   b. yet   c. still   d. anymore

6. Look at Yoko! She can _____ wear the same clothes she wore in high school ten years ago!
   a. already   b. yet   c. still   d. anymore

7. These shoes don't fit you _____. We need to buy you some that don't hurt your feet.
   a. already   b. yet   c. still   d. anymore

8. Are you finished with dinner _____?
   a. already   b. yet   c. still   d. anymore

9. Children, please sit down. It's not time to go home _____.
   a. already   b. yet   c. still   d. anymore

10. Oh my! I need to wake up Paul. I'm surprised his alarm clock hasn't gone off _____.
    a. already   b. yet   c. still   d. anymore

Directions: *Complete the sentences. Use **already**, **yet**, **still**, or **anymore**.*

1. I expected Mike to come home an hour ago, but he didn't.
   In other words, he _____ isn't home.
   In other words, he isn't home _____.

2. I was hungry an hour ago, but I didn't eat anything.
   In other words, I'm _____ hungry.

3. Erica used to work at the drugstore, but she quit her job.
   In other words, she doesn't work there _____.

4. We're late. The movie started an hour ago.
   In other words, the movie has _____ started.

5. Greg started smoking four years ago. He hasn't stopped.
   In other words, he _____ smokes.
   In other words, he hasn't quit _____.

6. We studied Chapter 6 last week.
   In other words, we've studied Chapter 6. We haven't studied Chapter 8 _____.

7. When I was a child, I used to read comic books. But they're for kids.
   In other words, I don't read comic books_____.

8. We started this exercise ten minutes ago.
   In other words, we have _____ started this exercise.
   In other words, we are _____ doing this exercise.

Directions: Complete the sentences with words in parentheses. Use the past perfect.

1. I got off work late. By the time I got to the bus stop, the bus (**leave, already**)

    _____ .

2. We (**think, not**) _____ of moving until we found out that the schools in the neighboring district were much better.

3. Jerry and Diane asked me to join them for dinner, but I (**eat, already**) _____

    _____ .

4. We wanted to build a campfire when we got to our campsite, but the camp ranger (**put up,**

    already) _____ a sign saying "No Fires."

5. Pedro planned to get an autograph from one of the baseball players, but by the time he

    arrived, the players (**start**) _____ the pre-game practice.

6. My in-laws were interested in buying the Clark's house on 5th Street, but when they went to

    look at it, it (**sell, already**) _____ .

7. Joe was about to pay his credit card bill when he saw that his wife (**pay, already**)

    _____ it.

8. Jan was going to talk to her secretary about the importance of arriving at work on time, but

    her manager (**met, already**) _____ with him.

9. Ellen sat down on the sofa and began to read the mystery novel her sister had given her. After

    a few pages, she realized she (**read, already**) _____ it.

Directions: Choose the correct completion.

1. I looked for Janet, but she _____ for work.
    a. has left   b. had left

2. As soon as I got home, I gave Mary her gift. I _____ to bring her some perfume from Paris.
    a. have promised   b. had promised

3. Grandma _____ her medicine yet. Maybe she forgot.
    a. hasn't taken   b. hadn't taken

4. Our electric bill was very high this month because we _____ some lights on in the house while
    we were away on vacation.
    a. have left   b. had left

5. The mattress from the store still _____. Do you want me to call the manager?
    a. hasn't arrived   b. hadn't arrived

6. Mrs. Jones wasn't happy when she got home. Her husband _____ the children build a tent in
    the backyard with her best sheets.
    a. has helped   b. had helped

7. The phone _____ several times today, but when I answer it, no one is there.
    a. has rung   b. had rung

8. We _____ this rice dish until Dick's sister came to live with us. Now we eat it all the time.
    a. haven't tried   b. hadn't tried

Past progressive vs. past perfect *(Chart 4-9)*

Directions: Choose the correct completion.

1. When the school bell rang, all the children _____ quietly in their chairs. Their teacher was very surprised.

    a. were sitting   b. had sat

2. I kept trying to go back to sleep this morning, but I couldn't. The crows in the trees _____ too much noise.

    a. were making   b. had made

3. Amy and Don _____ before at a soccer game, but they didn't remember. There were so many people there at the time.

    a. were meeting   b. had met

4. While my breakfast _____, I decided to go for a short walk on the beach.

    a. was cooling   b. had cooled

5. The restaurant had so much cigarette smoke that we wanted go to another one, but the waitress _____ our order.

    a. was taking   b. had already taken

6. When my sister's old car broke down, she wanted to buy a new one, but she couldn't because she _____ enough money.

    a. hadn't saved   b. wasn't saving

7. I _____ dinner for twenty guests, but because of the snowstorm, only ten people showed up.

    a. was preparing   b. had prepared

8. We _____ on the beach yesterday when an eagle flew overhead with a small bird in its mouth.

    a. were relaxing   b. had relaxed

Present perfect, past progressive, and past perfect *(Chart 4-9)*

Directions: Check the correct sentence in each pair.

1. _____ The cake didn't bake because I had forgotten to turn on the oven.

    _____ The cake didn't bake because I have forgotten to turn on the oven.

2. _____ The dog was barking at a squirrel when I left for work.

    _____ The dog has barked at a squirrel when I left for work.

3. _____ The automotive company was knowing about the defects in their cars for years.

    _____ The automotive company has known about the defects in their cars for years.

4. _____ My brother changed his major and has decided to become a software engineer.

    _____ My brother changed his major and had decided to become a software engineer.

5. _____ The rain had started by the time we arrived at the picnic area.

    _____ The rain has started by the time we arrived at the picnic area.

6. _____ When we got to the theater to buy concert tickets, at least a hundred people were already waiting in line.

    _____ When we got to the theater to buy concert tickets, at least a hundred people have already waited in line.

Directions: *Complete the sentences with the correct form (affirmative or negative) of the words in parentheses. Use the present perfect, past progressive, or past perfect.*

1. I didn't tell Omar that you were getting married. I (**tell**) _____ anyone yet. You told me you wanted to let everyone know the good news yourself.

2. Rita e-mailed me that she had finally reached Manila. She (**arrive**) _____ _____ there a few days late.

3. When Mike got to the office to pick up Liz, she was on the phone. She (**talk, still**) _____ an hour later.

4. The stores were very crowded yesterday. I (**want**) _____ to get a few things on sale, but I couldn't even find a parking spot.

5. Tony falls asleep so easily. He (**go, even**) _____ to sleep while driving! He needs to see a doctor.

6. While I (**try**) _____ on shoes at the store yesterday, another customer asked my salesperson for help. I thought that she was very impolite to interrupt.

7. By the time Marta noticed that her vanilla sauce was boiling over on the stove, it was too late. The sauce (**burn, already**) _____ .

8. Sara (**have**) _____ nightmares about bears since she was a child. Her parents can't figure out why.

CHAPTER 4 PRACTICE TEST

Directions: *Write the past participle.*

1. pay _____
2. swim _____
3. know _____
4. wait _____
5. study _____

6. grow _____
7. leave _____
8. cut _____
9. begin _____
10. eat _____

Part II Present perfect vs. present perfect progressive

Directions: *Complete the sentences with the words in parentheses. Use the present perfect or the present perfect progressive.*

1. A: (**you, try, ever**) _____ to make homemade candy?

   B: No, I _____ . But I (**make**) _____
   chocolate sauce several times. It was delicious.

2. A: Your eyes are red. (**you, cry**) _____?

   B: No, I have dust allergies.

3. A: The cat (**scratch**) _____ at the door for 10 minutes.

   B: I think she wants to go outside.

4. A: (**Anna, stay**) _____ home alone yet?

   B: No, she _____ . She's still too young.

5. A: (**you, finish**) _____ your homework yet?

   B: Yes, we _____ . We just finished.

Part III SINCE vs. FOR

Directions: *Complete the sentences with* **since** *or* **for**.

1. I swam in the lake _____ two hours. I was quite cold when I got out.

2. We haven't seen the dog _____ yesterday. I hope she didn't run away.

3. You have looked tired _____ Monday. Are you getting enough sleep?

4. My parents have worked together _____ twenty years. They're going to retire together, too.

5. I haven't talked to Ben _____ last week. I hope everything is OK.

6. You have worked for the same company _____ such a long time. Don't you
   want a change?

Part IV Present perfect vs. present perfect progressive

Directions: Choose the correct completion.

1. What a mess! It looks like the dog _____ in the garden since this morning.
   a. has dug   b. has been digging

2. A gopher _____ a hole, too. Now he's hiding in it.
   a. has dug   b. has been digging

3. Since this morning, I _____ six dozen cookies. Now I need to wrap them up.
   a. have baked   b. have been baking

4. Heidi likes to play dress-up. She _____ her princess costume since we bought it yesterday. She even slept in it!
   a. has worn   b. has been wearing

Part V YET, ALREADY, STILL, ANYMORE

*Directions: Complete the sentences with **yet**, **already**, **still**, or **anymore**.*

1. The baby has been in her crib for an hour and she _____ hasn't gone to sleep.

2. The clock used to chime every hour, but last week the chime stopped working. It doesn't ring

   _____ .

3. The school bus is coming, and you're not ready _____ .

4. This math class is going to be easy. I've _____ studied algebra in my country.

5. I think I'll order another hamburger. I'm _____ hungry.

Part VI Tense review (past progressive, present perfect, past perfect)

Directions: Choose the correct completion.

1. Look! The storm _____ branches from the trees onto our lawn. It will take a long time to clean up.
   a. was blowing   b. has blown   c. had blown

2. Susie was upset. Another child _____ her toy train. She found it on the floor in several pieces.
   a. was breaking   b. has broken   c. had broken

3. I _____ really tired all week. I've been getting enough sleep, so maybe I should see a doctor.
   a. was feeling   b. have felt   c. had felt

4. I'm sorry I don't have any ice cream to offer you. The trunk of the car was so hot that by the time I got home, it _____.
   a. was melting   b. has melted   c. had melted

Directions: Correct the errors.

1. Since we have moved to this neighborhood, we made many new friends.

2. Francisco have attended the opera since he took a music class in high school.

3. Nadia hadn't finished her dinner yet. She can't have dessert until she does.

4. Gary is at work since 5:00 this morning.

5. We have been owning our home since five years ago.

6. It has been raining on my birthday every year for the last ten years.

7. My parents and I don't anymore write letters to each other. We send e-mails.

8. Already I have decided to major in marine biology.

CHAPTER 4 FINAL TEST

Part I Past participles

Directions: *Write the past participle.*

1. visit _____
2. speak _____
3. think _____
4. write _____
5. stand _____

6. buy _____
7. win _____
8. read _____
9. teach _____
10. sell _____

Part II Present perfect vs. present perfect progressive

Directions: *Complete the sentences with the words in parentheses. Use the present perfect or the present perfect progressive.*

1. A: (**you, wear, ever**) _____ a tuxedo?

   B: No, I _____ . They don't look very comfortable.

2. A: Billy, your clothes are all dirty. (**you, jump**) _____ in mud puddles?

   B: Yes, I _____ . I'm sorry.

3. A: This bee (**fly**) _____ around me for ten minutes.

   B: Why don't we go inside?

4. A: (**you, get, ever**) _____ a speeding ticket?

   B: Yes, I _____ . I (**get**) _____ two tickets.

5. A: (**you, do**) _____ the wash yet?

   B: Yes, I _____ . I just finished.

Part III SINCE vs. FOR

Directions: *Complete the sentences with **since** or **for**.*

1. I'm trying to lose weight. I haven't eaten sweets _____ a week.

2. The storm is so noisy that we've been awake _____ several hours.

3. Erica has been upset _____ she got to work. I wonder what's going on.

4. Rick has been running marathons _____ five years, but now his knees are starting to hurt.

5. We haven't heard from Sara _____ she moved. And she never sent us her new address.

6. _____ last year, our sales for the company have increased 30 percent.

7. The employees have been waiting for their paychecks _____ April. The company says it can't pay.

8. Our water bill has stayed the same _____ a long time. We'll probably have a large increase soon.

Present perfect vs. present perfect progressive

Directions: Choose the correct completion.

1. Oh no! I _____ my contact lens again.
   a. have lost   b. have been losing

2. I'm so tired of this rain. It _____ nonstop for two days.
   a. has rained   b. has been raining

3. The Smiths know a lot about other cultures. They _____ to many countries since they retired.
   a. have traveled   b. have been traveling

4. Since we started dinner, the phone _____ at least five different times.
   a. has rung   b. has been ringing

5. Karen _____ for 10 minutes, but Bob isn't listening. In fact, I think he's fallen asleep.
   a. has talked   b. has been talking

6. I don't think your baby feels well. She _____ for the past hour. I think she's getting sick.
   a. has cried   b. has been crying

Part V   YET, ALREADY, STILL, ANYMORE

Directions: Complete the sentences with **yet**, **already**, **still**, *or* **anymore**.

1. We can't leave for work because I haven't found my keys _____ .

2. Sally, Daddy will read you a story as soon as you're ready for bed. Did you brush your teeth _____ ?

3. I've been doing the laundry all morning. I've _____ finished four loads.

4. I took an aspirin, but I _____ have a headache. I think I'll lie down.

5. We love this woodstove, but we can't use it. It's so old that the company doesn't make replacement parts for it _____ .

6. Sorry. Your order isn't ready _____ .

7. It's _____ snowing. Will it ever stop?

8. Steve doesn't drive to work _____ . He rides his bike and finds it much more relaxing than driving.

Part VI   Tense review (past progressive, present perfect, past perfect)

Directions: Choose the correct completion.

1. Our school bus broke down. While we _____ for another bus, we sang songs and told stories.
   a. were waiting   b. has waited   c. had waited

2. I woke up tired, but I didn't take a nap because I _____ for ten hours.
   a. was sleeping   b. have already slept   c. had already slept

3. Jason _____ without a lifejacket. He's going to try tomorrow.

   a. has never swum   b. wasn't swimming   c. had never swum

4. The teacher _____ a poem when the fire alarm went off. Everyone left the classroom quickly.

   a. was explaining   b. has explained   c. had explained

5. Dennis _____ his ankle again. He needs to be more careful when he plays soccer.

   a. was hurting   b. has hurt   c. had hurt

6. I wanted to buy some new dishes, but I decided I _____ too much money on clothes yesterday.

   a. was spending   b. have spent   c. had spent

7. There was a lot of activity in the park this afternoon. Some children _____ on the monkey bars and swings, while others _____ a soccer ball on the field.

   a. were playing   d. were kicking
   b. have played   e. have kicked
   c. had played   f. had kicked

8. Dr. Brooks treats patients, and she _____ two medical devices that help people with heart disease.

   a. was inventing   b. has invented   c. had invented

Part VII Error analysis

Directions: Correct the errors.

1. Sandy have been trying to call you. Did she reach you yet?

2. Ted hadn't called yet. I wonder if he lost our phone number.

3. Still I don't understand the problem.

4. Andy is on vacation since Saturday.

5. Already the rain has stopped.

6. I have been knowing about those problems for a few weeks.

7. Chris has been starting his Ph.D. thesis several times. He's not sure about his topic.

8. My elderly mother doesn't anymore drive. She can't see very well.

9. William went to the same summer camp since he was eight years old. He really enjoys it.

10. Beth wanted to move to a bigger apartment since her mother has come to live with her.

ASKING QUESTIONS

Short answers to yes/no questions *(Chart 5-1)*

Directions: Answer the questions.

Example:
Are you ready? No, I 'm not _____.

1. Is dinner ready? Yes, it _____.

2. Will you leave soon? Yes, we _____.

3. Is John leaving soon? Yes, he _____.

4. Did it rain last night? No, it _____.

5. Has the mail come yet? Yes, it _____.

6. Have you seen Paul? Yes, I _____.

7. Do fish jump? Yes, they _____.

8. Will Mr. and Mrs. Johnson be at the wedding? No, they _____.

9. Are they going to be out of town? Yes, they _____.

10. Did we already tell you that? Yes, you _____.

Questions with DO, DOES, IS, and ARE *(Chart 5-1)*

*Directions: Complete the sentences with **Do, Does, Is, Are**.*

1. _____ Bill like fish?

2. _____ he like to catch fish?

3. _____ he going fishing tomorrow?

4. _____ you going to go also?

5. _____ you good at catching fish?

6. _____ the weather going to be nice tomorrow?

7. _____ there clouds in the sky right now?

8. _____ it look cloudy?

9. _____ you have plans for today?

10. _____ you going to be busy?

Directions: Choose the correct information word.

1. _____ does the party start? (At 9:30.)
   a. What time   b. Where   c. Why

2. _____ will the party be? (At Sue's.)
   a. What time   b. Where   c. Why

3. _____ can I find out my test results? (Tomorrow morning.)
   a. When   b. Where   c. Why

4. _____ did Jeff quit his job? (Because he wanted more of a challenge.)
   a. What time   b. Where   c. Why

5. _____ is a good place for us to meet? (At the Mountain View café.)
   a. When   b. Where   c. Why

6. _____ shall we meet? (10:00 A.M.)
   a. What time   b. Where   c. Why

7. _____ are you leaving? (Because I have a class in 10 minutes.)
   a. When   b. Where   c. Why

8. _____ did Dr. Smith call? (About an hour ago.)
   a. When   b. Where   c. Why

*Directions: Create information questions with **who, who(m),** or **what.***

1. _____? Henry. (Bill saw Henry.)

2. _____? Bobby. (Bobby saw the fox.)

3. _____? Mary. (Mary placed an order.)

4. _____? An order. (Mary placed an order.)

5. _____? Joan's parents. (Joan's parents bought a car.)

6. _____? Mr. and Mrs. Brown. (Mr. and Mrs. Brown came.)

7. _____? A dog. (Bill brought home a dog.)

8. _____? Susie's toy train. (Susie's toy train broke.)

Directions: *Create questions with* **what** + *a form of* **do** *to complete the dialogues. Use the same verb tense or modal that is used in the parentheses.*

1. A: _____?
   B: They study rocks. (Geologists study rocks.)

2. A: _____ when you turn 65?
   B: Retire. (I will retire when I turn 65.)

3. A: _____ to help you?
   B: Dry the dishes. (You can dry the dishes to help me.)

4. A: _____ when his car broke down?
   B: Called a tow-truck. (Carl called a tow-truck when his car broke down.)

5. A: _____ if it snows?
   B: Stay home. (You should stay home if it snows.)

6. A: _____?
   B: Trying to catch a butterfly. (Caroline is trying to catch a butterfly.)

7. A: _____?
   B: Go to the opening of the art museum. (We would like to go to the opening of the art museum tomorrow.)

8. A: _____?
   B: Study for his final exams. (David is going to study for his final exams this weekend.)

9. A: _____ when you heard the siren?
   B: Stopped my car. (I stopped my car when I heard the siren.)

10. A: _____ when your baby cries?
    B: Sing to her. (I sing to my baby when she cries.)

Directions: *Complete the questions with* **which** *or* **what**.

1. There are three different hamburgers on the menu. _____ one do you want?

2. All four dresses look nice on you. I don't know _____ one you should buy.

3. At _____ temperature does water boil?

4. _____ should I buy for Eric's birthday? He has so many toys already.

5. I have red, green, and blue marking pens. _____ one would you like?

6. Tom has lost so much weight that I don't know _____ size he wears.

7. There are two local newspapers we can subscribe to. _____ one would be best?

8. _____ color eyes do you have? They seem to change color with the clothes you wear.

9. I know you can write with both your left and right hands, but _____ do you prefer to use?

10. _____ score did you get on your driving test?

Directions: *Choose the correct word.*

1. _____ told you about my new job?
   a. Who   b. Whose

2. _____ coat is this?
   a. Who   b. Whose

3. _____ papers are on your desk?
   a. Who   b. Whose

4. _____ met you at the airport?
   a. Who   b. Whose

5. _____ picked you up?
   a. Who   b. Whose

6. _____ lunch is that?
   a. Who   b. Whose

7. _____ took my lunch from the refrigerator?
   a. Who   b. Whose

8. _____ wrote this book?
   a. Who   b. Whose

9. _____ is going to help you with your homework?
   a. Who   b. Whose

10. _____ homework is on the table?
    a. Who's   b. Whose

QUIZ 8 WHO'S vs. WHOSE *(Chart 5-9)*

Directions: *Write complete questions using* **Who's** *or* **Whose**.

1. A: _____?
   B: Pat. (Pat's calling.)

2. A: _____?
   B: Pat's. (This is Pat's cell phone.)

3. _____?
   Joe. (Joe is skipping the meeting.)

4. _____?
   Brad's. (That's Brad's laptop computer.)

5. _____?
   Kim. (Kim is coming.)

6. _____?
   Beth. (Beth is the new student.)

7. _____?
   Beth's. (Those are Beth's parents.)

8. _____?
   The school's. (That's the school's rule.)

Directions: Match each question with the correct response.

1. _____ How tired are you?   a. Six feet.
2. _____ How old is he?   b. Three months.
3. _____ How tall is your father?   c. 20 miles.
4. _____ How big is your apartment?   d. Four rooms.
5. _____ How far away is the airport? e. Poorly.
6. _____ How do you get to work?   f. Very sleepy.
7. _____ How did you do on the test?   g. By car.

QUIZ 10 Questions with HOW *(Chart 5-10)*

Directions: Complete the sentences with the words from the list.

cold	fresh	hard	soon
expensive	happy	old	

1. A: How _____ was the test?
   B: It was very difficult.

2. A: How _____ is that tree?
   B: A farmer planted it around 1800.

3. A: How _____ is it outside?
   B: The snow is starting to melt, so it's above freezing.

4. A: How _____ is this bread? It looks a little old.
   B: We just baked it this morning.

5. A: How _____ is Ellen with her new job?
   B: She loves it.

6. A: How _____ is this car?
   B: Before I give you a price, let's talk about what you want.

7. A: How _____ does the movie start?
   B: In five minutes.

*Directions: Complete the questions with **often**, **far**, *or* **long**.*

1. A: How _____ do you see your grandchildren?
   B: About once a week.

2. A: How _____ away do they live?
   B: About 35 miles.

3. A: How _____ does it take to get to their house?
   B: If traffic isn't heavy, it takes about an hour.

4. A: How _____ do you exercise?
   B: Three to four times a week.

5. A: How _____ do you run?
   B: Just a few kilometers.

6. A: How _____ do you spend at the gym?
   B: Usually an hour.

7. A: How _____ is it from your home to your office?
   B: About three miles.

8. A: How _____ do you get together with friends?
   B: A few times a week.

9. A: How _____ does it take you to get to school?
   B: About 45 minutes.

10. A: How _____ is it from here to school?
    B: About 10 miles.

QUIZ 12 Questions with HOW *(Chart 5-14)*

*Directions: Write questions with **how**.*

1. A: How _____ "elephant"?
   B: E - L - E - P - H - A - N - T.

2. A: _____ ?
   B: I'm feeling great!

3. A: _____ ?
   B: I feel great!

4. A: _____ ?
   B: We're doing well, thank you.

5. A: _____ "good-bye" in French?
   B: *Au-revoir.*

6. A: _____ this word?
   B: "Ms." is an easy word to pronounce. You say "mizz."

Directions: Create questions with **how** for the given answers. *(The information in italics will help you.)*

1. This water is *very* cold. You can't swim in it.

   <u>How cold is this water?</u>

2. Julie is *5 feet* tall.

   _____

3. We go to the movies about *once a month.*

   _____

4. I came here *by bus.*

   _____

5. Our school is just *three blocks* away.

   _____

6. We need to leave *in ten minutes.*

   _____

7. My dentist appointment took *one hour.*

   _____

8. Jon's birthday was yesterday. He's *twenty.*

   _____

9. It takes me *three hours* to make bread.

   _____

10. Mr. Wang speaks English *perfectly.* He sounds like a native speaker.

    _____

Directions: Create questions. Use **where, when, what, who, whose, why, how far, how long,** *or* **how often**.

1. A: _____?
   B: At the store. (Mari is at the store.)

2. A: _____?
   B: Joe. (Joe is going to help with the party.)

3. A: _____?
   B: On Tuesday. (On Tuesday we went to the circus.)

4. A: _____?
   B: Because I was sick. (I was at home because I was sick.)

5. A: _____?
   B: Next week. (Mr. and Mrs. Jones will leave for vacation next week.)

6. A: _____?
   B: 20 minutes. (It takes 20 minutes to drive from here to school.)

7. A: _____?
   B: Carmen's. (That is Carmen's car.)

8. A: _____?
   B: A sofa. (David bought a sofa.)

9. A: _____?
   B: Ten miles. (It's ten miles from here to the airport.)

10. A: _____?
    B: Once a week. (We eat out once a week.)

11. A: _____?
    B: At the doctor's office. (I've been at the doctor's office.)

12. A: _____?
    B: In two days. (We fly home in two days.)

QUIZ 15 Tag questions *(Chart 5-16)*

Directions: Complete the tag questions.

1. It's raining, _____ it?

2. You have a coat on, _____ you?

3. You took an umbrella, _____ you?

4. You're not sick, _____ you?

5. You'll call soon, _____ you?

6. Pam called last night, _____ she?

7. Your answering machine doesn't work, _____ it?

8. The Petersons are leaving for vacation soon, _____ they?

9. They're going to travel to several different countries, _____ they?

Directions: Complete the tag questions.

1. They've been around the world twice, _____ they?

2. But they haven't been to New Zealand, _____ they?

3. It's been a cool summer, _____ it?

4. It should warm up soon, _____ it?

5. It won't rain tomorrow, _____ it?

6. You don't have to leave yet, _____ you?

7. They can understand the problem, _____ they?

8. Kim had to change her plans, _____ she?

9. You would like to help, _____ you?

10. I don't have all the answers, _____ I.

QUIZ 17 Error analysis *(Chapter review)*

Directions: Correct the errors.

1. Who's cell phone is that, mine or yours?

2. I was right about the price of the computer, didn't I?

3. What kind ethnic food you like to cook?

4. When your plane arrives from Paris?

5. Whom helped you prepare the dinner?

6. Why you leave without me?

7. Who you did take to work?

8. How much often do you see your family?

CHAPTER 5 PRACTICE TEST

Directions: Write the information words.

1. A: _____ do you like this town?
   B: We love it.

2. A: _____ is picking you up from school this afternoon?
   B: My older brother.

3. A: _____ lunch is this?
   B: It's Pam's. She'll be right back.

4. A: _____ are you doing?
   B: I'm trying to fix my glasses.

5. A: Traffic was terrible this morning. _____ did it take you to get to work?
   B: An hour.

6. A: These are the two mattresses we can afford. _____ one would be better?
   B: The softer one.

7. A: _____ is Johnny crying?
   B: He fell down and bruised his knee.

8. A: _____ do you go to the post office?
   B: About twice a week.

9. A: _____ is it from here to downtown?
   B: About six kilometers.

10. A: _____ do you plan to graduate?
    B: In two years.

Part II   Questions

Directions: Write complete questions.

1. Sara is a runner. She trains *one hour a day.*

   _____?

2. She runs *30 km. a week.*

   _____?

3. She runs *very* fast.

   _____?

4. She is going to run in a marathon *next week.*

   _____?

5. She will run with *several co-workers.*

   _____?

6. She plans *to win*.

_____?

7. She spells her name *S - A - R - A, not S - A - R - A - H.*

_____?

Part III Tag questions

Directions: Add tag questions.

1. You work outdoors, _____?

2. It didn't rain last night, _____?

3. Jane's been very busy, _____?

4. We can leave early, _____?

5. They don't have to attend the meeting, _____?

6. Sam had to go to the doctor again, _____?

Part IV Error analysis

Directions: Correct the errors.

1. What you know about the new department manager?

2. That dog is barking so loudly. Whose it belong to?

3. What means "besides"?

4. Marta changed jobs last month, wasn't she?

5. Which movie you see last night, *Monsters* or *Dragons?*

CHAPTER 5 FINAL TEST

Information questions

Directions: Write the information words.

1. A: _____ are you living right now?
   B: In an apartment near campus.

2. A: _____ is it from here to your apartment?
   B: About three miles.

3. A: _____ did it take you to get here?
   B: 20 minutes.

4. A: _____ did you come here?
   B: I wanted to study at a university.

5. A: _____ do you go back home?
   B: About once a month.

6. A: _____ do you like it here?
   B: I love it!

7. A: _____ is helping you pay for school?
   B: My parents.

8. A: _____ do you plan to graduate?
   B: In two years.

9. A: I've forgotten. _____ major did you decide on, math or business?
   B: Business.

10. A: _____ homework is this?
    B: It's mine.

Part II Writing questions

Directions: Write information questions.

1. Paul is going to go *to the Smith's wedding* tomorrow.

   _____?

2. He plans to wear *a tuxedo.*

   _____?

3. He is going to take *his girlfriend.*

   _____?

4. He is going to drive *her* car.

   _____?

5. They are going to stay *for three hours.*

   _____?

6. Jill got a new job *last month.*

_____?

7. She works *at an internet firm.*

_____?

8. She is going to *develop marketing plans* for the company.

_____?

9. She plans to be there *for at least two years.*

_____?

10. She drives to work *three times a week.*

_____?

11. She goes to work *by bus* on the other days.

_____?

12. She works *60 hours* a week.

_____?

Part III Tag questions

Directions: *Add tag questions.*

1. You got home late last night, _____ ?

2. It isn't raining right now, _____ ?

3. You will be there, _____ ?

4. Jan can help, _____ ?

5. We don't have to leave yet, _____ ?

6. Dr. Wilson had to leave early, _____ ?

7. Martha is going to pay me back, _____ ?

8. Your dog is friendly, _____ ?

9. We're not lost, _____ ?

10. You forgot the directions, _____ ?

Directions: *Correct the errors.*

1. I need help. How you spell "either"?

2. How you feel about the talk you had with Jeff yesterday?

3. Whose left their dirty dishes on the table?

4. What kind soup you want for lunch?

5. Sonya needs more time, isn't she?

6. What means "anyway"?

7. How long it takes to get from here to your home?

8. Whom told you about the party?

CHAPTER 6

NOUNS AND PRONOUNS

QUIZ 1 Pronunciation *(Chart 6-1)*

Directions: *Circle the correct pronunciation.*

1.	dishes	/s/	/z/	/əz/
2.	chairs	/s/	/z/	/əz/
3.	mistakes	/s/	/z/	/əz/
4.	colors	/s/	/z/	/əz/
5.	keys	/s/	/z/	/əz/
6.	cats	/s/	/z/	/əz/
7.	boxes	/s/	/z/	/əz/
8.	cups	/s/	/z/	/əz/
9.	computers	/s/	/z/	/əz/
10.	desks	/s/	/z/	/əz/

QUIZ 2 Plural nouns *(Chart 6-2)*

Directions: *Write the plural forms of the nouns.*

1. tooth _____

2. mouse _____

3. leaf _____

4. baby _____

5. video _____

6. box _____

7. voice _____

8. banana _____

9. table _____

10. child _____

11. woman _____

12. business _____

Directions: *Identify the subject and verb of each sentence. Also identify the object if there is one.*

1. Steve asked a question.

2. His question wasn't clear.

3. The phone rang three times.

4. I answered the phone.

5. The party started late.

6. Jenny loves horses.

7. The police stopped several cars.

8. The drivers looked surprised.

QUIZ 4 Objects of prepositions *(Chart 6-4)*

Directions: *Identify the preposition and the object of the preposition.*

1. The little boy ran loudly through the restaurant.

2. Two teenagers fell into an icy pond near their home.

3. Rescuers found them beneath the ice and pulled them out safely.

4. The sun sets early during the winter months.

5. The students are waiting for the bus at the bus stop.

6. My vacation begins in one hour.

7. The weather will be clear until Friday.

8. The sun is beginning to show through the fog.

Prepositions of time *(Chart 6-5)*

Directions: *Complete the sentences with the correct preposition.*

The earthquake occurred . . .

1. _____ midnight.

2. _____ 12:00.

3. _____ Saturday.

4. _____ May 24th.

5. _____ May.

6. _____ 2002.

7. _____ the twenty-first century

8. _____ Saturday night.

9. _____ the spring.

10. _____ the early morning.

QUIZ 6 **Word order** *(Chart 6-6)*

Directions: *Complete the sentences. Put the italicized phrases in the correct order.*

   Example: We always eat   *at home*   *at 1:00*   *lunch*

        → *We always eat lunch at home at 1:00.*

1. Bobby found   *at the playground*   *last weekend*   *a diamond ring*

2. Tom bought   *on Saturday*   *a car*   *at a used car dealer*

3. Our cat left   *a mouse*   *on our doorstep*   *last evening*

4. The children blew   *in the park*   *yesterday afternoon*   *bubbles*

5. Our teacher corrected   *at lunch time*   *our papers*   *outdoors*

6. The new librarian put   *on the wrong shelves*   *the books*   *yesterday*

7. The dog barked   *on the road*   *this morning*   *at cars*

8. Rachel collected   *all afternoon*   *on the beach*   *shells*

QUIZ 7 Subject–verb agreement *(Chart 6-7)*

Directions: *Underline and identify the subject (**S**) and the verb (**V**).*
                  S   **V**
    Example: <u>Eileen and Jerry</u> <u>live</u> *on a farm.*

1. Every teacher needs to have patience.

2. There are several holidays in the next three months.

3. People in our neighborhood are friendly to each other.

4. Everyone had a wonderful time at your party.

5. The pronunciation of many English words does not match the spelling.

6. There is just one mistake in your paragraph.

QUIZ 8 Subject–verb agreement *(Chart 6-7)*

Directions: *Circle the correct verb.*

1. Every student at the university *lives / live* in the dorm for the first year.

2. The snow on the trees *is / are* sparkling in the sunlight.

3. Here *is / are* some used computers for sale.

4. Do you agree that everyone *needs / need* friends to be happy?

5. Some spellings in English *doesn't / don't* seem to make sense.

6. People around the world *wants / want* the best for their children.

7. The mountains in the distance *is / are* popular with climbers.

8. Parents of teenagers *has / have* many worries and many joys.

9. *Does/Do* your mother and father make major decisions together or separately?

10. There *is / are* at least twenty-eight moons around Jupiter.

QUIZ 9 Adjectives *(Chart 6-8)*

Directions: Underline the adjectives.

1. The TV and DVD player are new.

2. Here's a comfortable chair.

3. The coffee is weak. I'll make a fresh pot.

4. A strong storm is coming toward our area.

5. Please fill the empty bucket with some warm water.

6. Sometimes during hot weather we sleep in the basement because it is cool there.

QUIZ 10 Adjectives and nouns *(Chart 6-8)*

Directions: The following list contains adjectives and nouns. Write the words under the correct headings.

curly	old	house	toy	fun	day
easy	drink	quiet	happy	cloth	
dishes	clean	newspaper	book	interesting	

Nouns   **Adjectives**

Example:

____dishes____   ____curly____

_____   _____

_____   _____

_____   _____

_____   _____

_____   _____

_____   _____

_____   _____

Directions: *Check the incorrect sentences and correct them.*

1. _____ Your flowers garden has many unusual flowers.

2. _____ Mosquito bites itch.

3. _____ There is customers parking in front of the store.

4. _____ I see three spiders webs in the bathroom.

5. _____ All the computer printers in the library are new.

6. _____ Three people in our office are celebrating their birthdays tomorrow. There will be a lot of birthdays cake to eat.

7. _____ Don't throw away the eggs cartons. The children can use them at school for art projects.

8. _____ I love all the noodles in this soup. It's great noodle soup.

QUIZ 12 Personal pronouns: subjects and objects *(Chart 6-10)*

Directions: *Complete the sentences with the subject pronoun or object pronouns:* **she, her, they, them, we, us,** *or* **it.**

1. Mr. and Mrs. O'Brien celebrated their 50th wedding anniversary. Their children had a party for _____ . More than 100 people came to celebrate with _____ . _____ enjoyed sharing this special occasion with their friends.

2. My twin brother and I are very similar. _____ have the same friends and enjoy the same activities. _____ wear the same style of clothes. Sometimes our friends and teachers get _____ mixed up. _____ have a good time fooling _____ .

3. Cars drive too fast on our road. _____ have almost hit children a few times. The neighborhood needs to meet with the safety officials from the city government and talk with _____ about lowering the speed.

4. Sara got a new car last week. _____ planned to drive _____ to a friend's house, but on the way, a tree branch fell on _____ . The roof of the car was damaged. Sara was sad, but also very happy that it only hit the car and not _____ .

Possessive nouns *(Chart 6-11)*

Directions: *Use the correct possessive form of the nouns in* **bold** *to complete the sentences.*

1. (**earth**) The _____ orbit around the sun takes 366 days in a leap year.

2. (**Jones**) Let's see if we can stay at the _____ summer house during vacation.

3. (**wife**) My _____ brother is doing research in the Sahara desert.

4. (**student**) The teacher handed back the _____ papers and told them she was very pleased with their work.

5. (**theater**) The movie _____ sound system was scratchy.

6. (**actor**) It was hard to hear the _____ voices.

7. (**grandson**) We will be attending our _____ graduation next week. He finished his university studies in three years.

8. (**teacher**) The _____ mailboxes are near their classrooms.

9. (**hospitals**) The _____ nurses have voted against 12-hour shifts.

10. (**city**) The two _____ mayors reached an agreement to reduce air pollution.

Review: nouns and possessives *(Charts 6-1 → 6-11)*

Directions: *Make the nouns plural where necessary. Add apostrophes to possessive nouns as appropriate.*

1. Dolphin are intelligent.

2. The leaf of many tree change color in the fall.

3. My daughter boyfriend gave her a diamond ring for her birthday.

4. The tomato plant in my garden are not doing well in the cool weather.

5. I need to wash these knife and fork before we can use them.

6. Some people prefer taking shower, while others enjoy bath more.

7. Three goose at the pond in the park ran after some child. They were afraid and ran to their parent.

8. I bought several box of match at Bob store. They were on sale.

Directions: Circle the correct words in italics.

1. Could I borrow your pen? *My / mine* is out of ink.

2. Ingrid left *hers / her* car at school last night, and it was gone this morning.

3. A friend of *my / mine* sent flowers to my office today.

4. You have *your / yours* opinion and we have *our / ours*.

5. I haven't spoken to the Johnsons. What are *their / there / they're* thoughts on the matter?

6. Chris says the smoke is from a forest fire, but I think *its / it's* actually from burning trash.

7. Newlyweds Emily and Dennis work at the same company in the same department. *Their / There / They're* desks are next to one another. *Their / There / They're* happy to be so close. Friends of *their / theirs* wonder about this, but Rita and Tom think *its / it's* good for *their / there / they're* relationship.

8. A: Look at this wonderful dessert! Kelly made it for *our / ours* party tonight.

   B: I know. *Its / It's* very rich. I think it has three kinds of chocolate in *it / its*.

Directions: Complete the sentences with reflexive pronouns.

1. Luis works 60-hour weeks. He needs to take care of _____ .

2. You two have a good time at the party. Enjoy _____!

3. When Yoko was cutting vegetables, she accidentally cut _____ with the paring knife.

4. My dream is to own my own company and work for _____ .

5. When little Ella wakes up from her nap, she likes to play in her room and talk to

   _____ .

6. Before we begin the meeting, let's all introduce _____ .

7. Eric saw _____ in the mirror, but thought it was another baby boy.

8. The cat is licking _____ clean.

9. The children played by _____ in the park while their mothers watched.

10. Bill, you need to have more confidence. You need to believe in _____ .

Directions: *Complete the sentences with* **another** *or* **the other**.

1. I didn't understand the explanation. Could you give me _____ ?

2. This is a dangerous intersection. Last night there was _____ car accident.

3. We calculated the amount twice. The first result seems incorrect, but _____ looks OK.

4. One sandwich didn't fill me up. I think I'll order _____ .

5. I live in the desert. June is a hot month. August is _____ .

6. Benito has experienced three earthquakes. One was in Turkey, _____ was in Italy, and _____ was in Japan.

7. Brown paint is too dark for this room. Let's choose _____ color.

8. We had a windstorm yesterday, and the weather forecaster says there will be _____ tomorrow.

9. This word has four definitions. I understand the first three, but not _____ .

10. The boots I bought weren't comfortable, so I took them back and got _____ pair.

Directions: *Complete the sentences with* **other(s)** *or* **the other(s)**.

1. Plants need different environments to grow in. For example, some plants prefer shade and lots of water, while _____ grow best in full sun and a dry climate.

2. Juan speaks Portuguese and Spanish. Does he speak any _____ languages?

3. Some groups of stars in the sky are easy for me to identify, but many _____ are more difficult.

4. I had five homework assignments for the weekend. I've finished two, but now I have to complete _____ before school tomorrow.

5. Scientists have discovered a dinosaur fossil in this area. They are looking for _____ .

6. The morning flight to London is booked, but two _____ flights are open in the afternoon.

7. There are four pears in the dish. Two of them aren't ripe yet, but _____ ones are good.

8. The Italian flag has three colors. One color is red, and _____ are green and white.

9. There is only one baked potato left. All of _____ were eaten at lunch.

10. The teacher caught five students cheating. One student seemed embarrassed, but _____ didn't.

Directions: *Complete the sentences with correct forms of other:* **another, other, others, the other, the others.**

1. You have one idea about how to solve the problem, and I have _____ .

    Since we can't agree, let's keep looking for _____ ideas.

2. Oh, no. Look. I found _____ gray hair on my head!

3. Out of all the vegetables I planted this spring, only the peas did well.

    _____ died.

4. These jeans have a small hole in them. Do you have any _____ in

    this size?

5. The bus I was waiting for broke down, so I had to catch _____ one.

6. Let's order two pizzas. One will be vegetarian. What shall we put on

    _____ one?

7. I burned your hamburger. I'll make you _____ one.

8. The dog ran away with my only pair of dress shoes. I found one in the garden and

    _____ under the front porch.

9. Some people need eight hours of sleep, but _____ need less.

10. I can give you only one reason why Carl was asked to leave the company.

    _____ reasons are confidential.

Directions: *Correct the errors.*

1. There are thirty day in the month of April.

2. Our apartments manager is out of town this week.

3. The bird has brought some worms to feed it's young.

4. The mountains look beautifuls against the clear, blue sky.

5. I broke my right hand, so I need to write with the another one.

6. The cars in the city produces a lot of pollution.

7. One hundred people are waiting in the rain to buy ticket for the concert. Everyone seem patient, but cold.

8. The childrens swimming pool in the city is open to all children aged three to seven.

9. Mr. James company recycles old computer.

10. The dancers practiced all morning in the studio their dance steps.

CHAPTER 6 PRACTICE TEST

Part I   Nouns

Directions: Make the nouns plural where appropriate. Some words may need to be made possessive.

1. My children name are Emma and Ellen.

2. My sister has twins. Her baby name are Tyler and Spencer.

3. The new computer aren't working properly. The instruction aren't clear.

4. Beth computer is similar to mine. She's going to let me use hers.

5. There are several article on woman and non-traditional job in today newspaper.

Part II   Pronouns

Directions: Circle the correct words in italics.

1. Did you know that the Smiths are cousins of *me / mine?*

2. Hamid called the company and asked to speak with *his / him* manager.

3. Gary and *I / me* are vacationing in Mexico next month.

4. A: Are these sunglasses *your / yours?*

   B: No, they're *hers / she's.*

5. The Bakers invited Graciela and *I / me* to a piano concert in the city.

6. You're bleeding. How did you cut *you / yourself ?*

Part III   Forms of OTHER

*Directions: Complete the sentences with correct forms of **other**: **another, other, others, the other, the others**.*

1. Alex found several colorful shells on the beach. He brought one home, but left

   _____ on the sand.

2. After the Blakes got a kitten, they decided they needed _____ one
   so it would have a playmate.

3. We're sorry we can't attend your party. We have _____ plans.

4. I have several friends with unusual pets. One has an iguana. _____

   has a python snake. One _____ even has a baby alligator.

Part IV Error analysis

Directions: Check the incorrect sentences and correct them.

1. _____ Tony was born in April 2, 1998.

2. _____ In the past, students have done well on this test.

3. _____ Several languages schools offer university preparation.

4. _____ The bird's nest have several eggs in it.

5. _____ What are you doing in Thursday evening?

6. _____ Every student in the class is working hard and making progress.

CHAPTER 6 FINAL TEST

Directions: *Make the nouns plural where appropriate. Some words may need to be made possessive.*

1. Our dog had three puppy last night.

2. Whose book are these? I'd like to borrow them.

3. People at the lecture thought the speaker idea were fascinating even though she was still a high school student.

4. Professor Browns math class are very difficult.

5. The two other math teacher course are easier.

6. The university main computer is having technical problem, so student cannot register at this time.

Part II Forms of OTHER

Directions: *Complete the sentences with correct forms of* **other**: **another, other, others, the other, the others**.

1. My school offers instruction in several different sports. Golf is one, and swimming is

   _____ .

2. So far, your suggestions have been very helpful. What _____ ideas do you have?

3. Three-year-old Bobby needs _____ pocket in his pants to hold all his treasures.

4. If Matt gets _____ failing grade, he'll have to repeat the class.

5. My friends have given me three surprise birthday parties in the past. I was surprised by the

   first, but not by _____ .

6. Some people are early-risers, and _____ like to sleep until noon.

7. Andrew has transferred to _____ position in the company so he can

   get more experience in _____ areas.

8. Linda has four areas of study that she is interested in. One is biology, and

   _____ are related to computers.

9. The window washers need to wash only the windows on the front of the building.

   _____ windows are clean.

(continued on next page)

10. Judge White had already given the thief several chances to improve his life. After the last robbery, the judge told him he wasn't giving him _____ one, and put him in jail.

Part III Pronouns

1. The city bus was so full that it couldn't pick up my brother and *I / me*. *We / Us* had to wait an hour for another one. *It / It's* was pretty full, too.

2. Toshi is proud of *his / him* daughters. They did well in school, and now each one has *she / her* own company and works for *herself / herselves*.

3. The baby bird is chirping in *its / it's* nest, waiting for *its / it's* mother. *Its / it's* hungry.

4. My husband works at home. *His / Him* office is in the basement. *He / His* built it *himself, itself*. *He / His* enjoys working at home. *His / Him* manager is happy with the arrangement, also. *She / Her* says *he / his* is more productive now.

5. A: Which notebook is *your / yours?*
   B: *My / Mine* is the one with the star on the cover.

6. A: Whose seats are these?
   B: Those people over *their / there / they're*. *Their / There / They're* waiting in line for popcorn.

Part IV Error analysis

Directions: *Check the incorrect sentences and correct them.*

1. _____ We rented for one month a cabin in the mountains.

2. _____ Abdul spent the weekend trying to repair his father's cars.

3. _____ My apartments building is small. It has only eleven unit.

4. _____ Your appointment is scheduled for Monday in the afternoon.

5. _____ In the morning, I like to take in the park long walks.

6. _____ There is several car in our driveway. Who do they belong to?

7. _____ The table's surface have scratches on it from the children toys.

8. _____ In the future, every students will need to turn in typed assignments.

9. _____ I fell asleep nine o'clock last night.

10. _____ Be careful! The floors in the kitchen and dining room are wet and slippery.

CHAPTER 7

MODAL AUXILIARIES

QUIZ 1 The form of modal auxiliaries *(Chart 7-1)*

Directions: Add the word **to** *where necessary. If* **to** *is not necessary, write* **Ø**.

1. Do we have _____ leave right now?

2. The delivery driver couldn't _____ find our house.

3. You must not _____ touch the stove, Susie. It's very hot.

4. John isn't here. He must _____ be stuck in traffic.

5. You ought _____ try this dessert. It's delicious.

6. The weather reporter says it will _____ be sunny for several days.

7. You may _____ borrow my car if you are back by 6:00 P.M.

8. Shelley might _____ help if she has time.

9. I have got _____ get my hair cut. It's so long.

10. Farmer Peters had better _____ build a stronger fence. Some cows escaped from his field.

QUIZ 2 Expressing ability *(Chart 7-2)*

Directions: Write sentences with **can** or **can't** using the given words.

1. bees / sting _____

2. spiders / make / honey _____

3. snakes / talk / to people _____

4. computers / solve / math problems _____

_____

5. newborn babies / walk _____

6. bears / climb / trees _____

7. dogs / drive / cars _____

8. birds / fly / long distances _____

_____

Directions: *Decide if the meaning of the modal verb is possibility or permission. Write **1** for possibility and **2** for permission.*

> 1 = possibility
> 2 = permission

1. _____ You **may leave** now.

2. _____ I **might need** some help.

3. _____ You **can go** home early.

4. _____ I **may need** extra time.

5. _____ You **might not get** a seat in the theater.

6. _____ You **may not** sit there.

7. _____ You **can't eat** that candy.

8. _____ It **may be** nice tomorrow.

9. _____ We **can begin** work tomorrow.

10. _____ We **may start** work tomorrow.

QUIZ 4 Expressing possibility *(Chart 7-3)*

Directions: *Rewrite the sentences, using the words in parentheses.*

1. Maybe we'll go away this weekend. (**might**)

2. It might snow tomorrow. (**maybe**)

3. Our baseball team may win the championship. (**maybe**)

4. Joan may be in the hospital. (**might**)

5. David might take the driving test tomorrow. (**may**)

6. Maybe Sara will meet with us this afternoon. (**might**)

7. James may be late for the meeting. (**maybe**)

QUIZ 5 Meanings of COULD *(Chart 7-4)*

Directions: Decide if **could** *expresses past, present, or future.*

1. Just think! You could graduate in one year!
2. I could touch my toes when I was younger.
3. Traffic is a little heavy. There could be an accident.
4. Mr. Chu could speak fluent English a few years ago, but he's forgotten some now.
5. You could help me with the dishes after dinner.
6. There could be some damage from the earthquake.
7. I could be at work late. I've got a project to finish.
8. Katherine could tell time when she was three years old.

past	present	future

QUIZ 6 COULD and MIGHT *(Charts 7-3 and 7-4)*

Directions: Make guesses using **could** *and* **might**.

1. There are rain clouds overhead.

   It _____ soon.

2. Martin looks pale.

   He _____ .

3. Dr. Brooks is late.

   She _____ .

4. Our manager didn't come to work today.

   She _____ .

5. The temperature is below freezing.

   It _____ tomorrow.

Directions: *Check all the correct modals for each item.*

1. I have a headache. _____ I leave early?

    _____ May   _____ Could   _____ Can   _____ Would

2. I finished my homework. _____ you check it?

    _____ May   _____ Could   _____ Can   _____ Would

3. The copy machine is out of paper. _____ you refill it?

    _____ May   _____ Could   _____ Can   _____ Would

4. It looks like you have your hands full. _____ I help you carry your groceries?

    _____ May   _____ Could   _____ Can   _____ Would

5. This rice is delicious. _____ I have another bowl?

    _____ May   _____ Could   _____ Can   _____ Would

6. I need to make a call. _____ you let me know when you are off the phone?

    _____ May   _____ Could   _____ Can   _____ Would

7. Good morning. _____ I help you find something in the store?

    _____ May   _____ Could   _____ Can   _____ Would

8. _____ you hand me the phone, please?

    _____ May   _____ Could   _____ Can   _____ Would

9. Excuse me. _____ I sit here?

    _____ May   _____ Could   _____ Can   _____ Would

10. _____ you please tell me what happened?

    _____ May   _____ Could   _____ Can   _____ Would

Directions: Rewrite the sentences, using **should** or **shouldn't**.

    Example: It isn't OK for people to steal.

        People __shouldn't steal__ .

1. It's a good idea to dress warmly in cold weather.

    You _____ warmly in cold weather.

2. It's a good idea to say "please" and "thank you."

    You _____ "please" and "thank you."

3. It's not a good idea to drive over the speed limit.

    You _____ over the speed limit.

4. It's a bad idea to steal.

    People _____ .

Use **ought to**.

5. It's a good idea to call your parents.

    You _____ your parents.

6. It's a good idea to leave a generous tip for the waiter.

    You _____ a generous tip for the waiter.

7. It's a good idea to volunteer to help people in your free time.

    You _____ to help people in your free time.

Directions: Rewrite the italicized sentences. Use **had better** *or* **had better not**.

1. *We should clean up.* Our guests will be here soon.

    _____

2. *You should arrive early for your flight.* Otherwise you may not get there in time.

    _____

3. *Diane shouldn't leave.* She isn't finished.

    _____

4. *You shouldn't eat that chicken.* It doesn't smell good.

    _____

5. *Steve should hurry.* He's going to miss his bus.

    _____

6. *You shouldn't leave the garbage out.* Animals will get into it.

    _____

Directions: Make suggestions with **should**, **had better**, *or* **ought to**.

Example: Billy is walking on the carpet with wet shoes. His mother is upset.
→ Billy should take off his shoes. *or*
→ Billy ought to take off his shoes. *or*
→ Billy had better take off his shoes.

1. You just touched a hot pan and burned your finger.

   I _____ .

2. There is a snake in front of your door, and you need to leave your house.

   I _____ .

3. It's raining, and there's a leak in Sue's roof. Water is coming into her apartment.

   She _____ .

4. Mr. Smith finishes dinner at a restaurant and discovers that he has no money with him.

   He _____ .

Directions: *Circle the correct modal.*

1. Yesterday, our teacher *must / had to* leave school early.

2. We *had got to / had to* work quietly by ourselves until the end of class.

3. Why did she *have to / had to* leave early?

4. Did you *have to / had to* work late last night?

5. I *have got to / had to* get ready for the party. It starts in 15 minutes.

6. We *must / had to* be on time for this party. We were late for the last one.

Necessity: MUST, HAVE TO, HAVE GOT TO   *(Chart 7-9)*

Directions: Write the past tense of the verbs.

1. We **have to pay** a late charge on our credit card.

    We _____ a late charge on our credit card.

2. Jerry **must go** to bed at 9:00.

    Jerry _____ to bed at 9:00.

3. I **have to get** a flu shot.

    I _____ a flu shot.

4. Linda **must wait** for a doctor.

    Linda _____ for a doctor.

5. What **do you have to do**?

    What _____?

6. Who **has got to work** overtime?

    Who _____ overtime?

QUIZ 13 Expressing lack of necessity and prohibition   *(Chart 7-10)*

*Directions: Complete the sentences with **don't/doesn't have to** or **must not**.*

1. Those mushrooms are poisonous. You _____ eat them.

2. We _____ decide now. We can make a decision later.

3. You _____ tell anyone what I told you. It's a secret.

4. Sam _____ go to the office today. He can work at home if he

    wants.

5. You _____ throw your toys. They will break.

6. Thanks, but you _____ to pick up the baby's toys. I'll do it

    later.

7. Bill _____ go to the doctor. He's feeling better today.

8. The windows still look clean. I _____ wash them yet.

89

Directions: Write **1** *if the modal* **must** *expresses a logical conclusion. Write* **2** *if the modal expresses necessity.*

```
1 = logical conclusion
2 = necessity
```

1. _____ You must be John Jr. You look just like your father.

2. _____ You must wash your hands with warm water and soap.

3. _____ Ellen must know about the accident. She's a police officer.

4. _____ You don't look well. You must sit down for a minute.

5. _____ We must feed the animals before we leave for work.

6. _____ Julie must like school. She's ready an hour early every morning.

7. _____ I see lightning in the distance. There must be a storm approaching.

8. _____ Children, you must stay in your seats until the bell rings.

9. _____ You got 100 percent on the exam! You must feel wonderful.

10. _____ Your grades are low. You must not study much.

QUIZ 15 Logical conclusions *(Chart 7-11)*

Directions: Make a logical conclusion about each of the situations. Use **must.**

Example: Jose isn't here yet.
→ He must be caught in heavy traffic.

1. Nancy has tears in her eyes. _____

2. Bobby is shivering. _____

3. The Nelsons' son is getting married. _____

4. Mr. Nasser is holding a can of bug spray. _____

_____

QUIZ 16 Imperative sentences (Chart 7-12)

Directions: *Check the incorrect sentences and correct them.*

1. _____ You have to wait here. Only patients are allowed in the X-ray room.

2. _____ Please you don't come in. I'm not ready yet.

3. _____ I hear a siren. Pull over to the side of the road.

4. _____ Please you dress quickly. We have to leave.

5. _____ This table is a mess. Please put away these papers.

6. _____ You need to help more with the housework. I can't do it all myself.

7. _____ Run and you get the mail. See if your package has come.

8. _____ This soup doesn't have much flavor. Hand me the salt, please.

QUIZ 17 Stating preferences (Chart 7-14)

Directions: *Complete the sentences with the correct verb form of* **prefer,** **like,** *or* **would rather**.

1. Tom _____ fish to red meat.

2. I _____ leave now than later.

3. The Wilsons _____ warmer climates to cooler ones.

4. Dr. Smith _____ see his hospital patients in the morning than

   in the evening.

5. Joanne _____ smaller cars better than bigger ones.

6. My father _____ reading novels to watching TV.

7. Look at Jeannie! She _____ walk than crawl.

8. John and Jeff _____ to swim in salt water better than fresh water.

9. I _____ pens to pencils.

10. We _____ spend our vacations with our grandchildren than travel.

Directions: *Choose the correct completion.*

1. I'm not feeling well. _____ I lie down for a while on your sofa?
   a. Could   b. Would   c. Must

2. You _____ drive more slowly or you are going to get another speeding ticket.
   a. could   b. ought to   c. had to

3. _____ I borrow your pencil? Mine just broke.
   a. Would   b. May   c. Ought

4. You _____ finish your dinner. I gave you a lot to eat.
   a. must not   b. don't have to   c. couldn't

5. Jessica looks unwell. She _____ see a doctor.
   a. should   b. can   c. would

6. _____ you help me lift this box? It's heavier than I thought.
   a. Will   b. May   c. Should

7. I just heard a car door. Daddy _____ be home.
   a. would   b. can   c. might

8. Our dog _____ count! Listen to him bark as I say the numbers.
   a. should   b. can   c. must

9. You _____ be Sally. Mary told me you would be coming at 12:00.
   a. can   b. will   c. must

10. _____ you still be here when I get back?
    a. Will   b. Would   c. May

11. What can we do about Grandma? She _____ drive anymore. She's dangerous.
    a. doesn't have to   b. might not   c. shouldn't

12. I already paid the electric bill by phone. You _____ write a check.
    a. don't have to   b. shouldn't   c. can't

13. _____ you turn down the heat, please?
    a. Could   b. Should   c. May

14. When Kara was two years old, she _____ recognize letters and numbers.
    a. could   b. should   c. might

15. We _____ use our credit card at the store because their computers weren't working.
    a. shouldn't   b. wouldn't   c. couldn't

16. _____ you please repeat that?
    a. Could   b. May   c. Should

17. Your lips are blue and you're shivering! You _____ be freezing.
    a. ought to   b. must   c. will

18. You _____ turn off the T.V. right now. You need to finish your homework or you won't be ready for your exam tomorrow
    a. ought to   b. don't need to   c. would

19. I'm bored. _____ to the mall?
    a. Let's go   b. Why we don't go   c. Go

20. _____ we will come home from our vacation early. We haven't decided.
    a. May be   b. Might   c. Maybe

CHAPTER 7 PRACTICE TEST

Part I CAN, COULD, or MIGHT

Directions: Complete the sentences with **can**, **could**, *or* **might**. *In some cases, more than one answer is possible.*

1. Look at little Ben! He _____ walk!

2. I don't know where Pam is. She _____ be shopping.

3. When I was younger, I was in great shape. I _____ run for an hour.

Part II MAY, MAYBE, or MIGHT

Directions: Rewrite the sentences, using the given words.

1. Kathy / be / upset (**may**) _____

2. it / snow / today (**may**) _____

3. we / stay / home / for the holidays (**might**) _____

4. we / stay / home / for the holidays (**maybe**) _____

Part III SHOULD, HAD BETTER, OUGHT TO

Directions: Make suggestions, using the verbs in parentheses.

1. A: I'm tired. (**should**)

   B: You _____

2. A: I have a stomachache. (**ought to**)

   B: You _____

3. A: I brought another student's school books home by mistake. (**had better**)

   B: You _____

Part IV Modal verbs

Directions: Answer the questions. Use the modals in italics.

1. What is something you *must* do today?

   _____

2. What is something you *should* do when you are at school?

   _____

3. What is something that people *shouldn't* do?

   _____

4. What is something you *have to* do before you go to bed?

_____

5. What is something you *had to do* last week?

_____

Directions: Choose the correct completion.

1. I don't know if I can go to your meeting. I _____ have another meeting.
   a. maybe   b. might   c. will

2. Jenny _____ be more careful with her glasses. She has already broken them twice.
   a. have to   b. would rather   c. ought to

3. _____ you tell me the time, please?
   a. Should   b. Would   c. Must

4. You _____ use your cell phone while you are in the bathtub. You could get an electric shock.
   a. could not   b. don't have to   c. must not

5. I don't want to stay home this weekend. I _____ go hiking.
   a. let's   b. should   c. would rather

Directions: Correct the errors.

1. My grades are low. I had to better study more.

2. May you please open the window? It's hot in here.

3. I want to stay home tonight. Let invite some friends over.

4. We can't to come to your party. We will be out of town.

5. Susan maybe has a solution to the problem.

6. Jackie isn't here. She can be at home in bed.

7. You mustn't to walk in mud puddles.

8. Why we don't go out for dinner tonight?

CHAPTER 7 FINAL TEST

Part I CAN, COULD, or MIGHT

Directions: Fill in the blanks with **can**, **could**, *or* **might**. *In some cases, more than one answer is possible.*

1. These new glasses are much better. I _____ see much more clearly.

2. When I lived in Paris, I _____ speak fluent French.

3. I don't know why the Martins aren't here. They _____ have another party to go to.

4. I don't know if we have enough help. We _____ need to call more people.

5. When Dr. Kim was in medical school, he _____ work for days with very little sleep.

Part II MAY BE, MAYBE, or MIGHT

Directions: Write sentences. Use the given words.

1. the dog / be / hungry (**may**) _____

2. Jack / quit / his new job (**might**) _____

3. there / be / more news / today (**may**) _____

4. you / feel better / soon (**maybe**) _____

Part III SHOULD, HAD BETTER, OUGHT TO

Directions: Make suggestions using the modals in parentheses.

1. A: I have a cut on my hand. (**should**)

   B: You _____

2. A: I ate too much at dinner. (**ought to**)

   B: You _____

3. A: I got my second speeding ticket this month. (**had better**)

   B: You _____

4. A: I failed my math test. (**should**)

   B: You _____

5. A: I just told you a secret. (**had better not**)

   B: You _____

Directions: *Answer the questions, using the modal in italics.*

1. What is something you *had to* do yesterday?

   _____

2. What is something you *must* do before you can drive a car?

   _____

3. What is something that children *shouldn't* do?

   _____

4. What is something you *should* do when you don't feel well?

   _____

5. What is something you *have to* do before you go to school?

   _____

Part V Modal verbs

Directions: *Choose the correct completion.*

1. I need to make a call. _____ I borrow your phone for a minute?
   a. Would   b. Could   c. Must

2. Peter _____ not be sick anymore. I just saw him leave his house.
   a. must   b. maybe   c. will

3. The swimming pool provides towels. You _____ bring one.
   a. couldn't   b. don't have to   c. might not

4. We don't want to stay in hotels on our trip. We _____ go camping.
   a. had better   b. should   c. would rather

5. You _____ forget to pay your credit card bill or you will have a late fee.
   a. don't have to   b. couldn't   c. mustn't

6. We _____ hurry. The movie starts in ten minutes.
   a. prefer   b. had better   c. can

7. _____ meet at school. Then we can all go to the picnic in one car.
   a. Should   b. Let's   c. Why don't

8. Mom, _____ I sleep at Jennifer's house tonight? Please, please!
   a. may   b. will   c. should

9. Dinner's delicious, but I'm full. I _____ eat another bite!
   a. can't   b. might not   c. ought not to

10. Mrs. Wilson _____ change jobs. She'll wait a few weeks to decide.
    a. may   b. can   c. has to

CONNNECTING IDEAS

Punctuating with commas and periods *(Chart 8-1)*

Directions: Add commas or periods where appropriate. Capitalize as necessary.

1. Beth planned to serve pizza green salad and ice-cream at the party.

2. Sam Jeff and Ellen helped with the decorations Bob picked up the pizza and drinks.

3. The party started at 6:00 several guests were late.

4. A few people talked others played soccer and several people danced.

5. Everyone had a wonderful time no one wanted to go home.

Connecting ideas with BUT, AND, or OR *(Charts 8-1 and 8-2)*

*Directions: Add **but**, **and**, or **or** Add commas if necessary.*

1. Do you want to order dinner now _____ later?

2. I'd like rice, chicken _____ vegetables, please.

3. I mailed the letter two weeks ago _____ Pierre hasn't received it. Maybe it's lost.

4. Did you put one _____ two stamps on it?

5. My husband's favorite hobbies are gardening, boat building _____ bird watching.

6. Golf _____ snow skiing are expensive sports.

7. My favorite sports are soccer _____ swimming. They are more affordable.

8. Children, you can camp outside tonight _____ sleep in the family room. Which would be better?

9. Yoko decided to sleep in the tent _____ she got cold in the middle of the night and went inside.

10. I tried to start a campfire _____ the wood was too wet. I didn't succeed.

Directions: Correct the errors.

1. I'm feeling hot. I ought take my temperature.

2. Would I borrow your pen? Mine isn't working.

3. I don't feel like cooking. Let's we order a pizza.

4. We'll be free on Saturday. We could to meet then.

5. Look at the sky. Maybe it snow tomorrow.

6. Thomas is late. He can have car trouble again.

7. Children don't have to play with matches. They can start fires.

8. Why we don't go for a walk after dinner? It's such a nice evening.

QUIZ 3 SO vs. BUT *(Charts 8-2 and 8-3)*

Directions: *Complete the sentences with* **so** *or* **but.**

1. The game was on TV, _____ I didn't watch it.

2. The game wasn't on TV, _____ I listened to it on the radio.

3. Liz began to cry, _____ I hugged her.

4. Liz began to cry, _____ she wouldn't tell me why.

5. My father is sick, _____ I will stay with him for a few days.

6. My father is sick, _____ he doesn't want me to stay with him.

7. Twenty people were invited to the party, _____ only ten came.

8. The library closes in fifteen minutes, _____ we need to go there now.

9. I can't find my car keys, _____ you'll have to drive.

10. I don't have my library card, _____ Renee has hers.

QUIZ 4 Using auxiliary verbs after BUT *(Chart 8-4)*

Directions: *Complete the sentences with auxiliary verbs.*

Example: The peas in my garden are ripe, but the corn ___isn't___ .

1. Sara wants to buy a used car, but her husband _____ .

2. Fred isn't ready, but I _____ .

3. Khalid has finished his test, but the other students _____ .

4. Most of our class will graduate this year, but a few students _____ .

5. I haven't read that book, but most of my friends _____ .

6. These lights have fluorescent bulbs, but those lights _____ .

7. We aren't going to work this weekend, but a few co-workers _____ .

8. You won't have to wait, but other passengers _____ .

9. I heard from my parents, but the rest of the family _____ .

10. The children don't want to go to bed, but I _____ .

Directions: *Complete the sentences by adding appropriate auxiliary verbs. Add* **too** *and* **either** *as appropriate.*

1. Ray is a vegetarian, and his daughter _____.

2. Ray drinks milk, but his daughter _____.

3. Patricia sings in the school choir, and her brother _____.

4. This grammar book has an index, but that one _____.

5. Marco worked hard yesterday, but his assistant _____.

6. I didn't clean the apartment last week, and my roommate _____.

7. This offer has expired, and that one _____.

8. I can't speak fluent English yet, and my classmates _____.

9. We're going to celebrate New Year's in the city, and our friends _____.

10. We'll set off fireworks, but our friends _____.

Directions: *Combine the two sentences into one. Use the words in parentheses.*

Example: Mrs. Jones is a grandmother. Mrs. Smith is a grandmother.

    (so) _Mrs. Jones is a grandmother, and so is Mrs. Smith._

    (too) _Mrs. Jones is a grandmother, and Mrs. Smith is too._

1. James went skiing. Tom went skiing.

    (so) _____

    (too) _____

2. Eric won't help. Diane won't help.

    (either) _____

    (neither) _____

3. Judy has a cold. Her husband has a cold.

    (so) _____

    (too) _____

4. Mr. Thomas isn't going to retire. Mrs. Ellis isn't going to retire.

    (either) _____

    (neither) _____

Directions: *Complete the sentences by agreeing with Speaker A's idea. Use* **so** *or* **neither**. *Use* **I**.

   Example: A: I'm late.   B: So am I.

1. A: I can't find my keys.   B: _____

2. A: I wasn't hungry this morning.   B: _____

3. A: I've never met Janet.   B: _____

4. A: I enjoy flying.   B: _____

5. A: I don't like to wait at the airport. B: _____

6. A: I'll be gone next week.   B: _____

7. A: I'm going to be away on business. B: _____

8. A: I have a question.   B: _____

QUIZ 8 Connecting ideas with BECAUSE   *(Chart 8-6)*

Directions: *Write sentences with* **because** *using the given phrases. Pay special attention to the meaning. (Note:* **Because** *can come either at the beginning or in the middle of the sentence.) Add punctuation as necessary.*

1. I had a high fever / I went to the doctor

   _____

2. Cindy failed the class / she didn't study

   _____

3. we went to the beach / it was a beautiful day

   _____

4. I need to get new jeans / my old jeans have holes in them

   _____

   _____

5. my car is making strange noises / I feel uncomfortable driving

   _____

   _____

6. Andy is going to go shopping / his favorite store is having a sale

   _____

   _____

Directions: Check all the correct sentences.

1. _____ Because it was hot, I jumped in the cool water.

   _____ I jumped in the cool water because it was hot.

   _____ I jumped in the cool water, so it was hot.

   _____ It was hot, so I jumped in the cool water.

2. _____ My feet hurt, so I took off my uncomfortable shoes.

   _____ Because my feet hurt, I took off my uncomfortable shoes.

   _____ Because my feet hurt, so I took off my uncomfortable shoes.

   _____ I took off my uncomfortable shoes, so my feet hurt.

3. _____ Oscar began coughing because the restaurant was smoky.

   _____ Oscar began coughing, so the restaurant was smoky.

   _____ The restaurant was smoky because Oscar began coughing.

   _____ So the restaurant was smoky Oscar began coughing.

   _____ Because the restaurant was smoky, Oscar began coughing.

4. _____ The campers put away their food because there were bears nearby.

   _____ So there were bears nearby the campers put away their food.

   _____ There were bears nearby because the campers put away their food.

   _____ Because there were bears nearby, the campers put away their food.

QUIZ 10 EVEN THOUGH/ALTHOUGH and BECAUSE *(Charts 8-6 and 8-7)*

Directions: Complete the sentences with **even though/although** *or* **because**.

1. _____ his alarm clock rang, Paulo didn't get up.

2. _____ the bus was late, Lynn got to work late.

3. The bus was late _____ traffic was light.

4. My manager wants to begin a new project _____ we don't have any money for it.

5. _____ the economy is weak, I am worried about my job.

6. _____ our refrigerator is new, it isn't working properly.

7. The baby was crying _____ she was hungry.

8. I didn't enjoy the movie _____ I didn't understand it.

9. You can come to the party _____ you didn't get an invitation.

10. Benito is paying for dinner _____ he invited us.

Directions: *Check the correct sentences.*

1. ____ Although we try to save money, we always seem to spend more than we have.

   ____ Because we try to save money, we always seem to spend more than we have.

2. ____ The students stayed indoors at school even though there were storm clouds in the area.

   ____ The students stayed indoors at school because there were storm clouds in the area.

3. ____ The store is open at night even though it doesn't have many customers.

   ____ The store is open at night because it doesn't have many customers.

4. ____ Although the police could smell gas, they couldn't find a gas leak.

   ____ Because the police could smell gas, they couldn't find a gas leak.

5. ____ The kitchen smells delicious because we have been making cookies.

   ____ The kitchen smells delicious although we have been making cookies.

QUIZ 12 Punctuating adverb clauses *(Charts 8-6 and 8-7)*

Directions: *Add commas where necessary.*

1. Even though the roads were crowded we got home on time.
2. Alice can't eat peanut butter because she is allergic to nuts.
3. Because the students felt the building shake they got under their desks.
4. Erica can't figure out this puzzle even though she did it once before.
5. Brad's computer is slow even though he just upgraded the memory.
6. Although this TV is new the picture isn't very clear.
7. A lot of people are working even though it's a holiday.

QUIZ 13 Error analysis *(Charts 8-1 → 8-7)*

Directions: *Correct the errors.*

1. I enjoy science my favorite subjects are physics math and chemistry.

2. Julia doesn't participate in sports. Either her friends.

3. Our baseball team lost the game. Because not enough players showed up.

4. The downstairs phone isn't working properly and this one doesn't either.

5. I wore a hat and sunglasses so the sun was so bright.

6. My mother is Australian, my father is Brazilian.

7. Even though you're upset now, but you'll understand our decision in a few days.

CHAPTER 8 PRACTICE TEST

Part I Punctuation and capitalization

Directions: *Add commas, periods, and capital letters as appropriate. Don't change any words or the order of the words.*

Michelle decided the weather was too nice to stay at home so she packed a picnic lunch and drove to the beach even though it was crowded she found a place to sit she spread out her blanket and opened her lunch inside was a sandwich potato chips and an apple because she was still full from breakfast she ate only a little and saved the rest for later she took out a book and opened it minutes later she was asleep and she woke up just as the sun was going down

Part II Using AND, BUT, OR, SO, BECAUSE, EVEN THOUGH

Directions: *Complete the sentences with* **and, but, or, because, even though**.

1. Who's going to sing at your wedding, Kathy _____ Denise?

2. _____ there is a lot of construction in his neighborhood, Dick doesn't notice the noise and dust.

3. Your parents can see the children this Saturday _____ mine can see them next Saturday.

4. _____ Rita has had several operations, the doctors still don't know what is causing her illness.

5. _____ we have a large home, we'd like to invite all our relatives for the holiday dinner.

6. The spaghetti sauce didn't have enough flavor _____ I put extra garlic in it.

7. It looks like a long book, _____ it didn't take long to read.

8. _____ we drive small cars, we get good gas mileage.

Directions: *Complete the sentences with your own words. Add punctuation where necessary.*

1. _____ even though the test was easy.

2. I'm studying _____ _____ and _____ .

3. Because I have a lot of homework _____ .

4. _____ but I didn't.

5. Although Sandra wears glasses she _____ .

Part IV Error analysis

Directions: *Correct the errors.*

1. I study hard even my classes are very easy.

2. After the accident, my left arm hurt and too my right shoulder.

3. Blackberries, strawberries, blueberries. They all grow in our garden.

4. Because taxes were so high, and people refused to pay.

5. We were excited about the concert, but we got there early to get good seats.

CHAPTER 8 FINAL TEST

Directions: Add commas, periods, and capital letters as appropriate. Don't change any words or the order of the words.

Ron needs to decide if he is going to go to graduate school or if he is going to get a job he will finish business school in a few months although he has enjoyed being a student he wants to start earning his own money his parents want him to get a Master's degree they have said they will pay for it so they think he should agree to stay in school Ron appreciates their generosity but he also wants to be more independent at this time in his life

Part II Using AND, BUT, OR, SO, BECAUSE, EVEN THOUGH

Directions: Complete the sentences with **and, but, or, because, even though**.

1. Which would you like, fried _____ boiled eggs?

2. _____ the birds in the trees make a lot of noise in the morning, Joyce wakes up early.

3. Sometimes my parents take their early morning walk in the park, _____ sometimes they go to the mall.

4. I fell asleep at the train station, _____ I missed my train.

5. _____ Peter read the chapter several times, he still couldn't remember the important details.

6. _____ her son is in the hospital, Mrs. Davis has decided to take time off from work.

7. We went to several stores, _____ we couldn't find a birthday gift for Nathan. He's difficult to shop for.

8. _____ Melissa slept eight hours, she still felt tired in the morning.

9. Melissa slept eight hours, _____ she still felt tired in the morning.

10. The owner wanted too much money for his truck, _____ we decided not to buy it.

Directions: Complete the sentences with your own words. Add punctuation where necessary.

1. Because I am a student _____

2. _____ even though the food was expensive

3. Although the weather is nice the children _____

4. _____ but John did.

5. I saw _____ _____ and _____ at the park.

6. _____ so we hurried.

Directions: Correct the errors.

1. People couldn't describe the accident. Because it happened so quickly.

2. Even Nadia is a new student, but she has made many friends.

3. So a storm was approaching the sailors decided to go into shore.

4. You can either pay by cash and check. Which do you prefer?

5. Maria didn't understand the lecture. Neither I did too.

6. Sylvia worked because it was her day off.

7. Clams, prawns, and shrimp, they are seafood I enjoy.

8. My husband walks in his sleep, and so his brother, too.

COMPARISONS

Comparisons with AS . . . AS *(Chart 9-1)*

Directions: Compare the ages of the people, using **almost as . . . as** *or* **not as . . . as.**

John: 10 Paul: 43
Maria: 45 Rosa: 35

1. John _____ Paul.

2. Paul _____ Maria.

3. John and Rosa _____ Maria.

Compare the temperatures of the cities.

Yesterday's weather: Paris 70°F / 21°C
Athens 90°C / 32°C
Vienna 68°C / 20°C

4. Vienna _____ Paris.

5. Paris _____ Athens.

6. Vienna and Paris _____ Athens.

QUIZ 2 **Comparisons with AS . . . AS** *(Chart 9-1)*

Directions: Using the given words, complete the sentences with **just as . . . as** *or* **not as . . . as.** *Use a negative verb if appropriate.*

1. light chocolate / dark chocolate

_____ delicious _____

2. a bee sting / a mosquito bite

_____ painful _____

3. a sunrise / a sunset

_____ beautiful _____

4. a hard pillow / a soft pillow

_____ comfortable _____

5. a poisonous snake / a non-poisonous snake

_____ scary _____

6. eating / sleeping

_____ important _____

7. China/England

_____ large _____

8. a sports car / a school bus

_____ fast _____

Directions: Give the comparative and superlative forms of the following adverbs and adjectives.

1. sweet   _____sweeter_____   _____the sweetest_____

2. funny   _____   _____

3. dark   _____   _____

4. dangerous   _____   _____

5. sad   _____   _____

6. confusing   _____   _____

7. badly   _____   _____

8. carefully   _____   _____

9. busy   _____   _____

10. famous   _____   _____

QUIZ 4 Comparatives *(Charts 9-2 and 9-3)*

Directions: Complete the sentences with the correct comparative form (**more/-er**) of the given adjectives.

1. The Sahara desert is (**large**) _____ the Kalahari desert.

2. Brown rice is (**health**) _____ white rice.

3. Which is (**slow**) _____ : an elevator or an escalator?

4. A hardback book is (**heavy**) _____ a paperback book.

5. An essay is (**long**) _____ a paragraph.

6. Small grocery stores are usually (**expensive**) _____
   supermarkets.

7. Paying bills by phone can be (**convenient**) _____
   writing checks.

8. Fast-food restaurants serve food (**quick**) _____ sit-down restaurants.

9. I find classic movies (**interesting**) _____
   current ones.

10. Riding a bike with a helmet is (**safe**) _____ riding without one.

Directions: *Write comparative sentences using the given words.*

1. summer / winter (**warm**)

2. a turtle / a rabbit (**fast**)

3. a work day / a holiday (**enjoyable**)

4. air / rocks (**heavy**)

5. snow / ice (**soft**)

6. ice-cream / lemons (**tasty**)

7. a newspaper / a book (**expensive**)

8. vegetables / butter (**healthy**)

9. a CD player / a CD (**cheap**)

10. a month / a year (**long**)

QUIZ 6 FARTHER and FURTHER *(Chart 9-3)*

Directions: *Complete the sentences with* **farther** *and/or* **further**. *Use both if possible.*

1. If you need to discuss these matters _____ , give me a call.

2. The bus station is _____ from our house than the train station.

3. You can go now. We have no _____ need of your services.

4. If you don't get our plumbing fixed now, it may cause _____ problems later.

5. I was surprised we hiked all the way to the lake. We went _____ than we had

    planned.

6. If you need more information, please contact my lawyer. I have nothing _____

    to say.

7. My grandparents like their new retirement community, but it's _____ from

    town than they realized.

8. Since my surgery, I've begun taking walks. Every day, I try to walk a little _____ .

9. You'll need to take a train from the airport to your hotel. The airport is _____

    from the city than the travel brochures tell you.

10. We're almost home. We just have a little _____ to go.

Directions: Complete the sentences. Use the pronouns for formal English.

1. The Smiths have seven children. I have only two children. Their family is bigger than

   _____ .

2. Jose can count to one hundred in Spanish. The other children in his class can only count to

   twenty. Jose can count better than _____ .

3. I don't enjoy cooking. My husband loves to cook. His cooking is better than _____ .

4. Beth can run a mile in ten minutes. Susan can run a mile in eight minutes. Susan can run

   faster than _____ .

5. We bought a two-bedroom house. The Bakers bought a four-bedroom house. The Bakers

   bought a larger house than _____ .

6. Dr. Smith isn't an expensive dentist. The other dentists in the city are more expensive than

   _____ .

7. You can lift heavy weights. I can only lift light weights. I can't lift as much as _____ .

8. Gary is 33 years old. Annie is 30. Dan is 27. I am 22. Gary, Annie, and Dan are older than

   _____ . I am younger than _____ .

Directions: Circle the correct answer. More than one answer may be correct.

1. This fish is not _____ good. You don't have to eat it.
   A. very   B. a lot   C. much   D. far

2. My mother is _____ more active than my father.
   A. very   B. a lot   C. much   D. far

3. It's starting to snow. It must be _____ cold outside.
   A. very   B. a lot   C. much   D. far

4. Barbara has a sunny personality. She is _____ happier than most people I know.
   A. very   B. a lot   C. much   D. far

5. For me, math is _____ more difficult than a foreign language.
   A. very   B. a lot   C. much   D. far

6. You look _____ tired. Are you getting enough sleep?
   A. very   B. a lot   C. much   D. far

7. Susie's _____ excited about school. She will be in kindergarten this year.
   A. very   B. a lot   C. much   D. far

8. This painting is _____ prettier than I remembered.
   A. very   B. a lot   C. much   D. far

9. It's also _____ more expensive than I remembered.
   A. very   B. a lot   C. much   D. far

10. Janice is _____ older than her husband. They seem to have a happy marriage.
    A. very   B. a lot   C. much   D. far

Directions: Choose the correct answer. In some cases, both answers may be correct.

1. Green peppers are *less sweet than | not as sweet as* red peppers.

2. A shower is *less relaxing than | not as relaxing as* a bath.

3. High heels are *less comfortable than | not as comfortable as* slippers

4. Vegetables are *less fattening than | not as fattening as* sweets.

5. Taking a bus is usually *less fast than | not as fast as* taking a train.

6. This test is *less difficult than | not as difficult as* the last one.

7. My pillow is *less soft than | not as soft as* yours.

8. The fish from the grocery store is *less fresh than | not as fresh as* the fish from the fish market.

9. The air in the countryside is *less polluted than | not as polluted as* the air in the city.

10. Arithmetic is *less hard than | not as hard as* calculus.

Directions: Check the sentences that have unclear comparisons. Make the necessary corrections.

1. _____ Benito understands math better than his wife.

2. _____ The children like cold weather better than their parents.

3. _____ Ms. Wilson cooks more often than Ms. Davis.

4. _____ Khalid visits his parents more than his brothers and sisters.

5. _____ I watch TV more than my teenagers.

6. _____ Ernesto studies harder for his exams than Michael.

Directions: Complete the sentences with **more** *or* **Ø**.

1. I collect dolls. I have _____ dolls than my sisters.

2. Shelley runs _____ quickly than the rest of the track team.

3. The weather is _____ better today than yesterday.

4. The reading in our literature class is _____ harder than I expected.

5. You have 10 minutes left. Is that enough, or do you need _____ time?

6. A top-loading washing machine uses _____ water than a front-loading machine.

7. The last math test was pretty hard. I hope the next one is _____ easier.

8. The plants outside are so dry. We need _____ rain than we had last month.

9. This car has _____ miles on it than the salesperson told me.

10. The children are working _____ quietly today than they were yesterday.

QUIZ 12 Repeating a comparative *(Chart 9-9)*

Directions: Complete the answers by repeating the comparative in italics.

1. The weather will get *hot* in the next few days. In fact, the weather reporter says it will get

   _____ .

2. When I got my grades, I felt very *discouraged*. As the evening went on, I got

   _____ .

3. When we began our hike it was raining a little. As we continued to hike, it began to rain *hard*.
   We finally decided to quit because it rained _____ .

4. When Jerry starts to laugh, his face turns *red*. As he continues to laugh, he gets

   _____ .

5. Each term, my classes seem more *challenging*. I'm enjoying them even as they become

   _____ .

6. Oscar was not *relaxed* with his children when they were younger. But as they get older, he's
   becoming _____ .

7. My teacher can't explain geometry problems very well. I get *confused*. I don't ask for further
   explanations because I just get _____ .

8. Medical insurance continues to rise. It's very *expensive* for our family. It seems that every
   year, it gets _____ .

Directions: *Complete the sentences, using double comparatives and the ideas in parentheses.*

1. *(They argued. They became upset.)*

   As the couple argued, they became more upset. They tried to calm down, but

   _____.

2. *(The bus driver sang. The children laughed.)*

   The bus driver sang, and the children laughed. They enjoyed the bus ride because

   _____.

3. *(I was tired when I began to exercise. However, as I exercised, I began to feel energetic.)*

   _____.

4. *(My mom is cooking low-fat meals for me to help me lose weight. But her cooking is delicious, and*

   I'm eating a lot of food.) I'm finding that _____

   _____.

Directions: *Complete the sentences with superlatives and the appropriate word:* **in**, **of**, *or* **ever**.

1. The kitchen is (**warm**) _____ room _____ our house.

2. Heidi is (**fast**) _____ word-processor _____ our class.

3. There are several talented singers in our choir, but Marcos has (**beautiful**)

   _____ voice _____ all.

4. I had a terrible day at work yesterday. It was one of (**bad**) _____

   days I've _____ had.

5. Siberia is one of (**cold**) _____ places _____ the world.

6. My ears hurt! That was (**noisy**) _____ concert I've _____

   been to.

7. It's frustrating. Mr. Jones works (**hard**) _____

   all, but his managers don't seem to notice.

8. For their anniversary, Joanne and Ted decided to try (**expensive**) _____

   _____ restaurant _____ town.

9. When I gave my speech, my knees were shaking. It was (**less/confident**)

   _____ I've _____ felt.

10. _____ all the people in our class, Theresa is (**lazy**) _____ and

    (**lucky**) _____. She does very little work and always gets high

    grades.

THE SAME, SIMILAR, DIFFERENT, LIKE, ALIKE *(Chart 9-12)*

Directions: Complete the sentences with **as, to, from,** *or* **Ø.**

1. My three-year-old son thinks that donkeys look similar _____ zebras.

2. He says they look alike _____ because of their ears.

3. Sometimes, Spiro looks like _____ he's not listening, but actually he's just concentrating.

4. My new house is similar _____ my old house, but it's more updated.

5. Fortunately, the appliances are different _____ my old ones. They're much newer.

6. A panda is similar _____ a bear, but they are not the same _____ . Bears don't have thumbs, but pandas do.

7. Is the town where you grew up much different _____ this city?

8. The size of this town is the same _____ my hometown, but the architecture is very different _____ .

9. Toshi was much different _____ the description people gave me. Everyone said he would be shy, but I found him to be quite talkative.

10. People say my sister and I are similar _____ each other, but we don't think we are similar _____ at all. We have entirely different interests.

QUIZ 16 THE SAME, SIMILAR, DIFFERENT, LIKE, ALIKE *(Chart 9-12)*

Directions: Compare the size of the clouds. Use **the same, similar, different, like,** *or* **alike.**

A   B   C   D

1. Figure A is _____ Figure B.

2. Figure A and Figure B and _____ .

3. A and D are _____ .

4. A is _____ C.

5. C is _____ D.

6. All of the figures are _____ each other.

7. All of the figures are _____ .

Directions: Complete the sentences, using **the same**, **similar**, **different**, **like**, *or* **alike**.

1. Dick likes comedy, and Sharon likes drama. Their taste in movies is very

   _____ .

2. I'm sorry, but we can't accept your credit card. The signature on the card and the one on the

   receipt are not _____ .

3. Greg and Joe are cousins, but people think they are twin brothers. They have _____

   _____ facial features, and they talk and walk _____ .

4. "They're," "their," and "there" all have _____ pronunciation.

5. Doug wants to marry someone who thinks _____ him.

6. A chipmunk looks _____ to a squirrel.

7. The clouds in this city are very low in the sky. The clouds in my hometown seem higher.

   Even though both cities are very rainy, the weather patterns are not _____ .

8. How are queen bees _____ from worker bees?

QUIZ 18 Error analysis *(Chapter review)*

Directions: Correct the errors.

1. The most friendliest person in our class is Julie.

2. The food at the restaurant was less good than the last time we were there.

3. The movie was very funny than we expected. We laughed the whole time.

4. Anna washes her dog more often than her children.

5. Matt's behavior is embarrassing. He keeps acting alike a teenager, but he's 50.

6. I have a same bag as you. Where did you buy yours?

7. My grandfather always said that one of the biggest mistake in his life was spending too much

   time away from his family.

8. For Jon, the game of chess is alike an interesting math puzzle.

9. As the horse got tired, he began walking slower and more slow.

10. The driving test was hard, more than I expected.

CHAPTER 9 PRACTICE TEST

Part I   Comparatives and superlatives

Directions: Complete the sentences with the comparative form or the superlative form of the given adjectives.

1. Did you know that cold water is (**heavy**) _____ warm water?

2. In our town, December is very cold and windy. Sometimes, December is (**cold**)

   _____ January. Of all the months, August is (**hot**)

   _____ .

3. Which movies do you think are (**bad**) _____ for children:

   movies with violence or movies with bad language?

4. Some artists prefer to paint with watercolors, but I think oils are (**pretty**)

   _____ and (**elegant**) _____

   _____ watercolors.

5. Did you know that Greenland is (**big**) _____ island in the

   world?

6. The cheesecake was wonderful. It was one of (**delicious**) _____

   _____ cheesecakes I've ever eaten.

Part II   AS . . . AS, THE SAME, DIFFERENT, LIKE, -ER . . . THAN, THE . . . -EST

*Directions: Compare the following circles, using **big** or **small** where appropriate.*

A   B   C   D   E

1. (**as . . . as**) _____

2. (**not as . . . as**) _____

3. (**the . . . -est**) _____

4. (**like**) _____

5. (**-er . . . than**) _____

6. (the same) _____

7. (different) _____

Part III

Prepositions

Directions: Complete the sentences, using **in**, **of**, **as**, **to**, **from**, *or* **Ø**.

1. _____ all the tests we've taken, that was the most challenging.

2. White bread is not as nutritious _____ whole wheat bread.

3. Who is the funniest student _____ your class?

4. I think Professor Brown's teaching methods are very different _____ Professor Green's.

5. Mrs. Thompson thinks it's cute to dress her twins alike _____ .

6. A lake is similar _____ a sea, but it is smaller.

Part IV

Double comparatives

Directions: Create sentences, using double comparatives and the ideas in parentheses.

1. *(Rick sat in the hot tub for a long time. He became relaxed.)*

_____

2. *(Johnny made many mistakes in his homework. He became frustrated.)*

_____

3. *(If a ball falls far, it goes fast.)*

_____

Error analysis

Directions: Correct the errors.

1. Let's buy this chair. It's less expensive from that one.

2. My brother is smaller than mine.

3. Baby Danny's hair is long and curly, so many people think he look a girl.

4. I got enough sleep. I'm not as tired today than yesterday.

5. The budget department gave us a lot money this year than last year. We can sure use the extra money.

6. If you need farther assistance, please ask.

CHAPTER 9 FINAL TEST

Part I   Comparatives and superlatives

Directions: Complete the sentences with the comparative form or superlative form of the given adjectives.

1. It's (**easy**) _____ to drive on State Street _____ Park Avenue because

   there is less traffic.

2. We learned today that light travels (**fast**) _____ sound.

3. The train trip took (**long**) _____ we expected, but it was very scenic.

   We saw some of (**lovely**) _____ sights we have ever seen.

4. Mexico City is (**large**) _____ city in Mexico. It is also is one

   of the world's (**populated**) _____ cities.

5. Our debate topic for next month is (**bad**) " _____ person in history."

   I wish the teacher had assigned us (**famous**) " _____

   person in history."

6. I can read French (**good**) _____ I can speak it.

7. Which is (**small**) _____ : the moon or the earth?

8. The (**big**) _____ lake in the world is the Caspian Sea.

9. How much (**far**) _____ do we have to drive? I'm getting hungry.

Part II   AS . . . AS, THE SAME, SIMILAR, DIFFERENT, LIKE, -ER . . . THAN, THE . . . -EST.

*Directions: Compare heights of the following trees. Use **tall** or **short** where appropriate.*

A   B   C   D   E

1. (**like**) _____

2. (**similar**) _____

3. (**almost as . . . as**) _____

4. (**not as . . . as**) _____

5. (**-er . . . than**) _____

A   B   C   D   E

6. (the . . . -est) _____

7. (the same) _____

Part III Prepositions

Directions: Complete the sentences, using **in**, **of**, **as**, **to**, **from**, *or* **Ø**.

1. A maple tree does not grow as tall _____ a redwood tree.

2. What is the coldest place _____ the world?

3. The public transportation system in this city is very different _____ the system in my country. My country has more subways and buses.

4. How are a duck and a goose alike _____ ?

5. _____ all the cities I've traveled to, Kuala Lumpur was definitely the hottest.

6. The artist who did this painting has a style similar _____ the artist in the gallery, but he is not as well known.

7. Michelle is the most talented manager _____ the company.

8. _____ the three children, Mary looks the most like her mother.

9. The snow was not as good for sledding today _____ yesterday.

10. Henry is a fast worker, but he is the least dedicated _____ all the employees.

Part IV Double comparatives

Directions: Create sentences using double comparatives and the ideas in parentheses.

1. (*Emily works hard. She earns a lot of money.*)

_____

2. (*The water became rough. The children in the boat were scared.*)

_____

3. (*Karen played the piano loudly. The dog barked.*)

_____

4. (*The ideas came fast. The writer wrote many pages.*)

_____

Part V Error analysis

Directions: *Correct the errors.*

1. These peas are delicious. I didn't know that fresh peas tasted so much better as frozen peas.

2. The flu can be a dangerous illness. It's very dangerous to have the flu than a cold.

3. Who has a more good life: a married person or a single person?

4. The clouds look dark. Let's hope it's not as rainy this afternoon that it was this morning.

5. The nine planets, Pluto is the smallest.

6. What has been a happyiest day in your life so far?

7. The baby got tired and more tired at the park.

8. A largest bird is the ostrich, but elephants are the largest land animals.

9. One of the strongest metal in the world is titanium.

10. Mrs. Davis helps her children more than her husband.

THE PASSIVE

Active vs. passive *(Charts 10-1 and 10-2)*

Directions: Circle ACTIVE *if the sentence is active. Circle* PASSIVE *if it is passive.*

1. ACTIVE   PASSIVE   William brought gifts to the wedding.

2. ACTIVE   PASSIVE   The grass was cut by the gardener.

3. ACTIVE   PASSIVE   The teacher is looking for errors on the test.

4. ACTIVE   PASSIVE   The newspaper was delivered by the mail carrier.

5. ACTIVE   PASSIVE   Earthquakes are measured by seismographs.

6. ACTIVE   PASSIVE   The earthquake moved the road.

7. ACTIVE   PASSIVE   The flowers were eaten by deer

8. ACTIVE   PASSIVE   The cat has scratched the furniture.

9. ACTIVE   PASSIVE   The movie was written by the director.

10. ACTIVE   PASSIVE   The magician performs magic tricks at birthday parties.

Active vs. passive *(Charts 10-1 and 10-2)*

Directions: Change the verbs to the passive. Do not change the tense.

1. Amy writes the report.

   The report _____ by Amy.

2. The managers write reports.

   Reports _____ by the managers.

3. Amy wrote the report.

   The report _____ by Amy.

4. Amy has written the report.

   The report _____ by Amy.

5. The managers have written reports.

   Reports _____ by the managers.

6. Amy will write the report.

   The report _____ by Amy.

7. Amy is going to write the report.

   The report _____ by Amy.

8. The managers are going to write the reports.

   The reports _____ by the managers.

Review of past participles   *(Charts 2-6 and 2-7)*

Directions: Write the past participles of the verbs.

1. buy   bought   _____
2. explain   explained   _____
3. rent   rented   _____
4. make   made   _____
5. sell   sold   _____
6. eat   ate   _____
7. tell   told   _____
8. throw   threw   _____
9. know   knew   _____
10. grow   grew   _____
11. feed   fed   _____
12. cut   cut   _____
13. catch   caught   _____
14. shoot   shot   _____
15. lose   lost   _____
16. wear   wore   _____

QUIZ 4 Forms of the passive   *(Charts 10-1 and 10-2)*

Directions: Change the verbs to the passive. Do not change the tense.

1. Rob drove Martha to school.

    Martha _____ to school by Rob.

2. The builder will fix our roof.

    Our roof _____ by our builder.

3. Our gift is going to surprise you.

    You _____ by our gift.

4. The students clean the classrooms.

    The classrooms _____ by the students.

5. The manager has checked our room.

    Our room _____ by the manager.

6. Mr. Fernandez signed the checks.

    The checks _____ by Mr. Fernandez.

Active vs. passive *(Charts 10-1 and 10-2)*

Directions: *Change the sentences from active to passive.*

1. The hospital will open a clinic.

2. The doctors are discussing a new treatment.

3. The nurse has given an injection.

4. Patients speak several different languages.

5. Electricians are going to install televisions in the rooms.

6. Volunteers painted the rooms.

QUIZ 6 Active vs. passive: question forms *(Charts 10-1 and 10-2)*

Directions: *Change the sentences from active to passive.*

1. Did the other team win the game?

2. Do the police know the suspects?

3. Will Gary clean the garage?

4. Is the mechanic going to fix your car?

5. Has the union reached an agreement?

6. Does your accountant keep old financial records?

7. Are your parents going to sign the forms?

Directions: Circle the letter of the sentence that has the same meaning as the given sentence.

1. You will be told the news later.
   a. You will give someone the news.
   b. Someone will give you the news.

2. The stores are managed by the mall.
   a. The mall manages the stores.
   b. The store manages the mall.

3. The dog chased the mouse by the river.
   a. The mouse was chased by the dog.
   b. The dog was chased by the river.

4. The story has been read to the children several times.
   a. The children have read the story.
   b. Someone has read to the children.

5. Chef Daniel cooks the guests' meals by himself on Monday nights.
   a. The meals are cooked by Chef Daniel.
   b. Someone else cooks the guests' meals.

QUIZ 8 Passive to active *(Charts 10-1 and 10-2)*

Directions: Change the sentences from passive to active. Keep the same verb tense.

1. The book was discussed by the students.

2. The company's name has been changed by the management.

3. The thief was caught by the police.

4. The soldiers were given orders by the leaders.

5. We have been invited to the ceremony by our president.

6. The game is going to be won by our team.

7. The telephone lines have been cut by a repair person.

8. An award will be given to Mr. Reed by the city.

Directions: Circle TRANSITIVE *if the verb takes an object. Circle* INTRANSITIVE *if it does not.*

1. TRANSITIVE   INTRANSITIVE   Andy swam in the ocean.

2. TRANSITIVE   INTRANSITIVE   Julia met Antonio at the library.

3. TRANSITIVE   INTRANSITIVE   The lawyer considered the problem.

4. TRANSITIVE   INTRANSITIVE   The bus driver drove down the wrong street.

5. TRANSITIVE   INTRANSITIVE   The packages will arrive two weeks late.

6. TRANSITIVE   INTRANSITIVE   Gina eats eggs for breakfast every morning.

7. TRANSITIVE   INTRANSITIVE   Dick and Susan never agree with each other.

8. TRANSITIVE   INTRANSITIVE   The fish died after a week in the fish tank.

9. TRANSITIVE   INTRANSITIVE   Chemicals killed the fish.

10. TRANSITIVE   INTRANSITIVE   Mr. Park invited his parents to the theater.

11. TRANSITIVE   INTRANSITIVE   A storm hit the coast last night.

12. TRANSITIVE   INTRANSITIVE   The children broke the window with a ball.

QUIZ 10 Active and passive *(Charts 10-1 → 10-3)*

Directions: Change the sentences to passive if possible.

1. Jonathan was involved in a serious car accident last night.

2. The plumber has finally fixed our sink.

3. Pedro is going to leave before sunrise.

4. We rode in a limousine to our wedding.

5. The Tangs stayed at a friend's summer house last month.

6. Lightning struck one of the cows in the pasture.

7. The board of directors will sell the company next month.

8. The answering machine has recorded the conversation.

Directions: *Change the active sentences to passive. Use the **by**-phrase only if necessary.*

1. Someone gave me this sweater.

2. Bill Gates and Paul Allen created Microsoft.

3. People check out books at a library.

4. Has anyone ever lied to you?

5. Picasso painted the picture.

6. Someone will paint these walls tomorrow.

7. People speak French and English in Canada.

8. When did someone first use cell phones?

9. The horse kicked Mr. Hill.

10. The referee has stopped the basketball game.

QUIZ 12 **Progressive tenses in passive** (Chart 10-5)

Directions: *Complete the sentences with the passive forms of the present and past progressive.*

1. Jonathan is taking care of the children this afternoon.

   The children _____ by Jonathan this afternoon.

2. The president was presenting awards when the fire alarm went off.

   Awards _____ by the president when the fire alarm went off.

3. The police were directing traffic when a city bus ran a red light.

   Traffic _____ by the police when a city bus ran a red light.

4. Someone is helping Mrs. Henderson with her housecleaning.

   Mrs. Henderson _____ with her housecleaning.

5. The gardener is cutting the grass today instead of tomorrow.

   The grass _____ by the gardener today instead of tomorrow.

6. The fire chief is investigating the cause of the fire.

   The cause of the fire _____ by the fire chief.

7. A road crew was repairing the road when the tornado struck.

   The road _____ when the tornado struck.

8. Someone is filming a movie about our town.

   A movie about our town _____ .

9. Someone is wrapping your gifts. Your gifts _____ .

10. Everyone stood quietly while people were reading the names of the soldiers.

    Everyone stood quietly while the names of the soldiers _____ .

Stative passive *(Chart 10-7)*

Directions: *Complete the sentences with appropriate prepositions.*

1. Julie has been divorced _____ Fred for two years.

2. The teachers were disappointed _____ our test scores.

3. This pot is made _____ clay.

4. Nicole is engaged _____ Francisco.

5. Yolanda is devoted _____ her elderly mother.

6. You seem very qualified _____ the job.

7. Are you done _____ the computer yet?

8. We are acquainted _____ the Browns, but we don't know them well.

QUIZ 18 Stative passive *(Chart 10-7)*

Directions: *Complete the sentences with the bolded words. Use the passive form, simple present, or simple past. Include prepositions where necessary.*

1. (**excite**) We _____ our new jobs. They begin next week.

2. (**oppose**) The president _____ higher taxes right now.

3. (**interest**) The baby _____ the bright-colored toys you have.

4. (**relate**) You look like Mr. Miller. _____ you _____ him?

5. (**satisfy**) The doctor _____ your progress at this time.

6. (**involve**) The children _____ soccer and basketball practice yesterday.

7. (**exhaust**) When Ed got home, he _____ work.

8. (**crowd**) I'm afraid the mall _____ holiday shoppers today.

9. (**compose**) What _____ this material _____ ?

10. (**scare**) The dog's barking. She _____ loud noises.

Participial adjectives: -ED vs. –ING *(Chart 10-8)*

Directions: Complete the sentences with the appropriate **–ed** *or* **–ing** *form of the words in italics.*

1. Po watched the news. It *surprised* him.

   a. Po was _____ .

   b. The news was _____ .

2. I work in a bank. The work *interests* me.

   a. It is _____ work.

   b. I am _____ in the work.

   c. The work is _____ .

3. The team won the game 60 to 0. The score still *amazes* the players.

   a. The score was _____ .

   b. The players are _____ .

   c. It was an _____ score.

Participial adjectives: -ED vs. –ING *(Chart 10-8)*

Directions: Circle the correct adjective.

1. Babies are *interested / interesting* in black and white objects.

2. It's very stormy outside. The children are *frightened / frightening* by the wind and the thunder. The noise of the storm is *frightened / frightening* to them.

3. Mr. Peters gave a powerful speech. The audience was *fascinated / fascinating* by his insights.

4. Going to the dentist is *scary / scared* for a lot of people, but I am not *scary / scared* unless I need extensive work, like a root canal. In either case, I never feel completely *relaxed / relaxing*.

5. Watching gorillas interact with each other is *interesting / interested*. They seem to have a lot of behaviors similar to humans. I am so *interested / interesting* that I may study zoology in graduate school.

6. My grandfather's time as a soldier is still *terrified / terrifying* to him. He is *surprised / surprising* that he occasionally has flashbacks.

GET + adjective/past participle *(Chart 10-9)*

Directions: *Complete the sentences with an appropriate form of* **get.**

Example: Even though I had an umbrella, the rain was so strong that I still __got__ wet.

1. Dennis and Heidi _____ engaged last June and married in August.

2. You look tired. _____ you _____ sick? Let's take your temperature.

3. I'll take this bottle of water with me. I might _____ thirsty.

4. You're bleeding, and your hand is cut. How _____ you _____ hurt?

5. Please don't play in the dirt. I don't want you to _____ dirty before the party.

6. My father is bald. I wonder if I _____ bald later.

7. This room is hot and stuffy. I _____ sleepy.

8. When you eat so fast, you must _____ full very quickly.

GET + adjective and past participle *(Chart 10-9)*

Directions: *Complete the sentences with the appropriate form of* **get** *and a word from the list.*

arrest	dark	hungry	lost	rich	sunburn
confuse	fat	invite	nervous	serious	

Example: The Millers are having a party. Did you __get invited?__

1. Every time the teacher explains a new problem, I _____ . He needs to be clearer.

2. It took Sandy two hours to find our house. She said she _____ and had to ask someone for directions.

3. If you have chips and pop for breakfast every day, you will probably _____ .

4. Before Tom gives presentations at his company, he always _____ . His hands shake, and his mouth gets dry.

5. Children, come inside. It's _____ now, and soon you won't be able to see anything.

6. Steven wants to earn a lot of money and _____ . But he doesn't want to get a job! How will he do it?

7. Please put on some sunscreen. The last time you were in the sun, you _____ _____ .

8. You just had breakfast, and now you want a snack? You sure _____ quickly!

9. This situation isn't funny. We need to _____ and think of a solution.

10. The neighbor's son _____ last night for driving a stolen car.

Directions: Check the sentences that contain a completed activity or situation.

1. _____ I used to live by myself.

2. _____ I am accustomed to living by myself.

3. _____ I am used to living by myself.

4. _____ It used to snow more in the winter.

5. _____ People here are used to a lot of snow.

6. _____ Are you accustomed to the snow?

7. _____ Where did you used to live?

8. _____ Are you used to living here?

*Directions: Complete the sentences with **used to** or **be used to**.*

1. When I was younger, I (**travel**) _____ more.

2. I love learning about other cultures. When I traveled, I (**spend**) _____
_____ time in small cities rather than busy tourist areas.

3. My husband and I often cook ethnic foods, so we (**eat**) _____
_____ spicy foods.

4. My parents have traveled a lot since they retired. They (**be**) _____
_____ away from home for weeks at a time.

5. Our neighbors (**be**) _____ chefs in a famous
restaurant years ago.

6. Where (**you, live**) _____ before you moved
here?

7. (**you, live**) _____ here now?

8. What (**your husband, do**) _____ before he
became president of the company?

9. This town (**have**) _____ lots of greenery, but
now it is mostly housing developments.

10. I preferred it when it was rural. I (**be, not**) _____
all this growth.

Directions: Create sentences with a similar meaning by using **be supposed to**.

Example: The hospital expects doctors to work weekends once a month.
→ *Doctors are supposed to work weekends once a month.*

1. The electric company expects customers to pay their bills on time.

2. The law says ABC Cable Company can't charge a late fee.

3. The restaurant says customers are not expected to leave tips for service.

4. Employees expect the company president to retire next month.

5. School policy says students have to wear uniforms.

QUIZ 26 BE SUPPOSED TO *(Chart 10-12)*

Directions: Check the incorrect sentences and correct them.

1. ____ Drivers are suppose to drive more slowly in rainy weather.

2. ____ Employees are supposed to treat customers with respect.

3. ____ You not supposed to wear shoes in the house.

4. ____ I was supposing to pick up Carl, but he got a ride from someone else.

5. ____ What are we supposed to do about Graciela's situation?

6. ____ It is supposed to snow tonight.

7. ____ Didn't you supposed to go to school early today?

8. ____ The new grocery store is supposed to open next week.

Directions: Circle the correct answer.

1. A: Are you enjoying your time in Paris?
   B: Yes, but I ____ the time change yet.
      a. wasn't getting used to   c. haven't gotten used to
      b. didn't accustomed to   d. didn't used to get

2. A: Whose coat is this?
   B: It ____ to me.
      a. is belongs   c. belongs
      b. belong   d. is belonging

3. A: Where is your hometown?
   B: It ____ on the coast.
      a. is located   c. locates
      b. located   d. is being located

4. A: Your face is so red.
   B: I stayed in the sun so long yesterday that I ____ .
      a. was sunburn   c. was get sunburn
      b. got sunburned   d. sunburned

5. A: Why is Matt at the police station?
   B: He ____ for being in a stolen car.
      a. get arrest   c. got arresting
      b. got arrested   d. was gotten arrested

6. A: Where's your motorcycle?
   B: At the repair shop. It ____ .
      a. is repairing   c. is being repaired
      b. was repairing   d. will repair

7. A: Why don't you use fresh vegetables in your cooking?
   B: I really can't tell the difference between fresh and ____ vegetables.
      a. froze   c. freeze
      b. freezing   d. frozen

8. A. You look like you're in hurry.
   B. I am. This project ____ done by 5:00 P.M.
      a. has to been   c. has to be
      b. will to be   d. must to being

Directions: *Correct the errors.*

1. When you're done your toys, you need to put them away.

2. Vegetables are contain important nutrients for your health.

3. Unfortunately, my father was died when I was a young girl.

4. The student wasn't agree with the teacher about his test score.

5. The department was just getting used to work with Brian when he left the company.

6. The books that you ordered are arrived two days ago.

7. The plumber was suppose to come today. I wonder why he didn't.

8. The city is very noisy, but we are get used to it.

CHAPTER 10 PRACTICE TEST

Part I Verbs

Directions: Circle the correct answer.

1. A: What happened to the roof of your car?

   B: It _____ in the windstorm.

      a. damaged   c. been damaged

      b. was damaged   d. has damaged

2. A: Why is the dog shivering?

   B: She _____ into the river.

      a. was fallen   c. fell

      b. falling   d. was falling

3. A: The kitchen table isn't set for dinner.

   B: Dinner _____ in the dining room tonight.

      a. is being serving   c. served

      b. will being served   d. is being served

4. A: My patient is not in Room 303.

   B: He _____ to the second floor.

      a. has moving   c. is moved

      b. moves   d. has been moved

5. A: This sculpture is beautiful.

   B: Thank you. It _____ by one of our student artists.

      a. was made   c. was making

      b. is made   d. has made

Part II Passive vs. active

Directions: Complete the sentences with the correct forms (active or passive) of the verbs in parentheses.

Yesterday there (**be**) _____ almost a tragedy at the swimming pool. A young

boy who didn't know how to swim (**jump**) _____ into the deep end. He (**begin**)

_____ to splash and yell when he couldn't swim to the side of the pool. He (**save**)

_____ from drowning by a lifeguard at the pool. It's lucky that he (**see**)

_____ by her.

Directions: Choose the correct adjective.

1. A: That roller coaster ride was *thrilled / thrilling!* Let's go again.

   B: You can go, but not me. It was too *scared / scary* for me. I was really *frightened / frightening.*

2. A: I am *disappointed / disappointing* that the neighborhood library will close soon.

   B: Yes, that was *surprised / surprising* news. It's too bad they couldn't find the money to stay open. It's *confused / confusing* because government officials can find money for other items, like salary increases for themselves.

Part IV Error analysis

Directions: Correct the errors.

1. The Jeffersons have been married with each other for fifty years.

2. Mr. Allen is very interesting from your work experience.

3. My husband and I used to living on a houseboat. Now we rent an apartment downtown.

4. Dr. Barry was arrived two hours late and missed the meeting.

5. Where were you go after the movie? I couldn't find you.

6. The dog began to cross the highway, but there were so many cars that he get scare.

Part I   Verbs

Directions: *Circle the correct answer.*

1. A: Did you make your sweater?

   B: It _____ by hand, and a friend gave it to me.

   a. made   c. is made

   b. was making   d. was made

2. A: Jack looks different.

   B: He _____ his beard.

   a. shaved   c. is being shaved

   b. had been shaved   d. shaving

3. A: Did Romeo quit his job?

   B: I _____ that he took a leave of absence.

   a. telling   c. have told

   b. was told   d. tell

4. A: When can I pick up the car?

   B. It _____ by tomorrow afternoon.

   a. should be fixed   c. should have fixed

   b. should fix   d. should be fixing

5. A: The weather certainly is cold here.

   B: I don't think I'll ever _____ it.

   a. am used to   c. get used to

   b. be use to   d. got used to

6. A: Why is there such a long line of people?

   B: All passengers _____ before boarding their airplane.

   a. must check   c. must be checking

   b. must have checked   d. must be checked

7. A. Who are you waiting for?

   B: My mom _____ pick me up in a few minutes.

   a. is supposed to   c. supposed to

   b. will supposed to   d. supposes to

8. A: How do you like college?

   B: I like living in the dorm, but I _____ the food.

   a. am not use   c. didn't used to

   b. am not used to   d. didn't use to

Directions: Complete the sentences with the correct forms (active or passive) of the verbs in parentheses.

1. A community meeting (**hold**) _____ last night. People (**ask**)

   _____ by community leaders to discuss several issues. But the

   community (**want**) _____ to discuss only one issue: the construction of a

   supermall. Developers in the audience (**argue**) _____ that it would bring jobs

   to the town. But most people (**say**) _____ it would destroy the small-town

   feeling of the community. The discussion (**become**) _____ tense. It was clear

   that more time (**need**) _____ in the future for discussion of this

   matter.

2. When I (**return**) _____ from my business trip, I was pleasantly

   surprised. My husband (**decide**) _____ to present me with a

   "welcome-home" gift. The entire house (**clean**) _____ .

   The windows (**wash**) _____ , the furniture (**dust**)

   _____ , the floors (**polish**) _____ , and

   dinner (**make**) _____ . The house had never looked so beautiful. I

   (**thank**) _____ him for doing such a wonderful job. For a minute

   he (**look**) _____ embarrassed, and then he finally (**say**) _____ :

   "Honey, everything (**do**) _____ by a cleaning company. But I (**get**)

   _____ a great discount!"

Directions: Circle the correct adjective.

1. A: How was the movie?
   B: I was *disappointed / disappointing*. It was supposed to have new special effects, but they
      weren't new. They were just *bored / boring*.
   A: That's too bad. Would you like to try another movie tonight? I hear *Chaos* is pretty
      excited / exciting.
   B: Let's give it a try. I'd like to see an *excited / exciting* movie.
2. A: I read an *interested / interesting* article about the environment yesterday. It says that the
      global climate is gradually getting warmer.
   B: I know the one you're talking about. I felt pretty *discouraged / discouraging* after reading it.
      Scientists believe the polar ice cap is melting and oceans could rise. It's kind of *depressed /
      depressing* to think about.

A: I know. It says we need to reduce the level of carbon monoxide in the air. But it seems that people here are buying bigger cars and using more gas. It's very *frustrated / frustrating* to see huge cars on the freeway with only a driver in them.

B: Perhaps people will be *alarmed / alarming* enough by the news to change their driving habits.

Part IV Error analysis

Directions: Correct the errors.

1. Ben and Rachel were get engaged last month.

2. The government is opposed against lower taxes.

3. I heard my name. Who was called me?

4. Dogs in the park supposed be on a leash.

5. Your fax was come a few minutes ago. Shall I get it for you?

6. Our apartment must clean before the party next week.

7. I used to running, but now I walk for exercise. It doesn't hurt my knees so much.

8. The fish isn't ready yet. It should be to cook a little longer.

9. We enjoyed our time in Malaysia, but we exhaust from the heat.

10. My grandmother is still recovering from her illness. She can walk only a few steps before she get tiring.

CHAPTER 11 COUNT/NONCOUNT NOUNS AND ARTICLES

QUIZ 1 A vs. AN *(Chart 11-1)*

Directions: Circle the correct article: **a** or **an**.

1. a an apple
2. a an experience
3. a an glass
4. a an elevator
5. a an onion
6. a an island
7. a an wrong answer
8. a an hour
9. a an home
10. a an small flashlight
11. a an long illness
12. a an unique gift

QUIZ 2 A vs. SOME *(Chart 11-2)*

Directions: Write **a**, **an**, *or* **some** in the blanks.

1. _____ message
2. _____ car
3. _____ money
4. _____ dishes
5. _____ homework
6. _____ assignment
7. _____ vocabulary
8. _____ word
9. _____ furniture
10. _____ pillow
11. _____ medicine
12. _____ bottle

QUIZ 3 Count and noncount nouns *(Charts 11-2 and 11-3)*

Directions: Add final -s if possible. Otherwise, put a slash (/) in the blank.

1. Here's a vocabulary book ____ for you.

2. How many new word ____ did you learn today?

3. Chinese is a tonal language ____ .

4. The heavy smog ____ in the air makes me cough.

5. The library video ____ are overdue.

6. I gave Paul some suggestion ____ for finding a new job, but he didn't like my advice ____ .

7. The sauce ____ tastes strange. Did you put sugar ____ in it instead of salt ____ ?

8. The grammar ____ in your paragraph is excellent, but you need to remove the slang ____ .

9. Jacques can't decide whether to major in history ____ or in music ____ .

10. I had expected to see only a few car ____ on the road so early in the morning, but traffic ____ was surprisingly heavy.

QUIZ 4 Count and noncount nouns *(Charts 11-2 → 11-4)*

Directions: Add final -s if possible. Otherwise, put a slash (/) in the blank.

1. We need more chalk ____ . All the pieces are too small to use.

2. Good luck ____ with your project ____ . It sounds very interesting.

3. Happiness and sadness ____ are not necessarily permanent conditions.

4. Darkness ____ comes early during the winter months.

5. I accidentally put the butter ____ in the freezer. It's completely frozen.

6. Could you mail the letter ____ on the table? They need to go out today.

7. Every anniversary, Kevin gives his wife an expensive ring ____ , a bracelet ____ , or a necklace ____ . She loves jewelry ____ , but ring ____ are her favorite.

8. The lawyer asked to present several new fact ____ to the judge. He had some important information ____ about his client.

9. Knowledge ____ comes with experience ____ .

10. Billy wants to be a firefighter ____ when he grows up.

*Directions: Circle **much** or **many** for the given noun. Add **-s/-es** as necessary.*

1. much   many   computer _____
2. much   many   dress _____
3. much   many   thunder _____
4. much   many   letter _____
5. much   many   peace _____
6. much   many   information _____
7. much   many   honesty _____
8. much   many   assignment _____
9. much   many   banana _____
10. much   many   progress _____
11. much   many   sunshine _____

*Directions: Complete the sentences by using **a few** or **a little** and the given noun. Use the plural form of the noun when necessary.*

1. cloud   There are _____ in the sky.

2. music   Let's listen to _____ .

3. meat   There's _____ left from dinner.

4. apple   Could you pick up _____ at the store? I need about

    three or four.

5. suggestion   The teacher gave her students _____ for writing topics.

6. salt   This soup needs _____ , and then it will be ready.

7. sand   I'm afraid I got _____ on your carpet.

8. help   Would you like _____?

9. coin   Here are _____ old _____ for

    your collection. They're from the 1940s.

10. egg   I'm not very hungry. I'll just have _____ for dinner.

    Two should be enough.

Directions: *Circle the correct words for the given noun. More than one word may be correct.*

1. a few   much   several   people

2. much   many   a little   fun

3. some   much   a lot of   tests

4. several   some   many   pollution

5. a few   a little   a lot of   weeks

6. much   a lot of   a little   knowledge

7. many   several   some   seas

8. several   a few   a little   insects

9. some   much   a little   paint

10. much   a few   some   prices

QUIZ 8 Nouns that can be count or noncount *(Chart 11-6)*

Directions: *Circle the correct answer.*

1. Who would like *coffee / coffees* ? I just made a fresh pot.

2. We've had *chicken / chickens* every night for dinner this week. Let's have something different tonight.

3. The hotel provides clothes *iron / irons* for guests who forget to bring their own.

4. Professor Chang has a lot of *time / times* for his students outside of class.

5. There's a lot of *light / lights* in this house because there are so many windows.

6. Emma has bleached her *hair / hairs* so often that it's starting to fall out.

7. Dennis should try wearing contact lenses for a while. He's always losing his *glass / glasses*.

8. We need to get *a wrapping paper / some wrapping paper* to wrap birthday gifts.

9. The museum exhibit has several *work / works* of art by Monet.

10. Professor Reed assigns a lot of *paper / papers* for his students to write.

Directions: Complete the phrase with a unit of measure from the list. More than one answer may be correct.

bag	bottle	box	can	jar

At the store, I bought . . .

1. a _____ of potatoes

2. a _____ of crackers

3. a _____ of juice

4. a _____ of honey

5. a _____ of soup

bowl	cup	glass	piece	slice

For a snack, I had . . .

6. a _____ of ice-cream

7. a _____ of toast

8. a _____ of juice

9. a _____ of cheese

10. a _____ of tea

QUIZ 10 Units of measure with noncount nouns *(Chart 11-7)*

Directions: Check the phrases that are correct.

1. _____ a bottle of sugar

2. _____ a piece of soup

3. _____ a slice of bread

4. _____ a bag of potatoes

5. _____ a bowl of cereal

6. _____ a slice of peas

7. _____ a bag of noodles

8. _____ a can of toast

9. _____ a slice of cake

10. _____ a can of paint

Directions: Write **the** *or* **a/an** *in the blanks.*

1. A: Where's _____ newspaper?

   B: It's on _____ kitchen counter next to _____ phone.

2. A: Do you know _____ time?

   B: I'm sorry. I'm not wearing _____ watch.

3. A: I'm very cold.

   B: I have _____ sweater you can put on.

4. A: I brought you _____ present.

   B: What _____ surprise! It's not even my birthday.

5. A: Excuse me, I'm looking for _____ library.

   B: It's right over there, across from _____ hospital.

6. A: What would you like to drink?

   B: I'll just have _____ glass of water.

QUIZ 12 Making general statements *(Chart 11-8)*

Directions: Check the sentences that make general statements.

1. _____ Cougars are dangerous.

2. _____ The cougar in the zoo looks dangerous.

3. _____ A cougar is dangerous.

4. _____ An ocean is vast.

5. _____ The honey in the jar is made from blackberries.

6. _____ Insects have six legs.

7. _____ An elephant cannot jump.

8. _____ The lemons in the basket are from my lemon tree.

9. _____ Sports equipment can be expensive.

10. _____ The sports equipment you bought is expensive.

Directions: *Complete the sentences with* **the** *or* **Ø**.

1. Sue prefers _____ chicken to _____ fish.

2. I'm afraid _____ milk from _____ refrigerator is spoiled.

3. At what age can children begin to eat _____ solid food?

4. When _____ cars were first used, they were called "horseless carriages."

5. _____ car in back of mine is blocking my way. I need to find _____ owner.

6. _____ dolphins breathe through air holes on top of their heads.

7. Our water has a lot of fluoride in it. _____ water at your house tastes much better.

8. Andrew needs to change jobs. _____ work he is doing now is not challenging.

9. _____ DVDs you got from the library last week are due today.

10. _____ caterpillars become _____ butterflies.

QUIZ 14 Using THE for second mention *(Chart 11-8)*

Directions: *Complete the sentences with* **the** *or* **a**.

Yesterday, I decided to buy _____ digital camera as _____ birthday present for my

husband. _____ camera was expensive, so I didn't know if my husband would be pleased or not

with _____ present I had chosen. He was thrilled until he tried _____ camera and it didn't

work. We went back to the store to return it. Both of us felt embarrassed, however, when the

salesperson showed us that we had forgotten to put in AA batteries. He gave us _____ batteries

free of charge, and told us to have fun. We took _____ picture of _____ salesperson and

assured him we would.

*Directions: Complete with **the**, **a**, or **Ø**. Add capital letters as necessary.*

1. _____ eggs have cholesterol.

2. It looks like _____ fruit in the bowl is spoiled.

3. There's no wind right now. _____ trees aren't moving.

4. I prefer sleeping on _____ firm mattress.

5. _____ air smells fresh today.

6. _____ nurses need to study science.

7. Do e-mails save _____ time or create _____ work for us?

8. _____ skunk sleeps during the day and hunts for food at night.

9. _____ chairs in your living room are very comfortable.

10. Does _____ success always come with _____ hard work?

QUIZ 16 Summary *(Charts 11-1 → 11-8)*

Directions: Choose the correct answer.

1. There are different ideas about how _____ became extinct.
   a. the dinosaur   c. dinosaurs
   b. a dinosaurs   d. the dinosaurs

2. How _____ do you want, a half or a full glass?
   a. many milk   c. much milks
   b. much milk   d. many milks

3. I found _____ about the history of my country at the library.
   a. a little information   b. a few informations
   c. a few information   d. a little informations

4. Visiting the rainforest in Brazil is _____ experience.
   a. a unique   c. an unique
   b. unique   d. the unique

5. I have _____ to give away to charity.
   a. lots of stuffs   c. lot of stuff
   b. a lot of stuffs   d. a lot of stuff

6. _____ people attended the movie preview. There were no empty seats.
   a. Many   c. A little
   b. A few   d. Much

7. Mrs. Kim drinks _____ of hot tea with breakfast every morning.
   a. a jar   c. a can
   b. a cup   d. a bottle

8. I need to study _____ new vocabulary this weekend.
   a. several   c. some
   b. a   d. many

*Directions: Complete the sentences with **the** or Ø.*

1. _____ Professor Black is replacing _____ Dr. Davis for the rest of the term.

2. Did you know that _____ Thailand was formerly called _____ Siam?

3. _____ Caspian Sea is in _____ Russia.

4. Joel wants to climb _____ Mt. Everest. He already attempted K2, but failed.

5. _____ North America consists of _____ Mexico, _____ United States, and _____
   Canada.

6. _____ Mr. Assad would like to visit _____ Abu Dhabi in _____ United Arab Emirates
   after he finishes working on a project in _____ Egypt.

7. We plan to vacation in _____ New Zealand, but we'll visit relatives in _____ Philippines
   first.

8. Earthquakes are common on islands in _____ Pacific.

QUIZ 18 Capitalization *(Chart 11-10)*

Directions: Add capital letters where necessary.

1. Theresa can't decide whether to study japanese or chinese.

2. where are you going for the summer break?

3. the alps are in switzerland, austria, and france.

4. We're reading shakespeare's *romeo and juliet* for our literature class.

5. the directions say to turn on fifth street, but this is park avenue.

6. i.b.m. is a company, and its initials stand for international business machines.

7. the mississippi river flows into the gulf of mexico.

8. i was supposed to be born in april, but i was a month late, so my birthday is in may.

9. which instructor do you prefer: dr. costa or professor pierce?

10. my friend william lincoln is a descendant of abraham lincoln.

CHAPTER 11 PRACTICE TEST

Part I Count and noncount nouns with expressions of quantity

Directions: Choose the correct answer.

1. I broke _____ and had to replace them.
   a. several dishes   c. one dishes
   b. a little dishes   d. much dish

2. _____ of other people often causes conflict in the world.
   a. Ignorances   c. Ignorance
   b. Some ignorances   d. Several ignorance

3. How _____ do you have for the weekend?
   a. many homeworks   c. much homework
   b. much homeworks   d. many homework

4. What _____! It's cooked just right.
   a. delicious fish   c. a delicious fishes
   b. delicious fishes   d. an delicious fish

5. Can I offer you a _____ of warm home-made bread?
   a. slice   c. pieces
   b. glass   d. cup

Part II Articles

*Directions: Complete the sentences with **a, an, the,** or **Ø**.*

1. Look at _____ fog! I can hardly see _____ road.

2. _____ Dr. Powell called. She wants to discuss _____ results from your heart tests.

3. I hear _____ noise. Is there _____ animal outside?

4. _____ woman in the red hat has _____ question.

5. The Bakers have _____ daughter and _____ son. _____ son is away at college, but

   _____ daughter still lives at home.

6. Quick! Open _____ door. I'm going to drop this heavy box.

Part III Capitalization

Directions: Add capital letters where necessary.

1. what part of canada are you from?

2. the assignment for our literature class is to read the first chapter of shakespeare's *hamlet*.

3. I heard that my neighbors, tariq and ali, plan to visit england in may.

4. maria's parents are from mexico. she speaks spanish fluently.

5. there is a miami university in ohio.

6. the lake is too cold for swimming. How about going to the indoor pool at mountain view park?

Part IV Error analysis

Directions: Correct the errors.

1. Let's get a drink of water. I'm a thirsty.

2. A scenery in the mountains is beautiful.

3. Your hair looks great. Did you get haircut?

4. For breakfast, Thomas ordered two toasts and eggs.

5. Here's a map of Pacific. Do you see Tahiti?

6. I need to have my a car checked soon.

7. There are no fish in the dead sea.

CHAPTER 11 FINAL TEST

Part I   Count and noncount nouns with quantifiers

Directions: Choose the correct answer.

1. _____ with computer programming is necessary for this job.
   - a. Experiences
   - b. Experience
   - c. An experience
   - d. Some experiences

2. The weather forecast said there wouldn't be _____ thunder, but it was quite loud last night.
   - a. A few
   - b. several
   - c. many
   - d. much

3. Here's a _____ of hot chicken soup. It should help your cold.
   - a. bottle
   - b. bag
   - c. cup
   - d. box

4. Dr. Rodriguez tried to give her patient _____ , but she wouldn't listen.
   - a. some advices
   - b. an advice
   - c. a little advice
   - d. many advices

5. Professor Johnson encourages his students to ask _____ .
   - a. questions
   - b. lot of questions
   - c. some question
   - d. several question

6. There's only _____ in our garden, so plants don't grow well.
   - a. a little sunlight
   - b. a few sunlight
   - c. a few sunlights
   - d. a little sunlights

7. Many doctors believe _____ can help an ill person heal more quickly.
   - a. the laughter
   - b. many laughters
   - c. several laughters
   - d. laughter

8. The store was almost sold out of toys. There weren't _____ left.
   - a. many
   - b. much
   - c. one
   - d. a little

9. I'm thirsty. _____ would be fine.
   - a. A glass of water
   - b. Glass of water
   - c. Glasses of waters
   - d. Some glass of water

10. _____ can come from simple pleasures in life, such as watching a sunset.
    - a. Many happinesses
    - b. Much happiness
    - c. Much happinesses
    - d. Many happiness

Directions: Complete the sentences with **a, an, the,** *or* **Ø***.*

1. Monday is _____ holiday for _____ students and _____ government employees.

2. Oops. It looks like our waiter made _____ mistake with our bill.

3. What's _____ difference between _____ hotel and _____ motel?

4. _____ cost of gasoline could rise this summer.

5. _____ fish need _____ oxygen to breathe.

6. It can be dangerous for climbers to climb _____ mountains in _____ warm weather.

7. What brings more happiness: _____ health or _____ wealth?

8. Every day there are hundreds of _____ earthquakes around _____ world.

9. We painted _____ walls of our apartment. Now we need to finish _____ ceiling.

10. _____ vitamins in this bottle have _____ iron. The others don't.

11. As I get older, I'm less excited about _____ birthdays.

12. We're lost. Let's stop at a store and get _____ map. I'm sure _____ map will have the street we're looking for.

Part III   Capitalization

Directions: Add capital letters where necessary.

1. our anatomy class will be taught by dr. jones. he's a professor, not a medical doctor.

2. does your friend live in an apartment or does he own a home?

3. tomorrow there will be a concert at washington park, near broadway avenue. A music group from south africa will be playing.

4. the university plans to tear down brown hall and build a new library.

5. in my country, new year's is the biggest holiday of the year.

6. when did william begin working for sony corporation?

7. *war and peace* is a long novel. i hope i can finish it before summer is over.

8. would you be interested in going on a boat trip down the colorado river? we would see part of the grand canyon.

Directions: Correct the errors.

1. I don't need a help now, but I will later on.

2. There are a little people at work who would prefer not to work with Alan.

3. The water is necessary for survival.

4. I married my a brother's best friend from college.

5. Joseph reached the top of Mt. mcKinley in Alaska yesterday.

6. Some friends bicycled through Sahara Desert last summer.

7. Ed worked on his car for a hour before he realized it needed expensive repairs.

8. Honolulu is in the Hawaii, but it is not on the island of Hawaii. It is on Oahu.

9. Mark tried several time to reach his parents, but their phone wasn't working.

10. Jane has so much a homework that she doesn't know where to start.

11. We heard that aunt betsy and uncle joe are moving to a retirement home next month.

ADJECTIVE CLAUSES

Adjective clauses with WHO *(Charts 12-1 and 12-2)*

Directions: Combine the two sentences into one sentence. *"b" is the adjective clause. Use* **who**.

1. a. There's the little boy.   b. He lost his balloon in the wind.

2. a. I heard about an elderly man.   b. He takes gifts to children in hospitals.

3. a. I met a marine biologist.   b. She once swam with sharks.

4. a. The people practice fire drills twice a month.   b. They work on this boat.

5. a. I helped a man.   b. He was confused and lost.

6. a. The doctor is very famous.   b. She treated me.

Adjective clauses with WHO and WHOM *(Charts 12-1 and 12-2)*

Directions: Complete the sentences using **who** *or* **whom**.

1. Those are some of the students _____ got scholarships to college.

2. There is the police officer _____ is moving into the apartment next to us.

3. How do you know the man _____ is holding the baby?

4. Pat is a person _____ others like immediately.

5. Here's the boy _____ found your wallet.

6. Did you give the boy _____ found your wallet any money?

7. One of the people _____ I met at the party is going to be my new supervisor.

8. I know a man _____ has nine brothers and nine sisters.

9. Children _____ have no brothers or sisters are called "only children."

10. The sales clerk _____ we asked for help was rude and unhelpful.

Directions: Circle all the correct completions.

1. We enjoyed the singers _____ gave the concert.
   a. who   b. whom   c. that   d. Ø

2. The children _____ attend Mountain Academy are very intelligent.
   a. who   b. whom   c. that   d. Ø

3. The truck driver _____ I spoke to was acting strange.
   a. who   b. whom   c. that   d. Ø

4. I met the lifeguard _____ rescued my child from the water.
   a. who   b. whom   c. that   d. Ø

5. Do you trust the person _____ you bought this car from?
   a. who   b. whom   c. that   d. Ø

6. Students _____ come to class early can get extra help from the teacher.
   a. who   b. whom   c. that   d. Ø

7. Where is the woman _____ manages this apartment building?
   a. who   b. whom   c. that   d. Ø

8. The college student _____ I take to school every morning lives next door to me.
   a. who   b. whom   c. that   d. Ø

9. The teacher _____ the students like best is creative and funny.
   a. who   b. whom   c. that   d. Ø

10. Are you the nurse _____ I spoke to on the phone?
    a. who   b. whom   c. that   d. Ø

QUIZ 4 Adjective clauses with WHICH, THAT, or Ø *(Chart 12-4)*

Directions: Circle the correct completion. *In some cases, both answers are correct.*

1. The book _____ Joan received for a graduation present was published in 1850.
   a. which   b. Ø

2. The college _____ George attends offers scholarships to 80 percent of its students.
   a. which   b. Ø

3. Andreas studies languages _____ are no longer spoken.
   a. that   b. Ø

4. My grandfather builds cabins _____ can be transported to building sites later on.
   a. which   b. Ø

5. The furniture _____ my father designs is sold in art galleries.
   a. that   b. Ø

6. I just found out that the toys _____ we saw on sale are dangerous for children.
   a. which   b. Ø

7. We're having lunch at a restaurant _____ has a breathtaking view of the city.
   a. which   b. Ø

8. There's a car _____ runs on electricity.
   a. that   b. Ø

QUIZ 5 Review of adjective clauses (Charts 12-1 → 12-4)

Directions: *Complete the sentences. Choose from* **who(m)**, **that**, **which**, **whose**, *or* **Ø**.

1. Maria is the person ___who(m)___ ___that___ ___Ø___ I saw at the party.

2. The man _____ _____ owns the gas station repaired my car for free.

3. Where is the DVD movie _____ _____ _____ you rented for tonight?

4. Enrique is a man _____ honesty wins praise from co-workers.

5. There's the thief _____ _____ stole my wallet.

6. The boat _____ _____ _____ we rented had engine problems the first day.

QUIZ 6 Review of adjective clauses (Charts 12-1 → 12-4)

Directions: *Combine the two sentences into one sentence.* *"b" is the adjective clause. Supply all possible completions for each.*

Example: a. Where is the fruit?   b. It was on the counter.
  → Where is the fruit that was on the counter?
  → Where is the fruit which was on the counter?

1. a. Here is the book.   b. You asked me to order for you.

2. a. There is the man.   b. He found my diamond ring.

3. a. The ring was very expensive.   b. I lost it.

4. a. I spoke with a woman.   b. She has thirteen children.

5. a. The restaurant was very crowded.   b. We went to it last night.

6. a. The elderly man has no relatives.   b. He lives in the apartment next to me.

Subject–verb agreement in adjective clauses *(Chart 12-5)*

Directions: Circle the correct verb.

1. Do you know the woman that *is / are* waving to you?

2. The stories which my children *likes / like* best have surprise endings.

3. Many people who *works / work* the night shift often have sleep disturbances.

4. The woman who *sells / sell* flowers on the corner is marrying one of her customers.

5. The house which my parents *is / are* designing is very energy-efficient.

6. I know a man that *spends / spend* every summer sailing the Pacific Ocean.

7. The letters that my grandfather *writes / write* are funny and full of news.

8. I hope that the people who *calculates / calculate* our taxes are honest.

Prepositions *(Chart 12-6)*

Directions: Combine the two sentences into one. "b" is the adjective clause. Write four sentences for each item.

1. a. The taxi is coming.   b. I am waiting for it.

   _____

   _____

   _____

   _____

2. a. The radio station has 24-hour news.   b. We listen to it.

   _____

   _____

   _____

   _____

3. a. The school specializes in dance and drama instruction.   b. Helen goes to it.

   _____

   _____

   _____

   _____

4. a. Across from the park is the health club.   b. Sarah belongs to it.

   _____

   _____

   _____

   _____

Directions: *Complete the sentences wit them.*
Supply one possible completion.

1. The lake _____ you ar

2. The country _____ Ma

3. The job _____ Pierre i

4. The book club _____

5. Don't tell me about the leak in y
   complain _____ is the

6. The building _____ yo
   rent.

7. The young man _____
   Oxford University.

8. Ron doesn't always get along wit
   _____ .

9. The elderly woman _____
   inheritance when she died.

10. The woman _____ Bla
    degrees.

Directions: *Combine the sentences wi*

1. The little girl was sad for days.

2. I'm friends with a woman. Her

3. I met a man at the park. His par

4. The dog is being cared for by the

5. I enjoyed meeting the couple. Tl

6. I have a friend. Her sailboat is a

7. The couple wants us to buy the

8. I have a friend. Her work involv

I started it

d they were at

line can fly arou

h her 20 years ago.

n all year.

work at food banks

alks on her cell phone th

tients and rude to the nur

y about home exercise machi

Part I

Ad
Dir
1.

2

t, whose, *or* **Ø.** *Write*

with my yard work is

been translated into

oftware company has

ere delicious.

as.

his job.

Directions: *Complete the sentences. Supply one possible completion and the appropriate preposition.*

1. "President" of the company is the position _____ I am interested

_____ .

2. The motel _____ we stayed _____ was overpriced.

3. Cambridge is the university _____ Omar graduated _____ .

4. The person _____ I agree _____ most often is you.

5. Charles' parents think he has chosen a job _____ he may soon become tired

_____ .

Part V Error analysis

Directions: *Check the incorrect sentences and correct them.*

1. _____ The color of paint Sandra picked it for her bedroom walls was an unusual blue.

2. _____ The train that came through the tunnel blew its whistle several times.

3. _____ The radio carries overseas stations which I bought.

4. _____ The doctor whom operated on my father is very skilled.

5. _____ I work with a woman grew up in the same neighborhood as me.

6. _____ The ambulance driver that drove my husband to the hospital didn't turn on his siren.

CHAPTER 12 FINAL TEST

Part I Adjective clauses

Directions: Combine the sentences, using an adjective clause.

1. The garden is looking healthy again. It nearly died from lack of rain.

2. I work with a man. His wife trains police dogs.

3. The computer disks were defective. I bought them.

4. The deer are eating the flowers. They grow in my garden.

5. Barb is a manager. People like to work for her.

6. Some of the mail was addressed to our neighbor. It was delivered to our house.

Part II Adjective clauses

Directions: Complete the sentences. Choose from among **who, who(m), which, that, whose,** *or* **Ø.**
Write all possible choices.

1. The coin _____ John found is very valuable.

2. I met a woman _____ has two sets of twins.

3. Let's choose a movie _____ the whole family can watch.

4. I spoke with a man yesterday _____ brother is a psychologist
   for animals.

5. The forest _____ lies below my house provides a home for
   deer and other wildlife.

6. The dress _____ Ann chose to wear for her wedding was light
   blue.

Part III Subject-verb agreement

Directions: Circle the correct verb.

1. My husband and I have a friend who *designs / design* jewelry for movie stars.

2. That is the bike which Michelle *wants / want* for her birthday.

3. Where are the socks that *goes / go* with those pants?

4. I study with a professor who *speaks / speak* several languages fluently.

5. The neighbors whose dog *barks / bark* all night are difficult to talk to.

6. Those are the chairs which *is / are* the most comfortable.

Part IV Prepositions

Directions: *Complete the sentences. Supply one possible completion and the appropriate preposition.*

1. Rebecca is an employee _____ other workers can always depend

   _____ .

2. The man _____ is staring _____ me is making me nervous.

3. This is literature _____ all students should be familiar _____ .

4. Hans is a financial advisor _____ you should listen _____ .

5. I'm returning the books _____ I borrowed _____ you.

6. Our neighbor created a fenced area for the dog _____ the children were

   frightened _____ .

7. These are the jeans _____ everyone at school is crazy _____ .

8. M.I.T. is a school _____ is famous _____ its engineering program.

Part V Error analysis

Directions: *Check the incorrect sentences and correct them.*

1. _____ The firefighters who they put out the fire were exhausted and dirty.

2. _____ The digital camera we ordered it still hasn't arrived.

3. _____ The man whom for I work is blind.

4. _____ Here is the receipt which you asked for.

5. _____ The finger is healing well which I broke.

6. _____ I studied with a professor who his books are known around the world.

7. _____ I met a little girl whose favorite food is raw mushrooms.

8. _____ Here's some medicine which should make you feel better.

CHAPTER 13

GERUNDS AND INFINITIVES

QUIZ 1 Verb + gerund *(Chart 13-1)*

Directions: *Complete the sentences with a verb from the list.*

paint	drive	move	smoke
do	get	rain	turn down

1. Would you mind _____ the stereo? I'm trying to sleep.

2. It stopped _____ so the children could finally go out and play.

3. Richard put off _____ his homework all week. Now he doesn't have enough time to finish it.

4. My husband and I are considering _____ a puppy, but we're not sure if that's a good idea for a family with a small child.

5. Jeff took a wrong turn on the road, but he kept _____ because he didn't want his girlfriend to know he had made a mistake.

6. We finished _____ our apartment. Now we can decorate the walls.

7. The Davidsons have discussed _____ closer to the city so Mr. Davidson would have a shorter commute to work.

8. When did Phil quit _____? He looks much healthier than the last time I saw him.

QUIZ 2 Verb + GO + -ING *(Chart 13-2)*

Directions: *Complete the sentences with a form of* **go** *and one of the given words.*

1. Tomorrow, I (**shop**) _____ for new summer clothes.

2. Last weekend, we (**sail**) _____ in our new sailboat. It felt like we were on vacation.

3. Let's (**camp**) _____ this weekend. The weather is supposed to be quite warm.

4. For Mike's 75th birthday, he (**skydive**) _____. His wife thought he was crazy.

5. Mr. Clark knows a great lake nearby where we can (**fish**) _____ .

6. Rain or shine, Janet (**jog**) _____ every morning before work.

7. We didn't want to spend our money, so we just (**window shop**) _____ _____ downtown for a few hours.

8. Our class (**bowl**) _____ this weekend to celebrate the end of the term.

Directions: *Circle the correct verb.*

1. Do you know the woman that *is / are* waving to you?
2. The stories which my children *likes / like* best have surprise endings.
3. Many people who *works / work* the night shift often have sleep disturbances.
4. The woman who *sells / sell* flowers on the corner is marrying one of her customers.
5. The house which my parents *is / are* designing is very energy-efficient.
6. I know a man that *spends / spend* every summer sailing the Pacific Ocean.
7. The letters that my grandfather *writes / write* are funny and full of news.
8. I hope that the people who *calculates / calculate* our taxes are honest.

Directions: *Combine the two sentences into one. "b" is the adjective clause. Write four sentences for each item.*

1. a. The taxi is coming.   b. I am waiting for it.

   _____

   _____

   _____

   _____

2. a. The radio station has 24-hour news.   b. We listen to it.

   _____

   _____

   _____

   _____

3. a. The school specializes in dance and drama instruction.   b. Helen goes to it.

   _____

   _____

   _____

   _____

4. a. Across from the park is the health club.   b. Sarah belongs to it.

   _____

   _____

   _____

   _____

*Directions: Complete the sentences with **that**, **which**, **who**(m), or Ø and the appropriate preposition. Supply one possible completion.*

1. The lake _____ you are familiar _____ is famous for fishing.

2. The country _____ Marco escaped _____ is having a civil war.

3. The job _____ Pierre is qualified _____ pays very well.

4. The book club _____ my mother belongs _____ sells books about knitting.

5. Don't tell me about the leak in your plumbing. The person _____ you should complain _____ is the manager of your apartment building.

6. The building _____ your company is interested _____ is not available for rent.

7. The young man _____ Mark introduced you _____ is a professor at Oxford University.

8. Ron doesn't always get along with two of the roommates _____ he lives _____ .

9. The elderly woman _____ Marta was kind _____ left her a large inheritance when she died.

10. The woman _____ Blake is married _____ has both M.D. and Ph.D. degrees.

*Directions: Combine the sentences with **whose**.*

1. The little girl was sad for days. Her doll was taken.

2. I'm friends with a woman. Her daughter is training to be a professional boxer.

3. I met a man at the park. His parents know my grandparents.

4. The dog is being cared for by the staff. His owner left him outside a restaurant.

5. I enjoyed meeting the couple. Their children go to the same school as our children.

6. I have a friend. Her sailboat is also her office.

7. The couple wants us to buy the property next door. We rent their summer house.

8. I have a friend. Her work involves designing houses for people in wheelchairs.

Directions: Check the incorrect sentences and correct them.

Example: ___✓___ I can't stop reading the book I started ~~it~~ last night.

1. _____ The family whom arrived late discovered they were at the wrong party.

2. _____ A neighbor who his son works for an airline can fly around the world for free.

3. _____ I ran into a woman I went to school with her 20 years ago.

4. _____ Those are the students that volunteer to work at food banks on weekends.

5. _____ The potatoes aren't done which I baked.

6. _____ The woman whom I ride to work with talks on her cell phone the entire time.

7. _____ I work with a doctor he is nice to his patients and rude to the nurses.

8. _____ Here is the magazine which has the story about home exercise machines.

CHAPTER 12 PRACTICE TEST

Part I Adjective clauses

Directions: Combine the sentences, using an adjective clause.

1. The couple was surprised. Their horse won the race.

2. The manager treats me fairly. I work for him.

3. The bus is an express bus. I take it to work.

4. Trees and bushes are called "evergreens." Their needles remain green all year.

Part II Adjective clauses

Directions: Complete the sentences. Choose from **who, who(m), which, that, whose,** *or* **Ø.** *Write all possible choices.*

1. The boy _____ I asked to help me with my yard work is

   saving money for a trip to Nepal.

2. The book _____ you are reading has been translated into

   several languages.

3. I went to school with a man _____ software company has

   made him a multi-millionaire.

4. The sandwiches _____ you made were delicious.

Part III Subject-verb agreement

Directions: Circle the correct verb.

1. Have you met the people who *is / are* renting that house?

2. An astronomer is a scientist who *studies / study* stars and planets.

3. There are several students in my class whose families *lives / live* overseas.

4. The employee who *is / are* meeting with the supervisor is going to lose his job.

Part IV Prepositions

Directions: *Complete the sentences. Supply one possible completion and the appropriate preposition.*

1. "President" of the company is the position _____ I am interested

   _____ .

2. The motel _____ we stayed _____ was overpriced.

3. Cambridge is the university _____ Omar graduated _____ .

4. The person _____ I agree _____ most often is you.

5. Charles' parents think he has chosen a job _____ he may soon become tired

   _____ .

Part V Error analysis

Directions: *Check the incorrect sentences and correct them.*

1. ____ The color of paint Sandra picked it for her bedroom walls was an unusual blue.

2. ____ The train that came through the tunnel blew its whistle several times.

3. ____ The radio carries overseas stations which I bought.

4. ____ The doctor whom operated on my father is very skilled.

5. ____ I work with a woman grew up in the same neighborhood as me.

6. ____ The ambulance driver that drove my husband to the hospital didn't turn on his siren.

CHAPTER 12 FINAL TEST

Part I Adjective clauses

Directions: *Combine the sentences, using an adjective clause.*

1. The garden is looking healthy again. It nearly died from lack of rain.

2. I work with a man. His wife trains police dogs.

3. The computer disks were defective. I bought them.

4. The deer are eating the flowers. They grow in my garden.

5. Barb is a manager. People like to work for her.

6. Some of the mail was addressed to our neighbor. It was delivered to our house.

Part II Adjective clauses

Directions: *Complete the sentences. Choose from among* **who, who(m), which, that, whose,** *or* **Ø.**
Write all possible choices.

1. The coin _____ John found is very valuable.

2. I met a woman _____ has two sets of twins.

3. Let's choose a movie _____ the whole family can watch.

4. I spoke with a man yesterday _____ brother is a psychologist
   for animals.

5. The forest _____ lies below my house provides a home for
   deer and other wildlife.

6. The dress _____ Ann chose to wear for her wedding was light
   blue.

Part III Subject–verb agreement

Directions: *Circle the correct verb.*

1. My husband and I have a friend who *designs / design* jewelry for movie stars.

2. That is the bike which Michelle *wants / want* for her birthday.

3. Where are the socks that *goes / go* with those pants?

4. I study with a professor who *speaks / speak* several languages fluently.

5. The neighbors whose dog *barks / bark* all night are difficult to talk to.

6. Those are the chairs which *is / are* the most comfortable.

Directions: Complete the sentences with the gerund or infinitive form of **work**.

1. Hans wants _____ .

2. Ellen would like _____ .

3. Mr. Bennett enjoys _____ .

4. The teenagers discussed _____ .

5. The strikers refused _____ .

6. Marie hopes _____ .

7. The builder postponed _____ .

8. Dr. Charles thought about _____ .

9. Mrs. Ross intended _____ .

10. My brother expected _____ .

QUIZ 4 Verb + gerund or infinitive *(Charts 13-1 → 13-4)*

Directions: Check the correct sentence of each pair.

1. a. _____ Joey pretended to be a monster.

   b. _____ Joey pretended being a monster.

2. a. _____ Joanna and Ben hope to have 500 guests at their wedding.

   b. _____ Joanna and Ben hope having 500 guests at their wedding.

3. a. _____ Ron quit to do construction after he hurt his back.

   b. _____ Ron quit doing construction after he hurt his back.

4. a. _____ Would you mind to turn down the TV?

   b. _____ Would you mind turning down the TV?

5. a. _____ Jason has finally finished to write his short story.

   b. _____ Jason has finally finished writing his short story.

6. a. _____ The Warrens can't afford to fly their son home for vacation.

   b. _____ The Warrens can't afford flying their son home for vacation.

7. a. _____ Sandra refused to take her parents' advice.

   b. _____ Sandra refused taking her parents' advice.

8. a. _____ I meant to call you days ago.

   b. _____ I meant calling you days ago.

9. a. _____ Did you postpone to see the doctor again?

   b. _____ Did you postpone seeing the doctor again?

10. a. _____ At graduation, the class promised meeting every five years.

    b. _____ At graduation, the class promised to meet every five years.

Directions: *Circle the correct answer. In some cases, both answers are correct.*

1. I hope Gina didn't forget _____ the stove again when she left.
   a. to turn off   b. turning off

2. In the mountains, it continued _____ for a week.
   a. to snow   b. snowing

3. We have some free time before dinner. Let's go _____.
   a. to sightsee   b. sightseeing

4. From a distance, the bear appeared _____ smaller than he was.
   a. to be   b. being

5. Have you thought about _____ extra employees for the holiday season?
   a. to hire   b. hiring

6. Anita and Rob have decided _____ at the same company.
   a. to work   b. working

7. Pierre began _____ English six months ago.
   a. to study   b. studying

8. Mrs. Allen can't stand _____ in icy weather.
   a. to drive   b. driving

9. We can't wait _____ our cousins on the coast.
   a. to visit   b. visiting

10. Bobby learned how _____ a tractor on his grandfather's farm.
    a. to operate   b. operating

Directions: *Complete the phrases with the correct preposition.*

1. thank you _____ coming

2. be afraid _____ swimming

3. believe _____ having

4. be nervous _____ going

5. plan _____ coming

6. look forward _____ seeing

7. be excited _____ flying

8. don't feel _____ eating

9. be good _____ drawing

10. apologize _____ hurting

Directions: Complete the sentences with a preposition and the given words.

1. Are you worried   + lose your job

   _____

2. Beth is afraid   + go to the dentist

   _____

3. Ken dreamt   + live on a tropical island

   _____

4. The students are responsible   + keep the classroom clean

   _____

5. Management is interested   + promote Terry to marketing director

   _____

6. Barbara insisted   + invite her former boyfriends to her wedding

   _____

*Directions: Complete the sentences with **by** or **with**.*

1. We traveled around the country last summer _____ train.
2. My parents and I communicate _____ e-mail once a week.
3. The salesperson greeted us _____ a smile.
4. The carpet installer cut the carpet _____ special scissors.
5. The package went _____ land _____ mistake, and arrived late.
6. The nurse took the patient's temperature _____ a thermometer.
7. It's easy to get around Tokyo _____ subway.
8. You can pay _____ credit card, but not _____ check.
9. Marcos measured the paper _____ a ruler.
10. Even though the Andersons are married, they live in different cities _____ choice.

Directions: Complete the sentences with **by** + *a verb from the list.*

call	draw	exercise	promise
cut	do	paint	wash

1. Khalid stays in shape _____ three times a week.

2. You can help me _____ the windows that I can't reach.

3. We can make the apartment look better _____ the bedrooms.

4. Andy is going to earn extra money _____ grass for his neighbors this summer.

5. Students can improve their grades _____ extra work.

6. I finally reached the airline _____ every five minutes for an hour.

7. The politician won the election _____ to lower taxes.

8. The little girl got her mother's attention _____ pictures on the wall with a red pencil.

Directions: Create sentences with the same meaning by using a gerund as the subject.

> *Example:* It is important to get a good night's sleep.
> → *Getting a good night's sleep is important.*

1. It is fun to travel with friends.

2. It isn't O.K. copy another student's homework.

3. It is easy to telephone someone in another country.

4. It is difficult to be away from family and friends.

5. It is interesting to learn about other countries.

6. It is dangerous to ride a bike without a helmet.

7. It is important to recycle as much garbage as you can.

8. It is impossible to predict the future.

QUIZ 11 IT + infinitive *(Chart 13-8)*

*Directions: Rewrite the sentences using **it** + infinitive.*

1. Learning how to ride a motorcycle properly is important for motorcyclists.

2. Writing with their left hand is hard for right-handed people.

3. Mixing two colors to make a new color is interesting for children.

4. Taking off shoes before entering a house is customary for many people.

5. Sailing a boat in windy weather is exciting for sailors.

6. Eating a variety of fruits and vegetables is important for good health.

QUIZ 12 Using IN ORDER TO *(Chart 13-9)*

*Directions: Answer the questions with the words in parentheses and **in order to**.*

Example: Why did you go on a diet? (lose weight)
→ *I went on a diet in order to lose weight.*

1. Why did you turn down the T.V? (hear you better)

_____

2. Why did you wear socks to bed? (keep my feet warm)

_____

3. Why did you withdraw money from the bank? (buy a car)

_____

4. Why did you call the doctor? (ask if I needed a flu shot)

_____

5. Why did you turn off the phone? (get some sleep)

_____

Directions: Complete the sentences with **to** *or* **for**.

Last weekend, I went to the mountains . . .

1. _____ ski with friends.

2. _____ a ski trip.

3. _____ have fun with friends.

4. _____ spend time away from the city.

5. _____ some fresh air and relaxation.

Yesterday, I made an appointment . . .

6. _____ my husband.

7. _____ see our lawyer.

8. _____ a meeting with our lawyer.

9. _____ speak with our lawyer.

10. _____ get some legal advice.

QUIZ 14 Using IN ORDER TO *(Chart 13-9)*

Directions: Add **in order** *where possible.*

Example: Alison would prefer to stay home tomorrow. (no change)
in order
Bill called the drugstore ∧ to ask a question.

1. Kim applied to the university for next year.

2. Judy is moving to be closer to her elderly parents.

3. Tom got new glasses to read better.

4. I have to be sure to pay my bills today.

5. Francisco started a fire to warm up the house.

6. Fortunately, we remembered to stop our mail while we were on vacation.

Directions: Complete the sentences with the words in parentheses and **too** *or* **enough**.

1. It's hot outside. I can't work in the garden.

    (**hot**) It's _____ to work in the garden.

    (**cool**) It isn't _____ to work in the garden.

2. I can't eat plain yogurt.

    (**sour**) Plain yogurt is _____ for me to eat.

    (**sweet**) Plain yogurt isn't _____ for me to eat.

3. I'm not going to make an omelet for breakfast.

    (**eggs**) I don't have _____ to make an omelet.

    (**tired**) I'm _____ to make an omelet for breakfast.

4. The brakes on the car are bad. Don't drive it.

    (**safe**) The car isn't _____ to drive.

    (**dangerous**) The car is _____ to drive.

5. Your shirt still has ink spots on it. You can't wear it.

    (**clean**) The shirt isn't _____ to wear.

    (**dirty**) It's _____ to wear.

Directions: Complete the sentences with **too** *or* **enough**. *Choose one of the adjectives in parentheses.*

1. (*little/big*) The kitten isn't _____ to stay outside all night.

2. (*young/old*) Your little boy is smart, and he is _____ to understand the word *no*.

3. (*old/young*) Grandpa Smith is 98. He is _____ to drive now.

4. (*expensive/cheap*) I know the watch is on sale, but it's still _____ for me to buy.

5. (*warm/cold*) The children are hoping for snow, but it isn't _____ to snow.

6. (*long/short*) I'll never finish this book in one week. It's _____ to read in a week.

7. (*soft/hard*) This pillow is uncomfortable. It's not _____ for me to sleep on. It feels like a rock.

8. (*hungry/not hungry*) I've got to stop for lunch. I'm _____ to do any more work.

Directions: *Circle the correct answer. In some cases, both answers are corret.*

1. We plan _____ our ten-year-old car soon.
   a. to replace   b. replacing

2. Jason learned how _____ when he was three years old.
   a. to ski   b. skiing

3. Although Nancy is fifteen, she is afraid of _____ alone in her house when her parents are out.
   a. to stay   b. staying

4. Professor Dunn always wears a suit and tie to class _____ professional.
   a. to look   b. looking

5. I meant _____ you, but I misplaced your phone number.
   a. to call   b. calling

6. Even after the teacher asked them to stop, several students continued _____ during the art history film.
   a. to talk   b. talking

7. Tony prefers _____ the stairs in tall buildings.
   a. to use   b. using

8. He's afraid of _____ in elevators.
   a. to ride   b. riding

9. We'd love _____ together with you over the holidays.
   a. to get   b. getting

10. Tina doesn't mind _____ on weekends because she gets paid a higher wage.
    a. to work   b. working

11. Don't put off until tomorrow _____ what you can do today.
    a. to do   b. doing

12. Our sociology professor promised _____ extra credit to those students who volunteered to work with disabled or senior citizens in the community.
    a. to give   b. giving

13. It's important for children _____ the value of money.
    a. to learn   b. learning

14. Thank you for _____ with the chemistry project. We never could have finished it on time by ourselves.
    a. to help   b. helping

15. Susie and Scott arrived at the theater early _____ good seats.
    a. to get   b. getting

16. Chris left the key to his house at work. He got in by _____ through an open window.
    a. climb   b. climbing

17. The students searched the Internet _____ more information for their research projects.
    a. to get   b. getting

18. It takes patience _____ young children.
    a. to teach   b. teaching

19. Gary likes _____ to the radio at night because it helps him fall asleep.
    a. to listen   b. listening

20. Grace keeps her dog in a fenced area _____ him from running away.
    a. to stop   b. stopping

CHAPTER 13 PRACTICE TEST

Part I

Gerunds and infinitives

Directions: Complete the sentences with the words in parentheses: gerund or infinitive. Some answers may require a preposition.

1. James is nervous (**start**) _____ his new management job because most of the employees wanted another person for the position.

2. Glen just started his own company. He can't afford (**take**) _____ a vacation this year.

3. Sam called his accountant (**ask**) _____ for tax advice.

4. Joe insists (**get**) _____ to the airport at least five hours before his flight. He refuses (**arrive**) _____ any later. (**Be**) _____ in control relaxes him, and he's calmer about the flight.

5. The children would like (**build**) _____ a snowman today. It began (**snow**) _____ last night, and now the snow is up to the windows. They plan (**make**) _____ a snowman as tall as the tree outside their house. School has been canceled for the week, and they are excited (**have**) _____ _____ some time off. When they finish (**build**) _____ their snowman, they're going to go (**sled**) _____ near their house.

Part II

Prepositions

Directions: Complete the sentences with the correct prepositions.

1. Mr. Thomas is planning _____ attending the meeting, but he'll be few minutes late.

2. Brad and Heidi hadn't seen each other since high school. They met at the airport _____ chance.

3. Carlos takes a cruise once a year because he thinks traveling _____ sea is the most interesting way to see the world.

4. After working hard all year, Alex and Donna are looking forward _____ a family vacation.

5. Mr. Brown ran onto the sidewalk, picked up his little boy, and stopped him _____ being hit by a runaway car.

Directions: *Make complete sentences. Add* **too** *or* **enough**.

Example: Jenny is sick. She can't go to school.

    a. (**sick**) *Jenny is too sick to go to school.*

    b. (**well**) *Jenny isn't well enough to go to school.*

1. Don't walk on the ice in the lake. It's not very cold.

    a. (**soft**) The ice _____ to walk on.

    b. (**frozen**) The ice _____ to walk on.

2. Wait a few minutes before you touch the pan. It's still hot.

    a. (**cool**) The pan _____ to touch.

    b. (**hot**) The pan _____ to touch.

Part IV Error analysis

Directions: *Check the incorrect sentences and then correct them.*

1. _____ It is impossible to jump for an elephant.

2. _____ Jack can't stand to cook fish indoors because of the strong smell.

3. _____ I tried digging a hole with a broken shovel, but it didn't work.

4. _____ We can continue discussion this topic tomorrow.

5. _____ If we arrive at the resort before noon, we can go to hiking in the mountains.

6. _____ Toshi was surprised that the salesclerk apologized her rude behavior.

CHAPTER 13 FINAL TEST

Part I Gerunds and infinitives

Directions: Complete the sentences with the words in parentheses: gerund or infinitive. Some answers may require a preposition.

1. At first, John was afraid (**hold**) _____ his newborn son because he seemed so fragile. But he soon realized that his son was quite strong, and he learned (**relax**) _____ with him.

2. Pedro is good (**kick**) _____ a soccer ball with his left foot even though he is right-handed. (**Play**) _____ soccer is his favorite sport.

3. When she gets home from work, Liz doesn't feel (**cook**) _____ . She just wants (**lie**) _____ on the sofa with a good book or magazine.

4. A young couple is interested (**buy**) _____ our house. They intend (**start**) _____ a family, so they would like (**add**) _____ on a few rooms.

5. A truck driver called (**get**) _____ help for a young woman with car trouble on the highway.

6. Last night I dreamt (**fly**) _____ over Paris in a hot-air balloon. A tour guide told me it was the only way to go (**sightsee**) _____ in Paris, so I flew over the city for several hours. I almost touched the Eiffel Tower, but I was afraid (**pop**) _____ the balloon. Suddenly I felt very cold. I tried (**cover**) _____ myself with blankets, but I couldn't. As soon as I woke up, I discovered why. My younger brother had decided (**pull**) _____ off all my blankets.

Part II Prepositions

Directions: Complete the sentences with the correct preposition.

1. Do you believe _____ ghosts or other supernatural beings?

2. You can reach the top shelf _____ stepping on the small chair next to the table.

3. In some areas of my country, it's cheaper to travel _____ train than _____ bus.

4. Even though Mrs. Miller's children are all grown, she continues to worry _____ them.

5. We paid our electric bill _____ check, but the company has no record of it.

6. My mother-in-law made this baby blanket _____ hand.

7. Let me see if I can quickly repair your pants _____ a needle and thread.

8. I was going to cut the lettuce _____ a knife, but my sister showed me it was faster to do it _____ a pair of scissors.

9. The mother comforted her son _____ holding him very close for a few minutes.

10. Becky forgave her little brother _____ breaking her pearl necklace.

Part III TOO vs. ENOUGH

*Directions: Make complete sentences. Use **too** or **enough**.*

1. I can't hear the speaker's voice. It's so soft.

   a. (**loud**) The speaker's voice _____ to hear.

   b. (**soft**) The speaker's voice _____ to hear.

2. This chocolate tastes terrible. It's very bitter because it contains no sugar.

   a. (**sweet**) This chocolate _____ to eat.

   b. (**bitter**) This chocolate _____ to eat.

3. The sun is coming in through the window. It's so bright that we can't see the picture on the TV.

   a. (**bright**) It _____ to see the picture.

   b. (**dark**) It _____ to see the picture.

4. I let my coffee sit on the table too long. Now I don't want to drink it.

   a. (**warm**) It _____ to drink.

   b. (**cool**) It _____ to drink.

Part IV Error analysis

Directions: Check the incorrect sentences and then correct them.

1. _____ Eating popcorn and watching a video is a great way to relax in the evening.

2. _____ I need to stop at the bank for withdrawing some money.

3. _____ Are you responsible cleaning up after the party?

4. _____ Is relaxing to walk barefoot in the sand on the beach.

5. _____ Jeannie asked to left work early to take her children to the doctor's.

6. _____ William took photography lessons to learn how to develop his own pictures.

7. _____ Driving in heavy traffic it requires skill and patience.

8. _____ If we hurry, we still have time to go swimming in the lake before dark.

9. _____ It is sometimes scary to visit the doctor for young children.

10. _____ Helen enjoys to be the center of attention at a party.

NOUN CLAUSES

Information questions and noun clauses *(Chart 14-1)*

Directions: Add final punctuation—a period (.) or a question mark (?). Then circle whether it is an information question or a noun clause.

   Examples:
   → *I don't know. Why did Jacques leave*❓   (information question)   noun clause
   → *I'm not sure where the Browns live.*   information question   (noun clause)

1. What does Nate do for a living	information question	noun clause
2. Do you know what time it is	information question	noun clause
3. When does class start	information question	noun clause
4. Please tell me. Why are you late	information question	noun clause
5. I wonder what happened	information question	noun clause
6. Who is coming	information question	noun clause
7. Did you know what Katie said	information question	noun clause

Noun clauses that begin with a question word *(Chart 14-2)*

Directions: Complete the sentences, using noun clauses.

   1. (Where is he living?)

      I don't know _____

   2. (Where do we go next?)

      I'm not sure _____

   3. (When was the party?)

      I'd like to know _____

   4. (Where will the next party be?)

      Please tell me _____

   5. (How did Tony and Patricia meet?)

      Do you know _____

   6. (What happened?)

      I wonder _____

   7. (When will the show be over?)

      Do you know _____

   8. (Where are the Ross twins studying?)

      I'm not sure _____

Directions: *Complete the sentences, using noun clauses.*

1. (What is the matter?)

   Please tell me _____

2. (What time is it?)

   Could you tell me _____

3. (Whose seat is this?)

   Do you know _____

4. (Who is at the door?)

   I don't know _____

5. (Whose car is that?)

   I wonder _____

6. (What is the difference?)

   We don't understand _____

7. (Whose problem is it?)

   The government doesn't know _____

8. (Who is in your class?)

   Do you know _____

Directions: *Change the questions to noun clauses.*
   Example:
   Are you ready? I'd like to know if (whether) you are ready.

1. *Is the store open?* Do you know _____

2. *Did Rosa go to lunch?* I'm not sure _____

3. *Are the movers coming soon?* Do you know _____

4. *Can fish fly?* Do you know _____

5. *Does Tom have any advice?* I'm not sure _____

6. *Do you need anything else?* Please tell me _____

7. *Will Alice be here tomorrow?* Do you know _____

8. *Is there any dinner left?* I wonder _____

9. *Has the mail come yet?* I'm not sure _____

10. *Does Samir eat meat?* Do you know _____

Directions: Write noun clauses that combine a sentence in italics and a phrase in parentheses. Try to express your own opinion.

> *UFOs exist.*
> *Men are stronger than women.*
> *Is smoking harmful?*
> *Can people learn to live together peacefully?*
> *Taxes are necessary.*
> *How will I die?*
> *Will wars ever end?*
> *Watching TV is harmful for young children.*

1. (I believe / I don't believe) _____

2. (I feel / I don't feel) _____

3. (I agree / I don't agree) _____

4. (I know / I don't know) _____

5. (I hope) _____

6. (I'm sure / I'm not sure) _____

7. (I wonder) _____

8. (I would like to know / I wouldn't like to know) _____

*Directions: Add the word **that** in the appropriate place to mark the beginning of a noun clause.*

1. The police are trying to prove the suspect took the money.

2. At school, the children like to pretend they are princes and princesses.

3. We're disappointed you didn't believe us.

4. Did I tell you we are moving next week?

5. Our teacher really trusts us. I still can't believe she leaves the room during tests.

6. For centuries, people were convinced the earth was flat.

7. Is it true your diamond necklace is missing?

8. Can you believe it's summer already?

9. I'm positive "scissors" is spelled with four "esses."

10. Carlos was impressed Juan knew so much about chemistry.

Directions: Complete the sentences with **so** *or* **not**.

1. A: Are you ready for the test?

    B: I hope _____ . *(I am ready.)*

2. A: You have some money with you. Is it enough?

    B: I hope _____. *(It is enough money.)*

3. A: It's started to rain. Do you still want to go swimming?

    B: I guess _____. *(I don't want to go swimming.)*

4. A: Here's a map. Do you think you can find the street the Browns live on?

    B: I think _____. *(I can find it.)*

5. A: Did you forget your wallet?

    B: I hope _____. *(I didn't forget my wallet.)*

6. A: Is Sergei well enough to return to work?

    B: I don't think _____. (He isn't well enough.)

7. A: Would you like to come with us?

    B: I guess _____. *(I would like to go with you.)*

8. A: Have you learned the names of all your students yet?

    B: I hope _____. *(I have learned their names.)*

9. A: Would you like another cup of coffee?

    B: I don't think _____. *(I don't want another cup.)*

10. A: Is Amy going to visit us next month?

    B: I believe _____. *(She is going to visit us.)*

Directions: Add quotation marks and the appropriate punctuation.

1. Carmen asked do you have money for parking

2. The doctor said stop smoking today

3. My mother said I won't be home until 7:00 tonight could you get dinner started

4. Our teacher asked who knows the answer who would like to write it on the board

5. The policeman said may I see your driver's license, please

6. The Johnsons said we have to go now we have another party to attend tonight

QUIZ 9 **Quoted speech** *(Chart 14-8)*

Directions: Add quotation marks and the appropriate punctuation.

I don't like spiders my daughter said

Why not I asked

They're quite ugly she replied

Well, they might look unpleasant I said they're not as beautiful as butterflies, but they're good to have around. They eat ants and flies that you don't want to have in your house. Even though you don't like them I said try to think of them as a gift from nature.

QUIZ 10 **Quoted speech vs. reported speech** *(Chart 14-9)*

Directions: Complete the sentences with the correct pronouns.

1. Mrs. Diaz said, "My secretary is on vacation this week."

    Mrs. Diaz said that _____ secretary was on vacation this week.

2. My husband said to me, "Our children want us to take them to a movie tonight."

    My husband said that _____ children wanted _____ to take _____ to a movie tonight.

3. Joan said, "I can come over to your house tonight and help you and your brother with the science project."

    Joan said that _____ could come over to _____ house tonight and help _____ and _____ brother with the science project.

4. Mr. Owens said, "I want my children to be independent and think for themselves."

    Mr. Owens said that _____ wanted _____ children to be independent and think for _____ .

5. The woman at the bakery said, "I'm afraid that our customers bought all our fresh bread this morning. We're sold out."

    The woman at the bakery said that _____ was afraid that _____ customers had bought all _____ fresh bread this morning. _____ were sold out.

6. The teachers at the school said to the parents, "We have high standards for your children, and we will support their efforts to be successful."

    The teachers at the school said to the parents that _____ had high standards for _____ children, and _____ would support _____ efforts to be successful.

Directions: Complete each sentence with the correct form of the verb. Use formal sequence of tenses.

1. The teacher said, "The test will be on Friday."

   The teacher said that the test _____ on Friday.

2. The mail carrier said, "There was no mail delivery on Monday because of the holiday."

   The mail carrier said that there _____ no mail delivery on Monday
   because of the holiday.

3. The weather reporter said, "Yesterday's weather set record cold temperatures across the
   country."

   The weather reporter said that yesterday's weather _____ record cold
   temperatures across the country.

4. Junko said, "I don't understand the problem."

   Junko said that she _____ the problem.

5. The director said, "The actors haven't learned their lines yet."

   The director said that the actors _____ their lines yet.

6. Pedro said, "The movie is going to start in ten minutes. We need to leave."

   Pedro said that the movie _____ in ten minutes, and that they

   _____ to leave.

7. Marie said, "My English teacher has the flu."

   Marie said that her English teacher _____ the flu.

8. The Smiths said, "We can feed your cats while you are away."

   The Smiths said they _____ our cats while we _____
   away.

Directions: Change the quoted speech to reported speech. Use formal verb forms.

1. My father said, "We enjoyed our trip to Singapore."

2. Our friends said, "We want to give you a going-away party."

3. Abdul said, "I will be twenty-five on my next birthday."

4. My husband said, "I can pick up the kids after school. You don't need to be home."

5. The boy said, "The dog took my ball. He isn't coming back."

6. Dr. Wilson said, "I'm going to retire in a few years. My husband and I are planning to travel."

7. My grandmother said to me, "I have had a wonderful life."

Directions: Complete the sentences with **said**, **told**, *or* **asked**.

1. The teacher _____ me if I had done my homework.

2. I _____ her I had finished it last night.

3. Benito _____ us he could take us to school.

4. The manager _____ that all employees would get overtime pay for the holiday.

5. Scott _____ his parents that he had rented an apartment.

6. His parents _____ they were pleased that he had found one.

7. The recipe _____ to use one cup of sugar, but the children misread it and used two.

8. The security guard _____ that everyone needed an I.D. card to enter the building. I _____ him that I had left mine at home. I _____ him if I could show him my driver's license. He _____, "No." He _____ me I had to go home and get it. I _____ him I would be late for work. He _____, "Sorry," but he couldn't change the rules.

QUIZ 14 Error analysis *(Chapter review)*

Directions: Correct the errors.

1. I don't know yet the doctor can see you tomorrow or not.

2. Please tell me what did they do.

3. Do you know whose coat on the chair is?

4. Do you know if or not the bus has come?

5. We'd like to know if the subway stop here?

6. I hope so that I can come with you tonight.

7. Suzanne say me that she wasn't home last night.

8. I'm afraid, that we have to cancel our plans.

9. The dentist said Your teeth look very healthy. You are taking good care of them.

10. The teacher isn't sure whether Liz want help or not.

CHAPTER 14 PRACTICE TEST

Part I Noun clauses

Directions: Complete the sentences with noun clauses.

1. A: Mom, where's the milk?

   B: I don't know _____.

2. A: What time will we be done?

   B: I'm not sure _____.

3. A: Are there any eggs left?

   B: I don't know _____.

4. A: Whose work is this?

   B: I don't know _____.

5. A: Is someone knocking at the door?

   B: I'll go check _____.

6. A: Who just left?

   B: I'll find out _____.

Part II Quoted speech

Directions: Add quotation marks and the appropriate punctuation.

My mom came in the bedroom and opened the curtains. What time is it I asked her.

Time to get up she replied.

But Mom I said it's not a school day. Please let me sleep in I begged.

You can't sleep in today she said. It's a special day.

What special day I asked.

It's your birthday she said.

Oh my gosh! I forgot. I have to get up right away I said. I have so many things I want
to do today.

Part III Reported speech

Directions: *Change the quoted speech to reported speech. Use formal verb forms.*

1. Julia said, "The cookies are ready."

2. The librarian said, "The library is going to close early today."

3. Erica said, "The bank manager left town with the bank's money."

4. John asked, "How far away is the airport?"

5. The clerk asked me, "Do you want paper or plastic bags?"

6. Marika said, "The flight will arrive in 10 minutes."

7. The fire chief said, "The fire took a long time to put out."

8. Helen said, "I can juggle three balls in the air at the same time."

Part IV Error analysis

Directions: *Correct the errors.*

1. My friends understand what do I like.

2. I'd like to know does this computer work?

3. The teacher told that he would be at a conference tomorrow.

4. I want to know why did they come.

5. Is a fact that exercise makes us healthier.

6. Do you know if Rick live here.

7. I'm sure, that we will have a good time together.

8. A strange man asked me "Where I live."

CHAPTER 14 FINAL TEST

Directions: *Complete the sentences with noun clauses.*

1. A: What's the date today?

   B: I'm not sure _____ .

2. A: Who will be the new manager?

   B: We don't know yet _____ .

3. A: Did Ed and Irene get engaged last weekend?

   B: I have no idea _____ .

4. A: Whose car are we taking?

   B: We haven't decided _____ .

5. A: How many people knew about the problem?

   B: I'll find out _____ .

6. A: Does the weather change much or stay the same in this area?

   B: I don't know _____ .

7. A: Did Paula leave the company?

   B: I haven't heard _____ .

8. A: Has anyone requested help yet?

   B: I'll see _____ .

9. A: Do you know the year you were born?

   B: Of course I know _____ .

10. A: Does the copy machine work?

    B: I'll see _____ .

Part II Quoted speech

Directions: Add quotation marks and the appropriate punctuation.

Last week, my teacher and I were talking about my future. What do you want to do after you finish school he asked.

I'm not sure I said. I'd like to have a job that is interesting and pays well.

Everyone would like that said my teacher. Is there a specific area you see yourself working in?

Yes I replied. I love working with animals. Maybe I could be a veterinarian.

One way to find out said my teacher is to work with animals first. Volunteer at an animal shelter or zoo. See how you like it.

I told him I liked his suggestion and thanked him.

Part III Reported speech

Directions: Change the quoted speech to reported speech. Use formal verb forms.

1. The police officer said to me, "I am giving you a warning, not a ticket."

2. The teacher said, "The test is going to be on Friday."

3. The students replied, "We don't want a test."

4. Joe asked, "Who took my car?"

5. The manager said, "We have decided to move our offices to a new location."

6. Yolanda said, "The bus will be late."

7. Sally said, "I can fix that for you."

8. My parents said, "We were happy to hear about your job promotion."

9. The doctor asked me, "Have you been taking your medicine?"

10. The dancers said, "We have practiced our dance steps. We're ready for our show."

Directions: Correct the errors.

1. Can you tell me whose coat belongs to this?

2. I felt better when the doctor said, your daughter just has a bad cold. It's nothing serious.

3. My friends ask me that. "When will you get married."

4. Did my mom ask you if or not you could come to our party?

5. Hamid asked why did I always come late?

6. Mr. Hill told to me that he was feeling ill.

7. Could you tell me where Fred work in the evenings?

8. I think so that you will enjoy being on the soccer team.

9. I know, that this will be a good opportunity for us.

10. Professor Thomas told us he will be absent yesterday.

QUIZ 1   (Group A)

Directions: Complete the sentences.

1. Please don't wake me ___up___ tomorrow morning. I don't have to go to work until noon.

2. The baby took _____ her shoes. She likes to be barefoot.

3. How can we figure _____ this math problem? It's very difficult.

4. After I handed _____ my homework, I remembered that I didn't write my name on it.

5. I don't understand this word. I'll look it _____ in the dictionary.

6. The chairperson put _____ the meeting until Friday. She wanted more time to prepare.

7. Christie loves to make _____ stories. Yesterday she told one about a prince and a frog.

8. Our teacher hands _____ a lot of homework. It takes us three hours a night to do.

9. Let me write _____ your address. Then I can send you an invitation to the party.

10. It's too bright in here. I think I will turn _____ a few lights.

11. Why did you throw _____ your old school books? They might be valuable some day.

12. Could you help me? I can't pick _____ this heavy box.

13. The baby cries whenever I put her _____ . She always wants to be held.

14. Before you can turn _____ the copy machine, you need a key. It won't work without one.

15. Julia put _____ a hat to go outdoors, but then decided it was warm enough without one.

QUIZ 2   (Group B)

Directions: Complete the sentences.

1. Where do polar bears come _____ ?

2. The police have been looking _____ the crime for several months.

3. Jennifer had a serious illness. It took her months to get _____ it.

4. The teacher always calls _____ me when I haven't done my homework. How does she know?

5. We got _____ the plane just as it was leaving. We almost missed our flight.

6. Six people need a ride to the hotel. How many people can get _____ this taxi?

7. If you run _____ Adam at work, ask him if he wants to have dinner with us on Saturday.

8. When Isabelle got _____ _____ the car at the airport, she slid and fell on some ice.

9. If the students can get _____ the bus at Fifth Avenue, a teacher can be there to pick them up.

Directions: *Complete the sentences.*

1. Why did you hang _____ the phone? I wanted to talk to Yuko.

2. I'm not sure if these shoes fit. I'll try them _____ .

3. Could you shut _____ the lights when you leave?

4. Nicole never puts her clothes _____ . They're all over her bedroom floor.

5. Ted would like to ask Sally _____ , but he's shy. Maybe she'll ask him out instead.

6. Christopher left his number. You can call him _____ after 5 P.M.

7. I'm done with the tools you lent me. I'll give them _____ to you tomorrow.

8. Emily has borrowed a lot of money for graduate school. It's going to take her a long time to pay it _____ .

9. The children can use these new crayons, but they need to put them _____ in the box when they're finished.

10. A truck was on fire on the highway. Several fire trucks were needed to put it _____ .

11. Every time my husband, Jay, plays rock 'n roll, I turn it _____ because it hurts my ears. Sometimes I even want to turn it off.

12. When Jay drives by himself, he turns the music _____ . Once he got a ticket for playing music too loud.

13. Can you believe it? Anita called _____ her wedding one week before the date.

14. I'm surprised Steven called me _____ . I haven't spoken to him in years.

Directions: *Complete the sentences.*

1. My printer isn't working properly. It's printing _____ only half the page.

2. We're lost. Let's turn _____ and see if we can find someone to help us.

3. Sonya is upset. Someone tore several pages _____ _____ her notebook.

4. Don't pay attention to the paragraphs I crossed _____ . Just read the other ones.

5. If I take this automotive class, I can find _____ how to repair my car.

6. This picture might be famous. Why don't you turn it _____ and see if there's a signature on the back.

7. Rachel must be sleepy. She has _____ one blue shoe and one brown shoe.

8. At the restaurant, the waiter filled _____ my thermos with coffee, but the lid wasn't on tight and it spilled all over the table.

9. David wasn't happy when his secretary pointed _____ the spelling mistakes in his e-mail.

10. He said he had looked it _____ carefully after he wrote it.

11. The city is going to tear _____ those old buildings and put up low-income housing.

12. Why did you tear _____ your composition and throw it away? Were you upset about your grade?

13. As soon as you fill _____ these two blanks, you'll be finished.

14. I don't have much time. How long does it usually take to fill _____ all these forms?

(Group E)

Directions: *Complete the sentences.*

1. You look upset. What can we do to cheer you _____ ?

2. The Johnson's were unable to work _____ their problems with their neighbor. Now they need to get a lawyer.

3. There are 100 candles on this birthday cake! Scott will need help to blow them all _____ .

4. At Henry's school, all parents must help _____ in the classroom once a month.

5. We can take the children to the party if you can bring them _____ home.

6. Let's clean _____ your toys before Mommy comes home. She'll be so pleased.

7. Matt is worried. His company has laid _____ 20 percent of its workforce.

8. Before I say *yes*, I need to think _____ your offer. I'm not sure if I want to change jobs.

9. Mr. and Mrs. Kelly brought _____ two children whose parents died when they were young. The Kellys raised them as their own.

10. We're not sure if we're going to have a large or a small wedding. We still need to talk _____ a lot of the details.

11. Mrs. Peterson was very generous. She gave _____ most of her money to charity before she died.

12. You can leave the TV _____ . I'll turn it off when I go to bed.

13. Jerry would like to take Nadia _____ to dinner, but he hasn't asked her yet.

14. The customer wanted to take a pair of shoes _____ to the store after wearing them for a month. The store refused to accept them.

Directions: *Check all the correct sentences.*

1. ____ Julie sang a song. She made it up.

   ____ Julie sang a song. She made up it.

2. ____ Please wake me up soon.

   ____ Please wake up me soon.

3. ____ Let's get in this taxi.

   ____ Let's get this taxi in.

4. ____ You need to pay the loan back.

   ____ You need to pay back the loan.

5. ____ I ran into some college friends at the train station.

   ____ I ran some college friends into at the train station.

6. ____ The secretary wrote down the phone number.

   ____ The secretary wrote the phone number down.

   ____ The secretary wrote it down.

   ____ The secretary wrote down it.

7. ____ We should clean up the garage this weekend.

   ____ We should clean the garage up this weekend.

   ____ We should clean up it.

8. ____ We were the last passengers to get on the plane.

   ____ We were the last passengers to get the plane on.

9. ____ Professor Moore handed out a long assignment.

   ____ Professor Moore handed a long assignment out.

   ____ Professor Moore handed out it.

10. ____ Could you help me figure this puzzle out?

    ____ Could you help me figure out this puzzle?

    ____ Could you help me figure it out?

11. ____ The lights were off. I turned them on.

    ____ The lights were off. I turned on them.

12. ____ Rita got over the flu very quickly.

    ____ Rita got the flu over very quickly.

13. ____ Why did you put off the meeting?

    ____ Why did you put the meeting off?

    ____ Why did you put off it?

14. ____ The police are looking into the crime.

    ____ The police are looking the crime into.

15. ____ Sorry. I already tore the message up.

    ____ Sorry. I already tore up the message.

    ____ Sorry. I already tore up it.

***Directions**: Complete the sentences.*

1. Jimmy, if you take a short nap now, you can stay _____ an hour later tonight.

2. We're trying to save money. We only eat _____ on special occasions like birthdays.

3. You look like you've had a hard day. Why don't you sit _____ and relax.

4. Yesterday, our five-year-old son told us that when he grows _____, he will do whatever he wants.

5. The restaurant sounds expensive. Do you know if we need to dress _____?

6. The school bus broke _____ on the highway, so another one had to come and get the children.

7. I don't think Ron and Bonnie will break _____. They've been together fifteen years.

8. When I got _____ at 5 A.M., I couldn't find my glasses. I immediately tripped over a chair and fell _____.

9. There are a thousand pieces to this puzzle, but Helen will figure it out. She never gives _____.

10. It's cold outside. Why don't you come _____ and wait in the lobby until the bus comes?

11. We planned to go _____ Friday night, but we couldn't get someone to watch the children. We'll just stay home.

12. Several times last night, someone called and hung _____. It made me quite nervous.

13. When the cat showed _____ for dinner last night, it had a bird in its mouth.

14. It looks like someone is moving _____ to the apartment next to yours. Let's go meet your new neighbors.

15. When you have an idea in a meeting, you need to speak _____ if you want people to pay attention.

16. The storm delayed all the flights at the airport. We were lucky to be the first plane to take _____.

17. After you take this medicine, you should stand _____ slowly. You might be a little dizzy.

18. Ben slowed down to pick up a hitchhiker on the highway, but I told him to go _____. Picking up hitchhikers is dangerous.

19. After Jonathan lost his business, he decided to move to a new city and start _____.

20. When war broke _____, my father was in the army and my mother was in the air force. They didn't see each other for more than a year.

21. The previous renters of this house moved _____ without telling the landlord they were leaving.

Directions: *Complete the sentences.*

1. Watch _____ _____ holes in the ice. The lake is not completely frozen.

2. Hani speaks several languages because he grew _____ _____ several countries.

3. I've gotten _____ _____ all my roommates except the one I have now. We argue!

4. You can't drop _____ _____ school! You have only a few months before you graduate.

5. The night the Martins got _____ _____ their camping trip, they learned they were grandparents. Their daughter had had a baby while they were away.

6. The students can't finish their art projects because the teacher has run _____ _____ paper and paints.

7. I always like to call before I visit. I'm not comfortable dropping _____ _____ someone without telling them I'm coming.

8. Even though Marie's in college, she doesn't study much. She prefers to fool _____ _____ her roommates.

9. As soon as the volleyball players get _____ _____ their practice, the janitor can lock up the building.

10. People who sign _____ _____ the dance class after it begins must pay a late fee.

11. Deer cross this road often. You need to drive slowly and look _____ _____ them.

Directions: *Complete the sentences.*

1. Elizabeth found _____ _____ her mother's illness from her sister. Her mother didn't want to worry her.

2. The sailors set _____ _____ the island when the water was calm, but a storm soon made them turn back.

3. Can you come _____ _____ my house Saturday night? I'm having a dinner party.

4. Papa will be home late tonight. He's getting _____ _____ some old friends at a restaurant.

5. Ingrid went _____ _____ work one week after her surgery, but it was too soon and now she's back in the hospital.

6. My parents told me I had to get a job this summer. They said I can't sit _____ _____ my friends like I did last summer.

7. I'll keep this medicine _____ _____ the children. It looks like candy.

8. The kids in the neighborhood like to hang _____ _____ each other at the baseball field after school.

9. Liz asked me to coffee this morning, but when I went _____ _____ her house, she wasn't there. She probably forgot.

10. I cut this dessert recipe _____ _____ the newspaper. It looks delicious.

11. Jonas is too young to walk to school by himself. His mother always comes _____ _____ him.

APPENDIX 1 FINAL TEST

Directions: Choose the correct answer.

1. The dinner is formal. You'll need to dress _____ .
   a. on   b. down   c. up   d. with

2. We'd better not stay _____ too late tonight. We need to be at the airport early in the morning.
   a. down   b. in   c. up   d. back

3. The roads are icy. Watch out _____ slippery spots on the hills.
   a. from   b. for   c in   d. on

4. We'll be gone for a few days, but we'll leave _____ a few lights. That way it will look like we're home.
   a. on   b. out   c. of   d. in

5. When the teacher pointed _____ all the simple errors the students made on the test, they were embarrassed.
   a. out   b. in   c. on   d. over

6. The hikers have enough water for five days. They aren't worried about running _____ .
   a. down   b. away   c. out   d. to

7. If you forgot your homework, you can hand it _____ tomorrow.
   a. out   b. back   c. up   d. in

8. In your country, do you stand _____ when the teacher enters the room?
   a. on   b. in   c. up   d. away

9. Joe is not happy with his new radio. He plans to take it _____ to the store.
   a. back   b. on   c. away   d. into

10. Please speak _____ . No one in the back of the room can hear you.
    a. in   b. out   c. over   d. up

11. Heidi needs to be more serious about her studies. She likes to stay out late and fool _____ with her friends.
    a. around   b. away   c. over   d. down

12. There's a hole in the newspaper. Did you cut an article _____ of it?
    a. from   b. out   c. away   d. up

13. I'll start the cassette _____ . The beginning wasn't very clear.
    a. over   b. on   c. around   d. back

14. Every time Pat brings _____ the idea of marriage, his parents get nervous. They think he's too young.
    a. in   b. to   c. up   d. back

15. Nancy is doing great. This is her first time on ice skates, and she hasn't fallen _____ yet.

    a. up   b. down   c. around   d. out

16. Mr. and Mrs. Clark argue a lot, but they always manage to work _____ their disagreements.

    a. in   b. up   c. to   d. out

17. Howard gave _____ smoking a month ago, but it's been hard for him. He still wants to smoke.

    a. on   b. in   c. up   d. out

18. The firefighters spent several hours at the fire. They had a difficult time putting it _____ .

    a. out   b. up   c. in   d. off

19. Renters need to pay the first and last month's rent before they can move _____ an apartment in this building.

    a. on   b. with   c. back   d. into

20. You need to fill in only the second half of the application. I crossed _____ the first part.

    a. over   b. in   c. out   d. up

21. Marty often forgets to put her glasses _____ their case. Even though they're new, they have several scratches on them.

    a. back   b. in   c. up   d. on

22. When Joan feels lonely, she just calls _____ a friend and talks for a while. Her long distance phone bills are very high.

    a. to   b. up   c. out   d. over

23. Mark ran _____ an old friend from high school at the airport. They were very happy to see each other.

    a. over   b. from   c. off   d. into

24. Jeff dropped out _____ dental school, but he hasn't told his parents yet.

    a in   b. to   c. from   d. of

25. Do you think the teacher will believe me if I tell her my little sister tore _____ my homework?

    a. off   b. up   c. down   d. away

26. How did so many people find out _____ our engagement? Did you tell them?

    a. of   b. to   c. from   d. about

APPENDIX 2 PREPOSITION COMBINATIONS

QUIZ 1 (Group A)

Directions: Complete the sentences.

1. I've been walking on the beach. My shoes are full _____ sand.

2. Tracy's engaged to be married. Her friends are so happy _____ her.

3. After exercising for an hour, Juan was thirsty _____ a cold drink.

4. Mrs. Barry is angry _____ her son for taking her car keys without asking.

5. He knew when he got home that she was angry _____ that.

6. How many days were you absent _____ school last month?

7. The police officer was polite _____ me when I asked for directions to the museum.

8. Our dog is curious _____ the new kitten we brought home.

9. One kilometer is equal _____ .62 miles.

10. Even though school doesn't start for another month, Susie is ready _____ it.

11. The children love their neighbor Ms. Hughes. She's very kind _____ them.

12. When Jake was a baby, he got a lot of shots. Now he's afraid _____ doctors.

13. The electrician wasn't familiar _____ this type of light fixture, but she fixed it anyway.

14. The students are nice _____ their teacher, Ms. Adams. They help her clean up after class.

15. Ms. Adams is happy _____ that.

QUIZ 2 (Group B)

Directions: Complete the sentences.

1. I'm making a dessert. Could I borrow a few eggs _____ you?

2. One hundred people applied _____ the one position open in the company.

3. The Johnsons discussed a tax question _____ their lawyer.

4. She had helped them _____ another legal problem.

5. People admire Monica _____ her kindness, patience, and humor.

6. Do you have a minute? I'd like to introduce you _____ my fiancée, Joan.

7. What time are you leaving _____ work tomorrow? Do you need to get up early?

8. Please don't stare _____ me. It makes me nervous.

9. Let me know if you need help _____ dinner. I'm not busy.

10. Some people believe _____ UFOs. Do you?

11. Mark and Lydia never argue _____ each other _____ anything except where to spend their vacations.

12. What are you laughing _____? What's so funny?

Directions: *Complete the sentences.*

1. The kids in the neighborhood are crazy _____ soccer. They play it whenever they have free time.

2. Do you think that too much of anything can be bad _____ you?

3. Simon is nervous _____ his upcoming driver's test. He failed it the first time.

4. The government has created advertisements to make drivers aware _____ new seatbelt laws.

5. Even though Joan knows smoking isn't good _____ her, she's having trouble quitting.

6. The answer may be clear _____ you, but it isn't _____ me.

7. The weather on the south part of the island is very different _____ the weather on the north part. It's much warmer in the south.

8. Who is responsible _____ your medical bills, you or an insurance company?

9. Paris is famous _____ its art museums.

10. Pierre has just published his first short story in a magazine. He's very proud _____ it.

11. The customs officials were friendly _____ us when we entered the country.

12. Let's go to a fast-food restaurant. I'm hungry _____ a milkshake and french fries.

13. Mrs. Rose is interested _____ 18th century antiques.

14. In my country, the weather in June is similar _____ the weather in September.

15. The police weren't sure _____ the witnesses' stories. They all remembered the event so differently.

16. Christine has five young children, and she's always patient _____ them.

17. Rieko took her cat on a trip, and it ran away. She's very sad _____ that.

Directions: *Complete the sentences.*

1. The train arrived _____ New Delhi at 5:00 A.M.

2. The tour group arrived _____ the hotel an hour later.

3. This candy is very rich. It consists mostly _____ butter and chocolate.

4. My son is anxious to graduate _____ high school and start college.

5. Dr. John talks _____ her heart patients _____ healthier diets.

6. Shh! I'm listening _____ my favorite part of the symphony.

7. We'd love to eat at an expensive restaurant, but who is going to pay _____ it?

8. The children complain _____ their parents often _____ the cafeteria food at school.

9. Excuse me. I've been standing here at the counter for ten minutes, and no one has waited _____ me. I'd like to buy this shirt.

10. Let's have a New Year's party and invite all the neighbors _____ it.

11. The school kids play catch while they are waiting _____ the bus.

12. John agreed _____ his wife _____ the need to save money, but they disagreed _____ each other _____ ways to spend it.

Directions: *Complete the sentences.*

1. What's the matter _____ Tony? He hasn't said a word to anyone since he got here.

2. Sometimes in life, it's hard to separate fact _____ fiction.

3. The class began informally. The teacher asked the students _____ their weekend.

4. The students are looking forward _____ the end-of-the-year party.

5. People often tell me that my mother looked _____ a movie star when she was young.

6. The sheriff's department searched _____ the escaped prisoner with search dogs and a helicopter.

7. Does it matter _____ you if we eat out tonight? I don't feel like cooking.

8. The animal control officer warned the neighborhood _____ a dangerous dog in the area.

9. These sunglasses don't belong _____ me.

10. Do you know _____ your summer vacation plans yet?

11. Mrs. Lee is looking _____ her cat. He ran away this morning.

12. Bobby dreamt _____ kings and castles last night.

13. My husband and I went to Greenland for vacation. Would you like to look _____ some pictures of our trip?

14. At the restaurant, Diane wanted more coffee. She couldn't find her server, so she asked the manager _____ another cup.

Directions: *Complete the sentences.*

1. Beth wasn't feeling well. She excused herself _____ the meeting.

2. Your eye is bruised. What happened _____ it?

3. Thank you _____ the home repair book. It's been very helpful.

4. The judge insists _____ respect in his courtroom.

5. After Danny apologized, Mrs. Brennan excused him _____ throwing a baseball through her window.

6. Do you approve _____ the clothes teenagers are wearing to school?

7. The doctor found that his patient had died _____ natural causes.

8. Ellen apologized _____ her friend _____ hurting her feelings.

9. Use these special glasses to protect your eyes _____ the bright light.

10. Robert forgave his son _____ not being honest with him.

11. Mrs. Patterson relies _____ her son Andrew to take care _____ her finances.

12. We need to get rid _____ this garbage. It's beginning to smell.

13. Many students depend _____ their parents to pay their school tuition.

14. When you compare this diamond _____ that diamond, it's hard to tell which one is fake.

Directions: *Complete the sentences.*

1. Do you ever wonder _____ the size of the universe?

2. Driving in winter conditions scares me. I'm not accustomed _____ snow and ice on the road.

3. The children are working very quietly. They are concentrating _____ their art projects.

4. One of the prisoners escaped _____ jail by digging a tunnel.

5. He was able to hide _____ the police for only a few hours.

6. What happens if you multiply a number _____ zero? What about when you subtract zero _____ a number?

7. Mohammed is hoping _____ a job transfer to a town closer to his parents' home.

8. The teacher spoke _____ the parents _____ their children's progress in class.

9. The staff heard _____ Mr. Miller's heart surgery _____ his daughter.

10. If we divide this chocolate bar _____ eight pieces, we can all have some.

11. You just need to add a little more cream _____ the sauce, and it will be done.

APPENDIX 2 FINAL TEST

Directions: *Choose the correct answer.*

1. Hiroshi has applied _____ a scholarship to dental school.
   a. to   b. in   c. for   d. at

2. Before reporters write stories, they need to be sure _____ their facts.
   a. in   b. of   c. from   d. over

3. So many vitamins are on the market now. How do we know which ones are good _____ us?
   a. for   b. to   c. with   d. about

4. Before you add the egg to the dough, separate the white _____ the yolk.
   a. by   b. on   c. of   d. from

5. We've been working all day in the hot sun. We're thirsty _____ some soda pop.
   a. about   b. from   c. in   d. for

6. Everyone laughs _____ Tom's stories about his childhood. They're very funny.
   a. with   b. for   c. at   d. from

7. My parents are still crazy _____ rock-n-roll music.
   a. in   b. about   c. into   d. at

8. When Lawrence quit smoking, he got rid _____ all the cigarettes in his house.
   a. of   b. from   c. to   d. in

9. The salespeople are talking to one another, and no one is waiting _____ us. Let's leave this department and get help somewhere else.
   a. for   b. on   c. with   d. by

10. How long will it take you to get ready _____ the meeting?
    a. with   b. in   c. to   d. for

11. Medical students complain _____ their long hours.
    a. over   b. from   c. about   d. in

12. They are looking forward _____ graduation even though they know they will have to work long hours as doctors.
    a. to   b. with   c. in   d. of

13. Do you ever wonder _____ life on other planets?
    a. about   b. in   c. to   d. at

14. The guest bedroom is full _____ boxes of old clothes that I plan to give away.
    a. at   b. of   c. in   d. for

15. George used to work on a fishing boat in the Bering Sea. He is accustomed _____ freezing temperatures.
    a. in   b. with   c. by   d. to

(continued on next page)

16. The president insists _____ loyalty from his staff.

    a. with   b. on   c. to   d. at

17. The soccer team is hoping _____ one more win before the end of the season.

    a. from   b. for   c. to   d. from

18. The registration counter is divided _____ two sections: one for new students and one for returning students.

    a. with   b. from   c. into   d. to

19. The firefighters' dog Sparky died _____ old age.

    a. with   b. in   c. about   d. from

20. Anthony doesn't drive anymore. He depends _____ his son to take him to his appointments.

    a. on   b. for   c. of   d. in

ANSWER KEY

Chapter 1: PRESENT TIME

Quiz 1, p. 1.
1. eats
2. doesn't eat
3. enjoys
4. walk
5. take
6. drive
7. begins
8. rings
9. come
10. don't have

Quiz 2, p. 1.
is working
am studying
are driving
build
explains
are living
buys

Quiz 3, p. 2.
1. Is she
2. Does she
3. Does she
4. Does she
5. Is she
6. Does she
7. Is she
8. Is she

Quiz 4, p. 2.
1. is rarely / is seldom OR is sometimes (*Answer may vary depending on workplace rules or expectations.*)
2. always use
3. sometimes stops
4. always go
5. seldom/rarely see

Quiz 5, p. 3.
1. is relaxing
2. is reading
3. comes
4. gets, throws
5. A: is ringing
   A: is calling
6. rings, jump
7. are working, garden

Quiz 6, p. 3.
1. /z/
2. /z/
3. /s/
4. /z/
5. /əz/
6. /s/
7. /əz/
8. /z/
9. /s/
10. /s/
11. /z/
12. /z/

Quiz 7, p. 4.
1. visits — is visiting
2. stays — is staying
3. rents — is renting
4. sees — is seeing
5. goes — is going
6. finishes — is finishing
7. pays — is paying
8. touches — is touching
9. tries — is trying
10. does — is doing
11. polishes — is polishing
12. runs — is running
13. cries — is crying
14. mixes — is mixing
15. puts — is putting

Quiz 8, p. 4.
1. is helping, helps
2. speaks, is speaking, need
3. is flying
4. exercises, is working, isn't exercising
5. Do you like
6. is sleeping, needs

Quiz 9, p. 5.
1. need, are
2. understands
3. don't remember
4. belongs
5. am thinking
6. think
7. Are you having
8. do you know

Quiz 10, p. 5.
1. a, d
2. A: a, c
   B: b
3. b
4. a
5. a, c, e
6. a, c
7. A: b
   B: b
   A: a
   B: a

Quiz 11, p. 6.
Answers may vary.
1. begins, ends
2. are singing
3. A: is crying
   B: is
4. A: is
   B: am cooking
5. catches, walks
6. are painting / are drawing

Quiz 12, p. 6.
1. A: Are
   B: I am
2. A: Is
   B: it is
3. A: Do
   B: we don't
4. A: Does
   B: she does
5. A: Do
   B: they do
6. A: Does
   B: he doesn't
7. A: Is
   B: he is
8. A: Are
   B: they aren't

PRACTICE TEST, p. 7.

Part I, p. 7.
1. is beginning
2. works, teaches, like, is

Part II, p. 7.
has, picks, isn't, likes, repair, are working, needs

Part III, p. 7.
Answers may vary.
1. is, are sitting, are writing, is correcting
2. goes, plays, are running, are kicking

Part IV, p. 8.
1. b
2. a, c
3. b
4. a
5. a

Part V, p. 8.
1. The teacher never yells at her students.
2. What time do you leave school every day?
3. The Smiths don't have a car.
4. Does Jonathan own an apartment or a house?
5. Wait. The sandwiches are ready, but not the pizza.

FINAL TEST, p. 9.

Part I, p. 9.
1. is getting, is coming
2. need
3. plays, practices
4. is starting
5. A: Do you exercise
   B: run, lift

Part II, p. 9.
own, wake, feeds, takes, have, leaves, catches, are staying, enjoying

Part III, p. 9.
Answers may vary.
1. has
2. are washing, come
3. is cooking, smells
4. has
5. is lying, has

Part IV, p. 10.
1. a, c
2. A: a
   B: a
3. a, d
4. a, c

Part V, p. 10.
1. Do you always go to school by bus?
2. I don't like movies with sad endings.
3. A rat is playing in the garbage can.
4. Does Maria go to work on Saturdays?
5. The books are on sale, but not the magazines.
6. Michelle has a beautiful engagement ring
7. Mr. Green is elderly, but he doesn't want to live with his children.

Chapter 2: PAST TIME

Quiz 1, p. 11.
1. Andrew studied for two hours yesterday.
2. Mark and Jan went to bed at 10:00 last night.
3. The alarm clock rang at 6:00 yesterday morning.
4. My grandparents visited us last month.
5. I took a nap yesterday afternoon.
6. Dr. Hughes taught medical students last Tuesday evening.
7. Victoria bought coffee on her way to work yesterday.
8. Mr. Wilson shopped at Farmer's Market last Saturday.

Quiz 2, p. 11.
1. Did the plane arrive
   The plane didn't arrive
2. Was the restaurant
   The restaurant wasn't
3. Did Julie get
   Julie didn't get
4. Did the nurse take
   The nurse didn't take
5. Did Ben work
   Ben didn't work
6. Did Sara swim
   Sara didn't swim

Quiz 3, p. 12.
1. A: Did Julia eat
   B: she did, ate
2. A: Did you go
   B: I didn't, was
3. A: Did Beethoven write
   B: he did, wrote
4. A: Did the Warrens build
   B: they did, built

5. A: Did you sleep
   B: I didn't, heard, stayed
6. A: Did a fish jump
   B: it did, jumped
7. A: Did the monster movie scare
   B: it didn't, didn't scare, made
8. A: Did you attend
   B: we didn't, missed, decided

Quiz 4, p. 12.
1. didn't snow
2. didn't travel
3. didn't develop
4. didn't damage
5. didn't drive
6. didn't write

Quiz 5, p. 13.
1. Did
2. Did
3. Was
4. Were
5. Did
6. Did
7. Did
8. Were
9. Did
10. Did

Quiz 6, p. 13.
1. /d/
2. /t/
3. /d/
4. /t/
5. /t/
6. /əd/
7. /d/
8. /t/
9. /d/
10. /əd/

Quiz 7, p. 14.

	-ing	past tense
1.	studying	studied
2.	living	lived
3.	working	worked
4.	staying	stayed
5.	trying	tried
6.	sleeping	slept
7.	helping	helped
8.	swimming	swam
9.	thinking	thought
10.	knowing	knew
11.	stopping	stopped
12.	buying	bought
13.	typing	typed
14.	playing	played
15.	driving	drove
16.	cutting	cut

Quiz 8, p. 14.
1. ate
2. won
3. chose
4. left
5. spoke
6. became
7. paid
8. upset
9. put
10. said
11. saw
12. read
13. drank
14. forgot
15. kept

Quiz 9, p. 15.
1. A: did you wear
   B: was, wore
2. baked
3. A: did you lose
   B: left
4. A: Did you have
   B: did
   A: did she say
   B: told
5. A: did you graduate
   B: finished

Quiz 10, p. 15.

1. ran
2. didn't have
3. was
4. worked
5. weren't
6. understood
7. shook
8. had
9. cried
10. didn't yell
11. wasn't
12. hurt
13. knew
14. snored
15. cleaned

Quiz 11, p. 16.

1. worked
2. sent
3. took
4. got, went
5. shook
6. burned, didn't touch
7. A: did you buy
   B: picked up
8. asked, heard
9. A: did the glass break
   B: dropped
10. A: did you order
    B: ordered, were

Quiz 12, p. 16.

Note: Time expressions can go either at the beginning or at the end of the sentence.

1. Ben started a software company last month.
2. Jose ate two pizzas last night.
3. He didn't feel well later.
4. Betsy fell out of a tree last week.
5. She didn't go to the doctor.
6. Last year the Bakers borrowed money from their parents.

Quiz 13, p. 17.

Answers may vary.
was, didn't want, didn't tell, took, decided, rode, got, wasn't, was, shopped, bought, found, ordered, walked, bought, sat, enjoyed, was

Quiz 14, p. 17.

1. failed (OR didn't pass)
2. ate/had, went, slept
3. taught
4. was/worked, went
5. followed/chased, stopped

Quiz 15, p. 18.

1. decided
2. didn't hear
3. spent, were living, studied
4. planned
5. made, won
6. ran, was traveling, tried, returned, didn't have

Quiz 16, p. 18.

was walking, saw, were talking, joined, chatted, decided, didn't know, was, asked, wasn't, didn't help, pointed, hoped

Quiz 17, p. 19.

went, was, sat, watch, were, were walking, entertaining, was selling, bought, were serving, had, didn't want, closed

Quiz 18, p. 19.

1. A: a
   B: b
2. A: a
   B. b
3. A: a
   A: b
   B: b, e, g

Quiz 19, p. 20.

1. pays, paid
2. drives, drove, was driving, passed
3. wakes up, woke up, was getting, listened
4. catches, caught, was chasing, knocked
5. traveled, were traveling, visited, didn't stay
6. watch, watched

Quiz 20, p. 20.

1. A: do you get up
   B: wake up, rises, slept, felt
2. A: are you doing
   B: am cleaning, got, were sleeping, made
3. A: look
   B: am, was working, took
4. A: Did you see
   B: didn't
   A: went

Quiz 21, p. 21.

1. After Donna got a ticket for speeding, she drove home very slowly.
2. While Mary and Greg watched an exercise video, their two children watched cartoons on another TV.
   Mary and Greg watched an exercise video while their two children watched cartoons on another TV.
3. Until Joy got her driver's license, her parents drove her to school.
4. Eric took a shower after he got home.
5. While Rachel cooked dinner, Rick gave the children a bath.
   Rachel cooked dinner while Rick gave the children a bath.
6. As soon as I got home, I went to bed.

Quiz 22, p. 21.

1. used to sit
2. used to eat
3. used to stay
4. used to have
5. used to think
6. Did your wife use(d) to
7. did you use(d) to read

Quiz 23, p. 22.

1. used to eat
2. used to swim
3. used to be
4. used to drink
5. used to work
6. used to have
7. used to chase
8. used to wake up

Quiz 24, p. 22.

1. Joe didn't walk to work yesterday. He took the bus.
2. Mary went to the emergency room at midnight last night.
3. While Dr. Hughes was listening to his patient, his cell phone rang. He didn't answer it.
4. Marco didn't use(d) to swim, but now he does because he took / is taking swimming lessons.
5. Po celebrated his success with his friends after he got a new job.
6. When the phone rang at 11:00 last night, I was in a deep sleep. I almost didn't hear it.

Part II, p. 37.

1. will dry
2. A: am going to go
   B: am going to swim
3. are going to sell
4. will get it

Part III, p. 38.

1. A: is chasing
   A: sit, will sting
   B: flew
2. A: were you, waited
   B: was, needed
   A: Are you going to work / Will you work / Are you working
   B: intend, need, will call
3. A: are your neighbors going to return / will your neighbors return / are your neighbors returning
   B: are staying, leave, plan, are going to visit / will visit

Part IV, p. 38.

1. Correct
2. The business office will close for one week next month.
3. Dinner is almost ready. The oven timer is about go off.
4. Fortunately our teacher is not going to give us a quiz tomorrow.
5. Next Saturday, Boris will stay home and clean out his garage.
6. Are you going to play tennis during lunch today?
7. Correct
8. Our electric bill may increase next month. Maybe our electric bill is going to increase next month.
9. Masako is buying / is going to buy / will buy a new truck next week. She plans to drive it to work.
10. Tomorrow when Pierre gets to work, he will / is going to interview several candidates
11. You will / are going to pay a large fine
12. Correct

Chapter 4: THE PRESENT PERFECT AND THE PAST PERFECT

Quiz 1, p. 39.

1. wrote   written
2. saw   seen
3. tried   tried
4. did   done
5. stayed   stayed
6. was/were   been
7. said   said
8. had   had
9. finished   finished
10. slept   slept
11. put   put
12. opened   opened
13. flew   flown
14. ate   eaten
15. played   played

Quiz 2, p. 39.

1. haven't passed   5. haven't started
2. haven't come   6. haven't called
3. hasn't stopped   7. haven't met
4. haven't begun   8. hasn't gone

Quiz 3, p. 40.

1. Have they studied for the test already?
2. Have you lived here for a long time?
3. Has Ingrid ever visited?
4. Have I answered your question yet?
5. Have we gotten a response already?

Quiz 4, p. 40.

1. a	5. b	9. b
2. b	6. a	10. b
3. b	7. b	
4. b	8. a	

Quiz 5, p. 41.

1. one week ago.
2. for one week; since Tuesday.
3. six years ago.
4. since last year., for a long time.
5. two hours ago.
6. since he got his Ph.D., for his entire career.

Quiz 6, p. 41.

1. since	5. since	9. for
2. for	6. since	10. since
3. for	7. since	11. for
4. for	8. for	12. since

Quiz 7, p. 42.

1. was	4. received	7. took
2. took	5. has had	8. drove
3. have been	6. met	

Quiz 8, p. 42.

1. for	4. since	7. since	10. for
2. since	5. for	8. since	
3. for	6. since	9. for	

Quiz 9, p. 43.

1. has ridden   has been riding
2. has eaten   has been eating
3. have studied   have been studying
4. have learned   have been learning
5. have worked   have been working
6. have slept   have been sleeping
7. has taken   has been taking
8. hasn't read   hasn't been reading
9. hasn't driven   hasn't been driving
10. haven't written   haven't been writing

Quiz 10, p. 43.

1. has been barking   5. has been beeping
2. has been talking   6. has been trying
3. have been standing   7. has been speaking
4. have been exercising 8. have been driving

Quiz 11, p. 44.

1. How long have you been standing here?
2. I have been working since 10:00 A.M.
3. It has been snowing for two days.
4. How long have they been studying for the test?
5. Why have you been working so long?
6. The taxi has been waiting for ten minutes.
7. Rachel has been riding her horse all morning.

Quiz 12, p. 44.

1. a	4. b	7. a
2. b	5. a	8. a
3. b	6. a	

Quiz 13, p. 45.

1. c   5. c   9. b
2. d   6. c   10. b
3. b   7. d
4. a   8. b

Quiz 14, p. 45.

1. still   4. already   7. anymore
    yet   5. still   8. already
2. still   yet   still
3. anymore   6. yet

Quiz 15, p. 46.

1. had already left   6. had already been sold
2. had not thought   7. had already paid
3. had already eaten   8. had already met
4. had already put up   9. had already read
5. had already started

Quiz 16, p. 46.

1. b   4. b   7. a
2. b   5. a   8. b
3. a   6. b

Quiz 17, p. 47.

1. a   4. a   7. b
2. a   5. b   8. a
3. b   6. a

Quiz 18, p. 47.

1. The cake didn't bake because I had forgotten
2. The dog was barking at a squirrel
3. The automotive company has known about the defects
4. My brother changed his major and has decided to become
5. The rain had started by the time we arrived at the
6. at least a hundred people were already waiting in line.

Quiz 19, p. 48.

1. haven't told   5. has even gone
2. had arrived   6. was trying
3. was still talking   7. had already burned
4. had wanted   8. has had

PRACTICE TEST, p. 49.

Part I, p. 49.

1. paid   5. studied   9. begun
2. swum   6. grown   10. eaten
3. known   7. left
4. waited   8. cut

Part II, p. 49.

1. A: Have you ever tried
    B: haven't, have made
2. A: Have you been crying
3. A: has been scratching
4. A: Has Anna stayed
    B: hasn't
5. A: Have you finished
    B: have

Part III, p. 49.

1. for   4. for
2. since   5. since
3. since   6. for

Part IV, p. 50.

1. b   3. a
2. a   4. b

Part V, p. 50.

1. still   4. already
2. anymore   5. still
3. yet

Part VI, p. 50.

1. b   3. b
2. c   4. c

Part VII, p. 51.

1. Since we moved to this neighborhood, we have made many new friends.
2. Francisco has attended the opera since he took a music class
3. Nadia hasn't finished her dinner yet.
4. Gary has been at work since 5:00 this morning.
5. We have owned our home for five years.
6. It has rained on my birthday every year
7. My parents and I don't write letters to each other anymore.
8. I have already decided to major in marine biology.

FINAL TEST, p. 52.

Part I, p. 52.

1. visited   5. stood   9. taught
2. spoken   6. bought   10. sold
3. thought   7. won
4. written   8. read

Part II, p. 52.

1. A: Have you ever worn
    B: haven't
2. A: Have you been jumping
    B: have
3. A: has been flying
4. A: Have you ever gotten
    B: have, have gotten
5. A: Have you done
    B: have

Part III, p. 52.

1. for   4. for   7. since
2. for   5. since   8. for
3. since   6. Since

Part IV, p. 53.

1. a   4. a
2. b   5. b
3. a   6. b

Part V, p. 53.

1. yet   5. anymore
2. yet/already   6. yet
3. already   7. still
4. still   8. anymore

Part VI, p. 53.

1. a   4. a   7. a, d
2. c   5. b   8. b
3. a   6. c

Part VII, p. 54.

1. Sandy has been trying to call you.
2. Ted hasn't called yet.
3. I still don't understand the problem.
4. Andy has been on vacation since Saturday.
5. The rain has already stopped.
6. I have known about those problems for a few weeks.
7. Chris has started his Ph.D. thesis several times.

8. My elderly mother doesn't drive anymore.
9. William has gone to the same summer camp
10. Beth has wanted to move to a bigger apartment since her mother came to live with her.

Chapter 5: ASKING QUESTIONS

Quiz 1, p. 55.
1. is   5. has   9. are
2. will   6. have   10. did
3. is   7. do
4. didn't   8. won't

Quiz 2, p. 55.
1. Does   5. Are   9. Do
2. Does   6. Is   10. Are
3. Is   7. Are
4. Are   8. Does

Quiz 3, p. 56.
1. a   4. c   7. c
2. b   5. b   8. a
3. a   6. a

Quiz 4, p. 56.
1. Who(m) did Bill see?
2. What did Bobby see?
3. Who placed an order?
4. What did Mary place?
5. Who bought a car?
6. Who came?
7. What did Bill bring home?
8. What broke?

Quiz 5, p. 57.
1. What do geologists do
2. What will you do
3. What can I do
4. What did Carl do
5. What should I do
6. What is Caroline doing / trying to do
7. What would you like to do tomorrow
8. What is David going to do this weekend
9. What did you do
10. What do you do

Quiz 6, p. 57.
1. Which   5. Which   9. which
2. which   6. what   10. What
3. what   7. Which
4. What   8. What

Quiz 7, p. 58.
1. a   5. a   9. a
2. b   6. b   10. b
3. b   7. a
4. a   8. a

Quiz 8, p. 58.
1. Who's calling
2. Whose cell phone is this
3. Who is skipping the meeting
4. Whose laptop computer is that
5. Who is coming

6. Who is the new student
7. Whose parents are those
8. Whose rule is that

Quiz 9, p. 59.
1. f   4. d   7. e
2. b   5. c
3. a   6. g

Quiz 10, p. 59.
1. hard   4. fresh   7. soon
2. old   5. happy
3. cold   6. expensive

Quiz 11, p. 60.
1. often   5. far   9. long
2. far   6. long   10. far
3. long   7. far
4. often   8. often

Quiz 12, p. 60.
1. do you spell   4. How are you doing
2. How are you feeling   5. How do you say
3. How do you feel   6. How do you pronounce

Quiz 13, p. 61.
1. How cold is this water?
2. How tall is Julie?
3. How often do you go to movies?
4. How did you come here?
5. How far away is your school?
6. When do you need to leave?
7. How long did your dentist appointment take?
8. How old is Jon?
9. How long does it take you to make bread?
10. How well does Mr. Wang speak English?

Quiz 14, p. 62.
1. Where is Mari
2. Who is going to help with the party
3. When did you go to the circus
4. Why were you at home
5. When will Mr. and Mrs. Jones leave for vacation
6. How long does it take to drive from here to school
7. Whose car is that
8. What did David buy
9. How far is it from here to the airport
10. How often do you eat out
11. Where have you been
12. When do you fly home?

Quiz 15, p. 62.
1. isn't   4. are   7. does
2. don't   5. won't   8. aren't
3. didn't   6. didn't   9. aren't

Quiz 16, p. 63.
1. haven't   5. will   9. wouldn't
2. have   6. do   10. do
3. hasn't   7. can't
4. shouldn't   8. didn't

Quiz 17, p. 63.
1. Whose cell phone is that, mine or yours?
2. I was right about the price of the computer, wasn't I?

3. What kind of ethnic food do you like to cook?
4. When does your plane arrive from Paris?
5. Who helped you prepare the dinner?
6. Why did you leave without me?
7. Who(m) did you take to work?
8. How often do you see your family?

PRACTICE TEST, p. 64.
Part I, p. 64.
1. How
2. Who
3. Whose
4. What
5. How long
6. Which
7. Why
8. How often
9. How far
10. When

Part II, p. 64.
1. How often does she train / How much does she train
2. How far does she run / How much does she run
3. How fast does she run
4. When is she going to run in a marathon
5. Who(m) will she run with
6. What does she plan to do
7. How does she spell her name

Part III, p. 65.
1. don't you
2. did it
3. hasn't she
4. can't we
5. do they
6. didn't he

Part IV, p. 65.
1. What do you know about the new department manager?
2. That dog is barking so loudly. Who does it belong to? / Whose is it?
3. What does "besides" mean?
4. Marta changed jobs last month, didn't she?
5. Which movie did you see last night, *Monsters* or *Dragons*?

FINAL TEST, p. 66.
Part I, p. 66.
1. Where
2. How far
3. How long
4. Why
5. How often
6. How
7. Who
8. When
9. Which
10. Whose

Part II, p. 66.
1. Where is Paul going tomorrow
2. What does he plan to wear
3. Who is he going to take
4. Whose car is he going to drive
5. How long are they going to stay
6. When did Jill get a new job
7. Where does she work
8. What is she going to do for the company
9. How long does she plan to be there
10. How often does she drive to work
11. How does she go to work on the other days
12. How many hours a week does she work / How much does she work

Part III, p. 67.
1. didn't you
2. is it
3. won't you
4. can't she
5. do we
6. didn't he/she
7. isn't she
8. isn't he/she/it
9. are we
10. didn't you

Part IV, p. 68.
1. I need help. How do you spell "either"?
2. How do you feel about the talk you had with Jeff yesterday?
3. Who left their dirty dishes on the table?

4. What kind of soup do you want for lunch?
5. Sonya needs more time, doesn't she?
6. What does "anyway" mean?
7. How long does it take to get from here to your home?
8. Who told you about the party?

Chapter 6: NOUNS AND PRONOUNS

Quiz 1, p. 69.
1. /əz/
2. /z/
3. /s/
4. /z/
5. /z/
6. /s/
7. /əz/
8. /s/
9. /z/
10. /s/

Quiz 2, p. 69.
1. teeth
2. mice
3. leaves
4. babies
5. videos
6. boxes
7. voices
8. bananas
9. tables
10. children
11. women
12. businesses

Quiz 3, p. 70.
1. Steve (S), asked (V), a question (O)
2. question (S), wasn't (V)
3. the phone (S), rang (V)
4. I (S), answered (V), the phone (O)
5. The party (S), started (V)
6. Jenny (S), loves (V), horses (O)
7. The police (S), stopped (V), several cars (O)
8. The drivers (S), looked (V)

Quiz 4, p. 70.
	preposition	object of preposition
1.	through	the restaurant
2.	into, near	icy pond, their home
3.	beneath	the ice
4.	during	the winter months
5.	for, at	the bus, the bus stop
6.	in	one hour
7.	until	Friday
8.	through	the fog

Quiz 5, p. 71.
1. at
2. at
3. on
4. on
5. in
6. in
7. in
8. on
9. in
10. in

Quiz 6, p. 71.
1. a diamond ring at the playground last weekend.
2. a car at a used car dealer on Saturday.
3. a mouse on our doorstep last evening.
4. bubbles in the park yesterday afternoon.
5. our papers outdoors at lunch time.
6. the books on the wrong shelves yesterday.
7. at cars on the road this morning.
8. shells on the beach all afternoon.

Quiz 7, p. 72.
	Subject	Verb
1.	Every teacher	needs
2.	holidays	are
3.	People	are
4.	Everyone	had
5.	The pronunciation	does not match
6.	one mistake	is

Quiz 8, p. 73.

1. lives
2. is
3. are
4. needs
5. don't
6. want
7. are
8. have
9. Do
10. are

Quiz 9, p. 73.

1. <u>new</u>
2. <u>comfortable</u>
3. <u>weak</u>, <u>fresh</u>
4. <u>strong</u>
5. <u>empty</u>, <u>warm</u>
6. <u>hot</u>, <u>cool</u>

Quiz 10, p. 73.

Nouns: dishes, drink, house, newspaper, toy, book, cloth, day

Adjectives: curly, easy, old, clean, quiet, happy, fun, interesting

Quiz 11, p. 74.

1. Your **flower** garden has many unusual flowers.
2. Correct.
3. There is **customer** parking in front of the store.
4. I see three **spider** webs in the bathroom.
5. Correct.
6. There will be a lot of **birthday** cake to eat.
7. Don't throw away the **egg** cartons.
8. Correct.

Quiz 12, p. 74.

1. them, them, They
2. We, We, us, We, them
3. They, them
4. She, it, it, her

Quiz 13, p. 75.

1. earth's
2. Jones'/Jones's
3. wife's
4. students'
5. theater's
6. actors'
7. grandson's
8. teachers'
9. hospitals'
10. cities'

Quiz 14, p. 75.

1. Dolphins
2. leaves, trees
3. daughter's
4. plants
5. knives, forks
6. showers, baths
7. geese, children, parents
8. boxes, matches, Bob's

Quiz 15, p. 76.

1. Mine
2. her
3. mine
4. your, ours
5. their
6. it's
7. Their, They're, theirs, it's, their
8. A: our
   B: It's, it

Quiz 16, p. 76.

1. himself
2. yourselves
3. herself
4. myself
5. herself
6. ourselves
7. himself
8. itself
9. themselves
10. yourself

Quiz 17, p. 77.

1. another
2. another
3. the other
4. another
5. another
6. another, the other
7. another
8. another
9. the other
10. another

Quiz 18, p. 77.

1. others
2. other
3. others
4. the others
5. others
6. other
7. the other
8. the others
9. the others
10. the others

Quiz 19, p. 78.

1. another, other
2. another
3. The others
4. others
5. another
6. the other
7. another
8. the other
9. others
10. The other

Quiz 20, p. 78.

1. There are thirty days in the month of April.
2. Our apartment manager is out of town this week.
3. The bird has brought some worms to feed its young.
4. The mountains look beautiful against the clear, blue sky.
5. I broke my right hand, so I need to write with the other one.
6. The cars in the city produce a lot of pollution.
7. One hundred people are waiting in the rain to buy tickets for the concert. Everyone seems patient, but cold.
8. The children's swimming pool in the city is open
9. Mr. James'/James's company recycles old computers.
10. The dancers practiced their dance steps in the studio all morning.

PRACTICE TEST, p. 79.

Part 1, p. 79.

1. children's names
2. babies' names
3. computers, instructions
4. Beth's
5. articles, women, jobs, today's

Part II, p. 79.

1. mine
2. his
3. I
4. A: yours
   B: hers
5. me
6. yourself

Part III, p. 79.

1. the others
2. another
3. other
4. Another, other

Part IV, p. 80.

1. Tony was born on April 2, 1998.
2. Correct.
3. Several language schools offer university preparation.
4. The bird's nest has several eggs in it.
5. What are you doing Thursday evening?
6. Correct.

FINAL TEST, p. 81.

Part I, p. 81.

1. puppies
2. books
3. speaker's ideas
4. Brown's, classes
5. teachers', courses
6. university's, problems, students

Part II, p. 81.

1. another
2. other
3. another
4. another
5. the others
6. others
7. another, other
8. the others
9. The other
10. another

Part III, p. 82.

1. me, We, It
2. his, her, herself
3. its, its, It's
4. His, He, himself, He, His, She, he

5. A: yours
   B: Mine
6. A: there
   B: there, They're

Part IV, p. 82.

1. We rented a cabin in the mountains for one month.
2. Correct.
3. My apartment building is small. It has only eleven units.
4. Correct.
5. In the morning, I like to take long walks in the park.
6. There are several cars in our driveway. Who do they belong to?
7. The table's surface has scratches on it from the children's toys.
8. In the future, every student will need to turn in typed assignments.
9. I fell asleep at nine o'clock last night.
10. Correct.

Chapter 7: MODAL AUXILIARIES

Quiz 1, p. 83.

1. to
2. Ø
3. Ø
4. Ø
5. to
6. Ø
7. Ø
8. Ø
9. to
10. Ø

Quiz 2, p. 83.

1. Bees can sting.
2. Spiders can't make honey.
3. Snakes can't talk to people.
4. Computers can solve math problems.
5. Newborn babies can't walk.
6. Bears can climb trees.
7. Dogs can't drive cars.
8. Birds can fly long distances.

Quiz 3, p. 84.

1. 2
2. 1
3. 2
4. 1
5. 1
6. 2
7. 2
8. 1
9. 2
10. 1

Quiz 4, p. 84.

1. We might go away this weekend.
2. Maybe it will snow tomorrow.
3. Maybe our baseball team will win the championship.
4. Joan might be in the hospital.
5. David may take the driving test tomorrow.
6. Sara might meet with us this afternoon.
7. Maybe James will be late for the meeting.

Quiz 5, p. 85.

1. future
2. past
3. present
4. past
5. future
6. present
7. future
8. past

Quiz 6, p. 85.

Answers may vary.
1. might/could rain
2. might/could be sick
3. might/could be in heavy traffic
4. might/could be sick
5. might/could snow

Quiz 7, p. 86.

1. May, Could, Can
2. Could, Can, Would
3. Could, Can, Would
4. May, Could, Can
5. May, Could, Can
6. Could, Can, Would
7. May, Could, Can
8. Could, Can, Would
9. May, Could, Can
10. Could, Can, Would

Quiz 8, p. 87.

1. should dress
2. should say
3. shouldn't drive
4. shouldn't steal
5. ought to call
6. ought to leave
7. ought to volunteer

Quiz 9, p. 87.

1. We had better clean up.
2. You had better arrive early for your flight.
3. Diane had better not leave.
4. You had better not eat that chicken.
5. Steve had better hurry.
6. You had better not leave the garbage out.

Quiz 10, p. 88.

Answers will vary.
1. should put cold water on it
2. should call for help
3. should call the apartment manager
4. should call his friend

The above sentences can also be written with *had better* or *ought to.*

Quiz 11, p. 88.

1. had to
2. had to
3. have to
4. have to
5. have got to
6. must

Quiz 12, p. 89.

1. had to pay
2. had to go
3. had to get
4. had to wait
5. did you have to do
6. had to work

Quiz 13, p. 89.

1. must not
2. don't have to
3. must not
4. doesn't have to
5. must not
6. don't have to
7. doesn't have to
8. don't have to

Quiz 14, p. 90.

1. 1
2. 2
3. 1
4. 2
5. 2
6. 1
7. 1
8. 2
9. 1
10. 1

Quiz 15, p. 90.

Answers will vary.
1. She must be sad.
2. He must be cold.
3. They must be happy.
4. There must be bugs nearby.

Quiz 16, p. 91.
1. Correct.
2. Please don't come in.
3. Correct.
4. Please dress quickly.
5. Correct.
6. Correct.
7. Run and get the mail.
8. Correct.

Quiz 17, p. 91.
1. prefers
2. would rather
3. prefer
4. would rather
5. likes
6. prefers
7. would rather
8. like
9. prefer
10. would rather

Quiz 18, p. 92.
1. a	8. b	15. c
2. b	9. c	16. a
3. b	10. a	17. b
4. b	11. c	18. a
5. a	12. a	19. b
6. a	13. a	20. c
7. c	14. a	

PRACTICE TEST, p. 93.
Part 1, p. 93.
1. can
2. might/could
3. could

Part II, p. 93.
1. Kathy may be upset.
2. It may snow today.
3. We might stay home for the holidays.
4. Maybe we will stay home for the holidays.

Part III, p. 93.
Answers will vary.
1. should go to bed.
2. ought to take some medicine.
3. had better take them back to school.

Part IV, p. 93.
Answers will vary.
1. I must go to work.
2. I should work hard.
3. People shouldn't steal.
4. I have to brush my teeth.
5. I had to pay some bills.

Part V, p. 94.
1. b
2. c
3. b
4. c
5. c

Part VI, p. 94.
1. My grades are low. I had better study more.
2. Could/Would/Can you please open the window? OR Please open the window.
3. Let's invite some friends over.
4. We can't come to your party.
5. Maybe Susan has a solution to the problem.
6. Jackie isn't here. She must/might/could be at home in bed.
7. You mustn't walk in mud puddles.
8. Why don't we go out for dinner tonight?

FINAL TEST, p. 95.
Part I, p. 95.
1. can
2. could
3. could, might
4. might
5. could

Part II, p. 95.
1. The dog may be hungry.
2. Jack might quit his new job.
3. There may be more news today.
4. Maybe you will feel better soon.

Part III, p. 95.
Answers will vary.
1. should put a bandage on it.
2. ought to go for a walk.
3. had better drive more slowly.
4. should study more.
5. had better not tell anyone.

Part IV, p. 96.
Answers will vary.
1. I had to go to school.
2. I must get a driver's license.
3. They shouldn't play with medicine.
4. I should rest.
5. I have to eat breakfast.

Part V, p. 96.
1. b	5. c	9. a
2. a	6. b	10. a
3. b	7. b	
4. c	8. a	

Part VI, p. 97.
1. I ought to take my temperature.
2. Can/Could/May I borrow your pen?
3. Let's order a pizza.
4. We'll be free on Saturday. We could meet then.
5. Maybe it will snow tomorrow.
6. He may/might/could have car trouble again.
7. Children shouldn't play with matches.
8. Why don't we go for a walk after dinner?

Chapter 8: CONNECTING IDEAS

Quiz 1, p. 98.
1. Beth planned to serve pizza, green salad, and ice-cream at the party.
2. Sam, Jeff, and Ellen helped with the decorations.
3. The party started at 8:00. Several guests were late.
4. A few people talked, others played soccer, and several people danced.
5. Everyone had a wonderful time. No one wanted to go home.

Quiz 2, p. 98.
1. or	5. , and	9. , but
2. , and	6. and	10. , but
3. , but	7. and	
4. or	8. or	

Quiz 3, p. 99.
1. but	5. so	9. so
2. so	6. but	10. but
3. so	7. but	
4. but	8. so	

Quiz 4, p. 99.
1. doesn't	5. have	9. didn't
2. am	6. don't	10. do
3. haven't	7. are	
4. won't	8. will	

Quiz 5, p. 100.

1. is too
2. doesn't
3. does too
4. doesn't
5. didn't
6. didn't either
7. has too
8. can't either
9. are too
10. won't

Quiz 6, p. 100.

1. James went skiing, and so did Tom.
   James went skiing, and Tom did too.
2. Eric won't help, and Diane won't either.
   Eric won't help, and neither will Diane.
3. Judy has a cold, and so does her husband.
   Judy has a cold, and her husband does too.
4. Mr. Thomas isn't going to retire, and Mrs. Ellis isn't going to either. Mr. Thomas isn't going to retire, and neither is Mrs. Ellis.

Quiz 7, p. 101.

1. Neither can I.
2. Neither was I.
3. Neither have I.
4. So do I.
5. Neither do I.
6. So will I.
7. So am I.
8. So do I.

Quiz 8, p. 101.

1. Because I had a high fever, I went to the doctor.
   I went to the doctor because I had a high fever.
2. Because she didn't study, Cindy failed the class.
   Cindy failed the class because she didn't study.
3. Because it was a beautiful day, we went to the beach.
   We went to the beach because it was a beautiful day.
4. Because my old jeans have holes in them, I need to get new jeans.
   I need to get new jeans because my old jeans have holes in them.
5. Because my car is making strange noises, I feel uncomfortable driving.
   I feel uncomfortable driving because my car is making strange noises.
6. Because his favorite store is having a sale, Andy is going to go shopping.
   Andy is going to go shopping because his favorite store is having a sale.

Quiz 9, p. 102.

1. Because it was hot, I jumped in the cool water.
   I jumped in the cool water because it was hot.
   It was hot, so I jumped in the cool water.
2. My feet hurt, so I took off my uncomfortable shoes.
   Because my feet hurt, I took off my uncomfortable shoes.
3. Oscar began coughing because the restaurant was smoky.
   Because the restaurant was smoky, Oscar began coughing.
4. The campers put away their food because there were bears nearby.
   Because there were bears nearby, the campers put away their food.

Quiz 10, p. 102.

1. Even though/Although
2. Because
3. even though/although
4. even though/although
5. Because
6. Even though/Although
7. because
8. because
9. even though/although
10. because

Quiz 11, p. 103.

1. Although we try to save money, we always seems to spend
2. The students stayed indoors at school because there were storm clouds.
3. The store is open at night even though it doesn't have many customers.
4. Although the police could smell gas, they couldn't find a gas leak.
5. The kitchen smells delicious because we have been making cookies.

Quiz 12, p. 103.

1. Even though the roads were crowded, we got home on time.
2. no comma
3. Because the students felt the building shake, they got under their desks.
4. no comma
5. no comma
6. Although this TV is new, the picture isn't very clear.
7. no comma

Quiz 13, p. 103.

1. I enjoy science. My favorite subjects are physics, math, and chemistry.
2. Julia doesn't participate in sports, and neither do her friends.
   Julia doesn't participate in sports, and her friends don't either.
3. Our baseball team lost the game because not enough players showed up.
4. The downstairs phone isn't working properly, and this one isn't either.
5. I wore a hat and sunglasses because the sun was so bright.
6. My mother is Australian, and my father is Brazilian.
7. Even though you're upset now, you'll understand our decision

PRACTICE TEST, p. 104.

Part 1, p. 104.

Michelle decided the weather was too nice to stay at home, so she packed a picnic lunch and drove to the beach. Even though it was crowded, she found a place to sit. She spread out her blanket and opened her lunch. Inside was a sandwich, potato chips, and an apple. Because she was still full from breakfast, she ate only a little and saved the rest for later. She took out a book and opened it. Minutes later she was asleep, and she woke up just as the sun was going down.

Part II, p. 104.

1. or
2. Even though
3. , and
4. Even though
5. Because
6. even though
7. but
8. Because

Part III, p. 105.

Answers will vary.

1. Many students failed
2. English, math, and biology
3. , I don't have much free time.
4. My friends went to a party,
5. , she can't see very well.

Part IV, p. 105.
1. I study hard even though my classes are very easy.
2. After the accident, my left arm hurt, and my right shoulder did too.
   After the accident, my left arm hurt, and so did my right shoulder.
3. Blackberries, strawberries, and blueberries all grow in our garden.
4. Because taxes were so high, people refused to pay.
5. We were excited about the concert, so we got there early

FINAL TEST, p. 106.
Part I, p. 106.
  Ron needs to decide if he is going to go to graduate school or if he is going to get a job. He will finish business school in a few months. Although he has enjoyed being a student, he wants to start earning his own money. His parents want him to get a Master's degree. They have said they will pay for it, so they think he should agree to stay in school. Ron appreciates their generosity, but he also wants to be more independent at this time in his life.

Part II, p. 106.
1. or	5. Even though	9. but
2. Because	6. Because	10. so
3. and	7. but	
4. so	8. Even though	

Part III, p. 107.
Answers will vary.
1. , I have a lot of homework.
2. We went to the restaurant even though the food was expensive.
3. nice, the children want to play inside.
4. Cindy didn't go to the party,
5. I saw Mary, John, and George at the park.
6. We were late,

Part IV, p. 107.
1. People couldn't describe the accident because it happened so quickly.
2. Even though Nadia is a new student, she has made many friends.
3. A storm was approaching, so the sailors decided to go into shore.
4. You can pay either by cash or by check.
5. Maria didn't understand the lecture. Neither did I.
6. Sylvia worked even though it was her day off.
7. Clams, prawn, and shrimp are seafood I enjoy.
8. My father walks in his sleep, and so does his brother. / and his brother does too.

Chapter 9: COMPARISONS

Quiz 1, p. 108.
1. is not as old as	4. was almost as warm as
2. is almost as old as	5. was not as hot/warm as
3. are not as old as	6. were not as hot/warm as

Quiz 2, p. 108.
Answers may vary.
1. Light chocolate is just as delicious as dark chocolate.
2. A mosquito bite is not as painful as a bee sting.
3. A sunrise is just as beautiful as a sunset.
4. A hard pillow is not as comfortable as a soft pillow.
5. A non-poisonous snake is not as scary as a poisonous snake.

6. Eating is just as important as sleeping.
7. England is not as large as China.
8. A school bus is not as fast as a sports car.

Quiz 3, p. 109.
1. sweeter	the sweetest
2. funnier	the funniest
3. darker	the darkest
4. more dangerous	the most dangerous
5. sadder	the saddest
6. more confusing	the most confusing
7. worse	the worst
8. more carefully	the most carefully
9. busier	the busiest
10. more famous	the most famous

Quiz 4, p. 109.
1. larger than	6. more expensive than
2. healthier than	7. more convenient than
3. slower	8. more quickly than
4. heavier than	9. more interesting than
5. longer than	10. safer than

Quiz 5, p. 110.
Answers may vary.
1. Summer is warmer than winter.
2. A rabbit is faster than a turtle.
3. A holiday is more enjoyable than a work day.
4. Rocks are heavier than air.
5. Snow is softer than ice.
6. Ice-cream is tastier than lemons.
7. A book is more expensive than a newspaper.
8. Vegetables are healthier than butter.
9. A CD is cheaper than a CD player.
10. A year is longer than a month.

Quiz 6, p. 110.
1. further	6. further
2. farther, further	7. farther, further
3. further	8. farther, further
4. further	9. farther, further
5. farther, further	10. farther, further

Quiz 7, p. 111.
1. mine (ours)	5. we did
2. they can	6. he is
3. mine	7. you can
4. Beth can	8. I am, they are

Quiz 8, p. 111.
1. A	6. A
2. B, C, D	7. A
3. A	8. B, C, D
4. B, C, D	9. B, C, D
5. B, C, D	10. B, C, D

Quiz 9, p. 112.
1. not as sweet as	6. both
2. both	7. not as soft as
3. both	8. not as fresh as
4. both	9. both
5. not as fast as	10. not as hard as

Quiz 10, p. 112.
1. better than his wife does.
2. better than their parents do.
3. Clear.
4. more often than his brothers and sisters do.
5. more than my teenagers do.
6. Clear.

Quiz 11, p. 113.
1. more	5. more	9. more
2. more	6. more	10. more
3. Ø	7. Ø	
4. Ø	8. more	

Quiz 12, p. 113.
1. hotter and hotter
2. more and more discouraged
3. harder and harder
4. redder and redder
5. more and more challenging
6. more and more relaxed
7. more and more confused
8. more and more expensive

Quiz 13, p. 114.
1. the more they argued, the more upset they became
2. the more the bus driver sang, the more they laughed
3. The more I exercised, the more energetic I became
4. the more she cooks, the more I eat

Quiz 14, p. 114.
1. the warmest, in	6. the noisiest, ever
2. the fastest, in	7. the hardest of
3. the most beautiful, of	8. the most expensive, in
4. the worst, ever	9. the least confident, ever
5. the coldest, in	10. Of, the laziest, (the) luckiest

Quiz 15, p. 115.
1. to	5. from	9. from
2. Ø	6. to, Ø	10. to, Ø
3. Ø	7. from	
4. to	8. as, Ø	

Quiz 16, p. 115.
Some answers may vary.
1. the same as	5. different from
2. the same	6. similar to
3. different	7. similar, alike
4. similar to	

Quiz 17, p. 116.
Answers may vary.
1. different	5. like
2. the same	6. similar
3. the same, alike	7. alike
4. the same	8. different

Quiz 18, p. 116.
1. The friendliest person in our class is Julie.
2. The food at the restaurant was not as good as the last time.
3. The movie was funnier than we expected.
4. Anna washes her dog more often than her children do.

5. He keeps acting like a teenager, but he's 50.
6. I have the same bag as you.
7. My grandfather always said that one of the biggest mistake**s** in his life
8. For Jon, the game of chess is like an interesting math puzzle.
9. As the horse got tired, he began walking more and more slowly / slower and slower.
10. The driving test was harder than I expected.

PRACTICE TEST, p. 117.
Part 1, p. 117.
1. heavier than
2. colder than, the hottest
3. worse
4. prettier, more elegant than
5. the biggest
6. the most delicious

Part II, p. 117.
Answers may vary.
1. B is as big as D.
2. A is not as big as C.
3. E is the smallest. OR C is the biggest.
4. A is like E.
5. C is bigger than A.
6. B and D are the same.
7. E and C are different.

Part III, p. 118.
1. Of	4. from
2. as	5. Ø
3. in	6. to

Part IV, p. 118.
1. The more (OR longer) he sat in the tub, the more relaxed he became.
2. The more mistakes he made, the more frustrated he became.
3. The farther/further a ball falls, the faster it goes.

Part V, p. 118.
1. It's less expensive than that one.
2. My brother is smaller than me / I am.
3. Baby Danny's hair is long and curly, so many people think he looks like a girl.
4. I got enough sleep. I'm not as tired today as yesterday.
5. The budget department gave us more money this year than last year.
6. If you need further assistance, please ask.

FINAL TEST, p. 119.
Part I, p. 119.
1. easier, than	6. better than
2. faster than	7. smaller
3. longer than, the loveliest	8. biggest
4. the largest, most populated	9. farther
5. the worst, the most famous	

Part II, p. 119.
Answers may vary.
1. A is like E.
2. A and B are similar.
3. C is almost as tall as D.
4. E is not as tall as D.
5. C is taller than B.
6. A and E are the shortest. / D is the tallest.
7. A and E are the same.

Part III, p. 120.
1. as
2. in
3. from
4. Ø
5. Of
6. to
7. in
8. Of
9. as
10. of

Part IV, p. 120.
1. The harder Emily works, the more money she earns.
2. The rougher the water became, the more scared the children in the boat were.
3. The more loudly Karen played the piano, the more the dog barked.
4. The faster the ideas came, the more pages the writer wrote.

Part V, p. 121.
1. I didn't know that fresh peas tasted so much better than frozen peas.
2. It's more dangerous to have the flu than a cold.
3. Who has a better life: a married person or a single person?
4. Let's hope it's not as rainy this afternoon as it was this morning.
5. Of the nine planets,
6. What has been the happiest day in your life so far?
7. The baby got more and more tired at the park.
8. The largest bird is the ostrich.
9. One of the strongest metals in the world is titanium.
10. Mrs. Davis helps her children more than her husband does.

Chapter 10: THE PASSIVE

Quiz 1, p. 122.
1. ACTIVE
2. PASSIVE
3. ACTIVE
4. PASSIVE
5. PASSIVE
6. ACTIVE
7. PASSIVE
8. ACTIVE
9. PASSIVE
10. ACTIVE

Quiz 2, p. 122.
1. is written
2. are written
3. was written
4. has been written
5. have been written
6. will be written
7. is going to be written
8. are going to be written

Quiz 3, p. 123.
1. bought
2. explained
3. rented
4. made
5. sold
6. eaten
7. told
8. thrown
9. known
10. grown
11. fed
12. cut
13. caught
14. shot
15. lost
16. worn

Quiz 4, p. 123.
1. was driven
2. will be fixed
3. are going to be surprised
4. are cleaned
5. has been checked
6. were signed

Quiz 5, p. 124.
1. A clinic will be opened by the hospital.
2. A new treatment is being discussed by the doctors.
3. An injection has been given by the nurse.
4. Several different languages are spoken by patients.
5. Televisions are going to be installed in the rooms by electricians.
6. The rooms were painted by volunteers.

Quiz 6, p. 124.
1. Was the game won by the other team?
2. Are the suspects known by the police?
3. Will the garage be cleaned by Gary?
4. Is your car going to be fixed by the mechanic?
5. Has an agreement been reached by the union?
6. Are old financial records kept by your accountant?
7. Are the forms going to be signed by your parents?

Quiz 7, p. 125.
1. b
2. a
3. a
4. b
5. a

Quiz 8, p. 125.
1. The students discussed the book.
2. The management has changed the company's name.
3. The police caught the thief.
4. The leaders gave the soldiers orders.
5. Our president has invited us to the ceremony.
6. Our team is going to win the game.
7. A repair person has cut the telephone lines.
8. The city will give Mr. Reed an award.

Quiz 9, p. 126.
1. INTRANSITIVE
2. TRANSITIVE
3. TRANSITIVE
4. INTRANSITIVE
5. INTRANSITIVE
6. TRANSITIVE
7. INTRANSITIVE
8. INTRANSITIVE
9. TRANSITIVE
10. TRANSITIVE
11. TRANSITIVE
12. TRANSITIVE

Quiz 10, p. 126.
1. No change.
2. Our sink has finally been fixed by our plumber.
3. No change.
4. No change.
5. No change.
6. One of the cows in the pasture was struck by lightning.
7. The company will be sold by the board of directors next month.
8. The conversation has been recorded by the answering machine.

Quiz 11, p. 127.
1. This sweater was given to me.
2. Microsoft was created by Bill Gates and Paul Allen.
3. Books are checked out at a library.
4. Have you ever been lied to?
5. The picture was painted by Picasso.
6. These walls will be painted tomorrow.
7. French and English are spoken in Canada.
8. When were cell phones first used?
9. Mr. Hill was kicked by the horse.
10. The basketball game has been stopped by the referee.

Quiz 12, p. 127.
1. are being taken care of
2. were being presented
3. was being directed
4. is being helped
5. is being cut
6. is being investigated
7. was being repaired
8. is being filmed
9. are being wrapped
10. were being read

Quiz 13, p. 128.

1. can be reached
2. has to be picked up
3. shouldn't be eaten
4. ought to be questioned
5. has to be changed
6. should be started
7. could be stolen
8. must be told
9. might be started
10. may be reached

Quiz 14, p. 128.

1. This meat should be cooked.
2. Your wound ought to be looked at by a doctor.
3. The issue must be voted on by the entire community.
4. You may be contacted tomorrow.
5. You might be surprised by the news.
6. The public has to be warned.

Quiz 15, p. 129.

Passive sentences: 1, 2, 4, 7, 8, 9

Quiz 16, p. 129.

1. should be washed
2. has eaten
3. kicked
4. will be held
5. are putting out
6. can be contacted
7. is going to be painted
8. is being built
9. turned off
10. has to be paid

Quiz 17, p. 130.

1. from
2. in/with
3. of
4. to
5. to
6. for
7. with
8. with

Quiz 18, p. 130.

1. are excited about
2. is opposed to
3. is interested in
4. Are . . . related to
5. is satisfied with
6. were involved in
7. was exhausted from
8. is crowded with
9. is . . . composed of
10. is scared of

Quiz 19, p. 131.

1. a. surprised
   b. surprising
2. a. interesting
   b. interested
   c. interesting
3. a. amazing
   b. amazed
   c. amazing

Quiz 20, p. 131.

1. interested
2. frightened, frightening
3. fascinated
4. scary, scared, relaxed
5. interesting, interested
6. terrifying, surprised

Quiz 21, p. 132.

1. got
2. Are, getting
3. get
4. did, get
5. get
6. will get
7. am getting
8. get

Quiz 22, p. 132.

1. get confused
2. got lost
3. get fat
4. gets nervous
5. getting dark
6. get rich
7. got sunburned
8. get hungry
9. get serious
10. got arrested

Quiz 23, p. 133.

Checked sentences: 1, 4, 7

Quiz 24, p. 133.

1. used to travel
2. used to spend
3. are used to eating
4. are used to being
5. used to be
6. did you used/use
7. Are you used to living
8. did your husband used/use to do
9. used to have
10. am not used

Quiz 25, p. 134.

1. Customers are supposed to pay their bills on time.
2. ABC Cable Company isn't supposed to charge a late fee.
3. Customers are not supposed to leave tips for service.
4. The company president is supposed to retire next month.
5. Students are supposed to wear uniforms.

Quiz 26, p. 134.

1. Drivers are supposed to drive more slowly
2. Correct.
3. You are not supposed to wear shoes in the house.
4. I was supposed to pick up Carl,
5. Correct.
6. Correct.
7. Weren't you supposed to go to school early today?
8. Correct.

Quiz 27, p. 135.

1. c
2. c
3. a
4. b
5. b
6. c
7. d
8. c

Quiz 28, p. 136.

1. When you're done with your toys,
2. Vegetables contain important nutrients
3. Unfortunately, my father died when I was a young girl.
4. The student didn't agree with the teacher about his test score.
5. The department was just getting used to working with Brian when
6. The books that you ordered arrived two days ago.
7. The electrician was supposed to come today.
8. The city is very noisy, but we are getting used to it.

PRACTICE TEST, p. 137.

Part I, p. 137.

1. b
2. c
3. d
4. d
5. a

Part II, p. 137.

was, jumped, began, was saved, was seen

Part III, p. 138.

1. A: thrilling
   B: scary, frightened
2. A: disappointed
   B: surprising, confusing

Part IV, p. 138.

1. The Jeffersons have been married to each other
2. Mr. Allen is very interested in your work experience.
3. My husband and I used to live on a houseboat.
4. Dr. Barry arrived two hours late and missed the meeting.
5. Where did you go after the movie?
6. but there were so many cars that he got scared.

FINAL TEST, p. 139.

Part I, p. 139.
1. d
2. a
3. b
4. a
5. c
6. d
7. a
8. b

Part II, p. 140.
1. was held, were asked, wanted, argued, said, became, will be needed / is going to be needed
2. returned, decided, was cleaned, were washed, (was) dusted, (were) polished, (was) made, thanked, looked, said, was done, got

Past perfect could also be used for these verbs: had decided, had been cleaned, had been washed, (had been) dusted, (had been) polished, (had been) made

Part III, p. 140.
1. B: disappointed, boring
   A: exciting
   B: exciting
2. A: interesting
   B: discouraged, depressing
   A: frustrating
   B: alarmed

Part IV, p. 140.
1. Ben and Rachel got engaged last month.
2. The government is opposed to lower taxes.
3. I heard my name. Who called me?
4. Dogs in the park are supposed to be on a leash.
5. Your fax came a few minutes ago.
6. Our apartment must be cleaned before the party
7. I used to run, but now I walk for exercise.
8. It should be cooked a little longer.
9. but we were exhausted from the heat.
10. She can walk only a few steps before she gets tired.

Chapter 11: NONCOUNT NOUNS AND ARTICLES

Quiz 1, p. 142.
1. an
2. an
3. a
4. an
5. an
6. an
7. a
8. an
9. a
10. a
11. a
12. a

Quiz 2, p. 142.
1. a
2. a
3. some
4. some
5. some
6. an
7. some
8. a
9. some
10. a
11. some
12. a

Quiz 3, p. 143.
1. /
2. s
3. /
4. /
5. s
6. s, /
7. /, /, /
8. /, /
9. /, /
10. s, /

Quiz 4, p. 143.
1. /
2. /, /
3. /
4. /
5. /
6. s
7. /, /, /, /, s
8. s, /
9. /, /
10. /

Quiz 5, p. 144.
1. many, s
2. many, es
3. much, /
4. many, s
5. much, /
6. much, /
7. much, /
8. many, s
9. many, s
10. much, /
11. much, /

Quiz 6, p. 144.
1. a few clouds
2. a little music
3. a little meat
4. a few apples
5. a few suggestions
6. a little salt
7. a little sand
8. a little help
9. a few, coins
10. a few eggs

Quiz 7, p. 145.
1. a few, several
2. much, a little
3. some, a lot of
4. some
5. a few, a lot of
6. much, a lot of, a little
7. many, several, some
8. several, a few
9. some, much, a little
10. a few, some

Quiz 8, p. 145.
1. coffee
2. chicken
3. irons
4. time
5. light
6. hair
7. glasses
8. some wrapping paper
9. works
10. papers

Quiz 9, p. 146.
1. bag, can (*box* may be possible in some countries)
2. bag, box
3. bottle, box, can, jar (*bag* may be possible in some countries)
4. bottle, can, jar
5. can, box
6. bowl, cup
7. piece, slice
8. cup, glass
9. piece, slice
10. cup (*glass* is possible in some countries and is common with iced tea)

Quiz 10, p. 146.
Checked phrases: 3, 4, 5, 7, 9, 10

Quiz 11, p. 147.
1. A: the
   B: the, the
2. A: the
   B: a
3. B: a
4. A: a
   B: a
5. A: the
   B: the
6. B: a

Quiz 12, p. 147.
Checked sentences: 1, 3, 4, 6, 7, 9,

Quiz 13, p. 148.
1. Ø, Ø
2. the, the
3. Ø
4. Ø
5. The, the
6. Ø
7. The
8. The
9. The
10. Ø, Ø

Quiz 14, p. 148.
a, a, The, the, the, the, a, the

Quiz 15, p. 149.
1. Ø
2. the
3. The
4. a
5. The
6. Ø
7. Ø, Ø
8. A
9. The
10. Ø, Ø

Quiz 16, p. 149.
1. c   4. a   7. b
2. b   5. d   8. c
3. a   6. a

Quiz 17, p. 150.
1. Ø, Ø   5. Ø, Ø, the, Ø
2. Ø, Ø   6. Ø, Ø, the, Ø
3. The, Ø   7. Ø, the
4. Ø   8. the

Quiz 18, p. 150.
1. Theresa can't decide whether to study Japanese or Chinese.
2. Where are you going
3. The Alps are in Switzerland, Austria, and France.
4. We're reading Shakespeare's *Romeo and Juliet*
5. The directions say to turn on Fifth Street, but this is Park Avenue.
6. I.B.M. is a company, and its initials stand for International Business Machines.
7. The Mississippi River flows into the Gulf of Mexico.
8. I was supposed to be born in April, but I was a month late, so my birthday is in May.
9. Which instructor do you prefer: Dr. Costa or Professor Pierce?
10. My friend William Lincoln is a descendant of Abraham Lincoln.

PRACTICE TEST, p. 151.
Part I, p. 151.
1. a   4. a
2. c   5. a
3. c

Part II, p. 151.
1. the, the   4. The, a
2. Ø, the   5. a, a, The, the
3. a, an   6. the

Part III, p. 152.
1. What part of Canada are you from?
2. The assignment for our literature class is to read the first chapter of Shakespeare's *Hamlet*.
3. I heard that my neighbors, Tariq and Ali, plan to visit England in May.
4. Maria's parents are from Mexico. She speaks Spanish fluently.
5. There is a Miami University in Ohio.
6. The lake is too cold for swimming. How about going to the indoor pool at Mountain View Park?

Part IV, p. 152.
1. Let's get a drink of water. I'm thirsty.
2. The scenery in the mountains is beautiful.
3. Did you get a haircut?
4. For breakfast, Thomas ordered two pieces of toast and eggs.
5. Here's a map of the Pacific.
6. I need to have my car checked soon.
7. There are no fish in the Dead Sea.

FINAL TEST, p. 153.
Part I, p. 153.
1. b   5. a   9. a
2. d   6. a   10. b
3. c   7. d
4. c   8. a

Part II, p. 154.
1. a, Ø, Ø   5. Ø, Ø   9. the, the
2. a   6. Ø, Ø   10. The, Ø
3. the, a, a   7. Ø, Ø   11. Ø
4. The   8. Ø, the   12. a, the

Part III, p. 154.
1. Our anatomy class will be taught by Dr. Jones. He's a professor,
2. Does your friend live in an apartment
3. Tomorrow there will be a concert at Washington Park, near Broadway Avenue. A music group from South Africa will be playing.
4. The university plans to tear down Brown Hall
5. In my country, New Year's is the biggest holiday
6. When did William begin working for Sony Corporation?
7. *War and Peace* is a long novel. I hope I can finish it
8. Would you be interested in going on a boat trip down the Colorado River? We would see part of the Grand Canyon.

Part IV, p. 155.
1. I don't need help now,
2. There are a few people at work who would prefer
3. Water is necessary for survival.
4. I married my brother's best friend from college.
5. Joseph reached the top of Mt. McKinley
6. Some friends bicycled through the Sahara Desert
7. Ed worked on his car for an hour before he realized
8. Honolulu is in Hawaii, but it is not on the island
9. Mark tried several times to reach his parents,
10. Jane has so much homework that she doesn't know
11. We heard that Aunt Betsy and Uncle Joe are moving to a retirement home

Chapter 12: ADJECTIVE CLAUSES

Quiz 1, p. 156.
1. There's the little boy who lost his balloon in the wind.
2. I heard about an elderly man who takes gifts to children in hospitals.
3. I met a marine biologist who once swam with sharks.
4. The people who work on this boat practice fire drills twice a month.
5. I helped a man who was confused and lost.
6. The doctor who treated me is very famous.

Quiz 2, p. 156.
1. who   5. who   9. who
2. who   6. who   10. whom
3. who   7. whom
4. whom   8. who

Quiz 3, p. 157.
1. a, c   6. a, c
2. a, c   7. a, c
3. a, b, c, d   8. a, b, c, d
4. a, c   9. a, b, c, d
5. a, b, c, d   10. a, b, c, d

Quiz 4, p. 157.
1. a, b   4. a   7. a
2. a, b   5. a, b   8. a
3. a   6. a, b

Quiz 5, p. 158.

1. who(m), that, Ø
2. who, that
3. that, which, Ø
4. whose
5. who, that
6. that, which, Ø

Quiz 6, p. 158.

1. Here is the book that you asked me to order for you.
Here is the book which you asked me
Here is the book you asked me
2. There is the man who found my diamond ring.
There is the man that found
3. The ring which I lost was very expensive.
The ring that I lost
The ring I lost
4. I spoke with a woman who has thirteen children.
I spoke with a woman that has
5. The restaurant which we went to was very crowded.
The restaurant that we went to
The restaurant we went to
6. The elderly man who lives in the apartment next to me has no relatives.
The elderly man that lives in the apartment next to me

Quiz 7, p. 159.

1. is
2. like
3. work
4. sells
5. are
6. spends
7. writes
8. calculate

Quiz 8, p. 159.

1. The taxi which I am waiting for is coming.
The taxi that I am waiting for . . .
The taxi I am waiting for . . .
The taxi for which I am waiting
2. The radio station which we listen to has 24-hour news.
The radio station that we listen to has 24-hour news
The radio station we listen to
The radio station to which we listen
3. The school which Helen goes to specializes in dance and drama instruction.
The school that Helen goes to . . .
The school Helen goes to . . .
The school to which Helen goes . . .
4. The health club which Sarah belongs to.
that Sarah belongs to.
Sarah belongs to
to which Sarah belongs.

Quiz 9, p. 160.

1. that/which/Ø, with
2. that/which/Ø, from
3. that/which/Ø, for
4. that/which/Ø, to
5. who(m)/that, to
6. that/which/Ø, in
7. who(m)/that, to
8. who(m)/that, with
9. who(m)/that, to
10. who(m)/that, to

Quiz 10, p. 160.

1. The little girl whose doll was taken was sad
2. I'm friends with a woman whose daughter is training
3. I met a man at the park whose parents know my grandparents.
4. The dog whose owner left him outside a restaurant is being cared for by the staff.
5. I enjoyed meeting the couple whose children go to the same school

6. I have a friend whose sailboat is also her office.
7. The couple whose summer house we rent want us to buy
8. I have a friend whose work involves designing houses

Quiz 11, p. 161.

1. The family who arrived late discovered
2. A neighbor whose son works for an airline can fly
3. I ran into a woman who I went to school with 20 years ago.
4. Correct.
5. The potatoes which I baked aren't done.
6. Correct.
7. I work with a doctor who is nice to his patients
8. Correct.

PRACTICE TEST, p. 162.
Part I, p. 162.

1. The couple whose horse won the race was surprised.
2. The manager who(m)/that/Ø I work for treats me fairly.
The manager for whom I work treats me fairly.
3. The bus which/that/Ø I take to work is an express bus.
4. Trees and bushes whose needles remain green all year are called "evergreens."

Part II, p. 162.

1. who(m), that, Ø
2. that, which, Ø
3. whose
4. that, which, Ø

Part III, p. 162.

1. are
2. studies
3. live
4. is

Part IV, p. 163.

1. which/that/Ø, in
2. which/that/Ø, in/at
3. which/that/Ø, from
4. who(m)/that/Ø, with
5. which/that/Ø, of

Part V, p. 163.

1. The color of paint Sandra picked for her bedroom walls was an unusual blue.
2. Correct.
3. The radio which I bought carries overseas stations.
4. The doctor who operated on my father is very skilled.
5. I work with a woman who grew up in the same neighborhood as me.
6. Correct.

FINAL TEST, p. 164
Part I, p. 164.

1. The garden which/that nearly died from a lack of rain is looking healthy again.
2. I work with a man whose wife trains police dogs.
3. The computer disks which/that/Ø I bought were defective.
4. The deer are eating the flowers which/that grow in my garden.
5. Barb is a manager who(m)/that/Ø people like to work for.
Barb is a manager for whom people like to work.
6. Some of the mail which/that was delivered to our house was addressed to our neighbor.

Part II, p. 164.
1. which/that, Ø
2. who/that
3. which/that/Ø
4. whose
5. which/that
6. which/that/Ø

Part III, p. 164.
1. designs
2. wants
3. go
4. speaks
5. barks
6. are

Part IV, p. 165.
1. who(m)/that/Ø, on
2. who/that, at
3. which/that/Ø, with
4. who(m)/that/Ø, to
5. which/that/Ø, from
6. which/that/Ø, of
7. which/that/Ø, about
8. which/that, for

Part V, p. 165.
1. The firefighters who put out the fire
2. The digital camera we ordered still hasn't arrived.
3. The man who(m)/that/Ø I work for / for whom I work is blind.
4. Correct.
5. The finger which/that/Ø I broke is healing well.
6. I studied with a professor whose books are known
7. Correct.
8. Correct.

Chapter 13: GERUNDS AND INFINITIVES

Quiz 1, p. 166.
1. turning down
2. raining
3. doing
4. getting
5. driving
6. painting
7. moving
8. smoking

Quiz 2, p. 166.
1. am going shopping
2. went sailing
3. go camping
4. went skydiving
5. go fishing
6. goes jogging
7. went window shopping
8. is going to go / is going bowling

Quiz 3, p. 167.
1. to work
2. to work
3. working
4. working
5. to work
6. to work
7. working
8. working
9. to work
10. to work

Quiz 4, p. 167.
1. a
2. a
3. b
4. b
5. b
6. a
7. a
8. a
9. b
10. b

Quiz 5, p. 168.
1. a
2. a, b
3. b
4. a
5. b
6. a
7. a, b
8. a, b
9. a
10. a

Quiz 6, p. 168.
1. for
2. of
3. in
4. about
5. on
6. to
7. about
8. like
9. at
10. for

Quiz 7, p. 169.
1. Are you worried about losing your job?
2. Beth is afraid of going to the dentist.
3. Ken dreamt about living on a tropical island.
4. The students are responsible for keeping the classroom clean.
5. Management is interested in promoting Terry to marketing director.
6. Barbara insisted on inviting her former boyfriends to her wedding.

Quiz 8, p. 169.
1. by
2. by
3. with
4. with
5. by, by
6. with
7. by
8. by, by
9. with
10. by

Quiz 9, p. 170.
1. by exercising
2. by washing
3. by painting
4. by cutting
5. by doing
6. by calling
7. by promising
8. by drawing

Quiz 10, p. 170.
1. Traveling with friends is fun.
2. Copying another student's homework isn't O.K.
3. Telephoning someone in another country is easy.
4. Being away from family and friends is difficult.
5. Learning about other countries is interesting.
6. Riding a bike without a helmet is dangerous.
7. Recycling as much garbage as you can is important.
8. Predicting the future is impossible.

Quiz 11, p. 171.
1. It is important for motorcyclists to learn how to ride a motorcycle properly.
2. It is hard for right-handed people to write with their left hand.
3. It is interesting for children to mix two colors to make a new color.
4. It is customary for many people to take off shoes before entering a house.
5. It is exciting for sailors to sail a boat in windy weather.
6. It is important for good health to eat a variety of fruits and vegetables.

Quiz 12, p. 171.
1. I turned down the TV in order to hear you better.
2. I wore socks to bed in order to keep my feet warm.
3. I withdrew money from the bank in order to buy a car.
4. I called the doctor in order to ask if I needed a flu shot.
5. I turned off the phone in order to get some sleep.

Quiz 13, p. 172.
1. to
2. for
3. to
4. to
5. for
6. for
7. to
8. for
9. to
10. to

Quiz 14, p. 172.
1. no change
2. Judy is moving in order to be closer
3. Tom got new glasses in order to read better.
4. no change
5. Francisco started a fire in order to warm up the house.
6. no change

Quiz 15, p. 173.
1. too hot, cool enough
2. too sour, sweet enough
3. enough eggs, too tired
4. safe enough, too dangerous
5. clean enough, too dirty

Quiz 16, p. 173.
1. big enough
2. old enough
3. too old
4. too expensive
5. cold enough
6. too long
7. soft enough
8. too hungry

Quiz 17, p. 174.
1. a
2. a
3. b
4. a
5. a
6. a, b
7. a, b
8. b
9. a
10. b
11. b
12. a
13. a
14. b
15. a
16. b
17. a
18. a
19. a, b
20. a

PRACTICE TEST, p. 175.
Part 1, p. 175.
1. about starting
2. to take
3. to ask
4. on getting, to arrive, Being
5. to build, to snow/snowing, to make, about having, building, sledding

Part II, p. 175.
1. on
2. by
3. by
4. to
5. from

Part III, p. 176.
1. a. is too soft
   b. isn't frozen enough
2. a. isn't cool enough
   b. is too hot

Part IV, p. 176.
1. It is impossible for an elephant to jump.
2. Correct.
3. Correct.
4. We can continue to discuss / discussing this topic tomorrow.
5. If we arrive at the resort before noon, we can go hiking in the mountains.
6. Toshi was surprised that the sales clerk apologized for her rude behavior.

FINAL TEST, p. 177.
Part I, p. 177.
1. of holding, to relax
2. at kicking, Playing
3. like cooking, to lie
4. in buying, to start, to add
5. to get
6. about flying, sightseeing, of popping, to cover, to pull

Part II, p. 177.
1. in
2. by
3. by, by
4. about
5. by
6. by
7. with
8. with, with
9. by
10. for

Part III, p. 178.
1. a. isn't loud enough
   b. is too soft
2. a. isn't sweet enough
   b. is too bitter
3. a. is too bright
   b. isn't dark enough
4. a. isn't warm enough
   b. is too cool

Part IV, p. 178.
1. Correct.
2. I need to stop at the bank to withdraw some money.
3. Are you responsible for cleaning up
4. It is relaxing to walk barefoot in the sand
5. Jeannie asked to leave work early
6. Correct.
7. Driving in heavy traffic requires skill and patience.
8. Correct.
9. It is sometimes scary for young children to visit the doctor.
10. Helen enjoys being the center of attention

Chapter 14: NOUN CLAUSES

Quiz 1, p. 179.
1. question mark (?)   information question
2. question mark (?)   noun clause
3. question mark (?)   information question
4. question mark (?)   information question
5. period (.)   noun clause
6. question mark (?)   information question
7. question mark (?)   noun clause

Quiz 2, p. 179.
1. I don't know where he is living.
2. I'm not sure where we go next.
3. I'd like to know when the party was.
4. Please tell me where the next party will be.
5. Do you know how Tony and Patricia met?
6. I wonder what happened.
7. Do you know when the show will be over?
8. I'm not sure where the Ross twins are studying.

Quiz 3, p. 180.
1. what the matter is.
2. what time it is?
3. whose seat this is?
4. who is at the door.
5. whose car that is.
6. what the difference is.
7. problem it is.
8. who is in your class?

Quiz 4, p. 180.
1. if the store is open?
2. if Rosa went to lunch.
3. if the movers are coming soon?
4. if fish can fly?
5. if Tom has any advice.
6. if you need anything else.
7. if Alice will be here tomorrow?
8. if there is any dinner left.
9. if the mail has come yet.
10. if Samir eats meat?

Quiz 5, p. 181.
Answers will vary.
1. I don't believe (that) UFOs exist.
2. I don't feel (that) men are stronger than women.
3. I agree (that) taxes are necessary.
4. I know (that) watching TV is harmful for young children.

5. I hope (that) people can learn to live together peacefully.
6. I'm sure (that) smoking is harmful.
7. I wonder if wars will ever end.
8. I wouldn't like to know how I will die.

Quiz 6, p. 181.
1. trying to prove **that** the suspect
2. children like to pretend **that** they
3. We're disappointed **that** you didn't believe us.
4. Did I tell you **that** we are moving
5. I still can't believe **that** she leaves the room
6. people were convinced **that** the earth
7. Is it true **that** your diamond necklace
8. Can you believe **that** it's summer
9. I'm positive **that** "scissors" is spelled
10. Carlos was impressed **that** Juan knew so much

Quiz 7, p. 182.
1. so
2. so
3. not
4. so
5. not
6. so
7. so
8. so
9. so
10. so

Quiz 8, p. 182.
1. Carmen asked, "Do you have money for parking?"
2. The doctor said, "Stop smoking today."
3. My mother said, "I won't be home until 7:00 tonight. Could you get dinner started?"
4. Our teacher asked, "Who knows the answer? Who would like to write it on the board?"
5. The policeman said, "May I see your driver's license, please?"
6. The Johnsons said, "We have to go now. We have another party to attend tonight."

Quiz 9, p. 183.
"I don't like spiders," my daughter said.
"Why not?" I asked.
"They're quite ugly," she replied.
"Well, they might look unpleasant," I said. "They're not as beautiful as butterflies, but they're good to have around. They eat ants and flies that you don't want to have in your house. Even though you don't like them," I said, "try to think of them as a gift from nature."

Quiz 10, p. 183.
1. her
2. our, us, them
3. she, my/our, me, my
4. he, his, themselves
5. she, their, their, They
6. they, their, they, their

Quiz 11, p. 184.
1. would be
2. had been
3. had set
4. didn't understand
5. hadn't learned
6. was going to start, needed
7. had
8. could feed, were

Quiz 12, p. 184.
1. My father said that they had enjoyed their trip to Singapore.
2. Our friends said they wanted to give me/us a going-away party.
3. Abdul said that he would be twenty-five on his next birthday.
4. My husband said that he could pick up the kids after school, and that I didn't need to be home.

5. The boy said that the dog had taken his ball, and that he wasn't coming back.
6. Dr. Wilson said that she was going to retire in a few years, and that her husband and she were planning to travel.
7. My grandmother said to me that she had had a wonderful life.

Quiz 13, p. 185.
1. asked
2. told
3. told
4. said
5. told
6. said
7. said
8. said, told, asked, said, told, told, said

Quiz 14, p. 185.
1. I don't know yet if the doctor can see you tomorrow or not.
2. Please tell me what they did.
3. Do you know whose coat is on the chair?
4. Do you know if the bus has come or not?
5. We'd like to know if the subway stops here.
6. I hope that I can come with you tonight.
7. Suzanne told me / said to me that she wasn't / hadn't been home last night.
8. I'm afraid that we have to cancel our plans.
9. The dentist said, "Your teeth look very healthy. You are taking good care of them."
10. The teacher isn't sure whether Liz wants help or not.

PRACTICE TEST, p. 186.
Part I, p. 186.
1. where the milk is.
2. what time we will be done.
3. if there are any eggs left.
4. whose work this is.
5. if someone is knocking at the door.
6. who just left.

Part II, p. 186.
My mom came in the bedroom and opened the curtains. "What time is it?" I asked her.
"Time to get up," she replied.
"But Mom," I said, "it's not a school day. Please let me sleep in," I begged.
"You can't sleep in today," she said. "It's a special day."
"What special day?" I asked.
"It's your birthday," she said.
"Oh my gosh! I forgot. I have to get up right away," I said. "I have so many things I want to do today."

Part III, p. 187.
1. Julia said (that) the cookies were ready.
2. The librarian said (that) the library was going to close early today.
3. Erica said (that) the bank manager had left town with the bank's money.
4. John asked how far away the airport was.
5. The clerk asked if I wanted paper or plastic bags.
6. Marika said (that) the flight would arrive in 10 minutes.
7. The fire chief said (that) the fire had taken a long time to put out.
8. Helen said (that) she could juggle three balls in the air at the same time.

Part IV, p. 187.
1. My friends understand what I like.
2. I'd like to know if this computer works.

3. The teacher told me/us that he would be at a conference tomorrow.
   The teacher said that he would be at a conference tomorrow.
4. I want to know why they came.
5. It is a fact that exercise makes us healthier.
6. Do you know if Rick lives here?
7. I'm sure that we will have a good time together.
8. A strange man asked me where I lived.
   A strange man asked me, "Where do you live?"

FINAL TEST, p. 188.

Part I, p. 188.
1. I'm not sure what the date is today.
2. We don't know yet who the new manager will be.
3. I have no idea if Ed and Irene got engaged last weekend.
4. We haven't decided whose car we are taking.
5. I'll find out how many people knew about the problem.
6. I don't know if the weather changes much or stays the same in this area.
7. I haven't heard if Paula left the company.
8. I'll see if anyone has requested help yet.
9. Of course I know the year I was born.
10. I'll see if the copy machine works.

Part II, p. 189.
Last week, my teacher and I were talking about my future. "What do you want to do after you finish school?" he asked.

"I'm not sure," I said. "I'd like to have a job that is interesting and pays well."

"Everyone would like that," said my teacher. "Is there a specific area you see yourself working in?"

"Yes," I replied. "I love working with animals. Maybe I could be a veterinarian."

"One way to find out," said my teacher, "is to work with animals first. Volunteer at an animal shelter or zoo. See how you like it."

I told him I liked his suggestion and thanked him.

Part III, p. 189.
1. The police officer said that he was giving me a warning, not a ticket.
2. The teacher said that the test was going to be on Friday.
3. The students replied that they didn't want a test.
4. Joe asked who had taken his car.
5. The manager said (that) they had decided to move their offices to a new location.
6. Yolanda said that the bus would be late.
7. Sally said that she could fix that for me/us.
8. My parents said that they had been happy to hear about my job promotion.
9. The doctor asked me if I had been taking my medicine.
10. The dancers said that they had practiced their dance steps enough, and they were ready for their show.

Part IV, p. 190.
1. Can you tell me whose coat this is?
2. I felt better when the doctor said, "Your daughter just has a bad cold. It's nothing serious."
3. My friends ask me, "When will you get married?"
   My friends ask me when I will get married.
4. Did my mom ask you if you could come to our party?
5. Hamid asked why I always came late.
6. Mr. Hill told me that he was feeling ill.
7. Could you tell me where Fred works in the evenings?
8. I think that you will enjoy being on the soccer team.
9. I know that this will be a good opportunity for us.
10. Professor Thomas told us he would be absent yesterday.

Appendix 1: PHRASAL VERBS

Quiz 1, p. 191.
1. up	5. up	9. down	13. down
2. off	6. off	10. off	14. on
3. out	7. up	11. out	15. on
4. in	8. out	12. up	

Quiz 2, p. 191.
1. from	4. on	7. into
2. into	5. on	8. out of
3. over	6. into	9. off

Quiz 3, p. 192.
1. up	5. out	9. back	13. off
2. on	6. back	10. out	14. up
3. off	7. back	11. down	
4. away	8. back	12. up	

Quiz 4, p. 192.
1. out	5. out	9. out	13. in
2. around	6. over	10. over	14. out
3. out of	7. on	11. down	
4. out	8. up	12. up	

Quiz 5, p. 193.
1. up	5. back	9. up	13. out
2. out	6. up	10. over	14. back
3. out	7. off	11. away	
4. out	8. over	12. on	

Quiz 6, p. 194.
1. She made it up.
2. Please wake me up soon.
3. Let's get in this taxi.
4. Both are correct.
5. I ran into some college friends
6. The first three are correct.
7. The first two are correct.
8. We were the last passengers to get on the plane.
9. The first two are correct.
10. All are correct.
11. The lights were off. I turned them on.
12. Rita got over the flu very quickly.
13. The first two are correct.
14. The police are looking into the crime.
15. The first two are correct.

Quiz 7, p. 195.
1. up	7. up	13. up	19. over
2. out	8. up, down	14. into	20. out
3. down	9. up	15. up	21. out
4. up	10. in	16. off	
5. up	11. out	17. up	
6. down	12. up	18. on	

Quiz 8, p. 196.
1. out for	5. back from	9. through with
2. up in	6. out of	10. up for
3. along with	7. in on	11. out for
4. out of	8. around with	

Quiz 9, p. 196.

1. out about
2. out for
3. over to
4. together with
5. back to
6. around with
7. away from
8. out with
9. over to
10. out of
11. along with

FINAL TEST, p. 197.

1. c
2. c
3. b
4. a
5. a
6. c
7. d
8. c
9. a
10. d
11. a
12. b
13. a
14. c
15. b
16. d
17. c
18. a
19. d
20. c
21. a
22. b
23. d
24. d
25. b
26. d

Appendix 2: PREPOSITION COMBINATIONS

Quiz 1, p. 199.

1. of
2. for
3. for
4. at / with
5. about
6. from
7. to
8. about
9. to
10. for
11. to
12. of
13. with
14. to
15. about

Quiz 2, p. 199.

1. from
2. for
3. with
4. with
5. for
6. to
7. for
8. at
9. with
10. in
11. with, about
12. at

Quiz 3, p. 200.

1. about
2. for
3. about
4. of
5. for
6. to, to
7. from
8. for
9. for
10. of
11. to/with
12. for
13. in
14. to
15. about/of
16. with
17. about

Quiz 4, p. 201.

1. in
2. at
3. of
4. from
5. to, about
6. to
7. for
8. to, about
9. on
10. to
11. for
12. with, about, with, about

Quiz 5, p. 201.

1. with
2. from
3. about
4. to
5. like
6. for
7. to
8. about/of
9. to
10. about
11. for
12. of, about
13. at
14. for

Quiz 6, p. 202.

1. from
2. to
3. for
4. on
5. for
6. of
7. of/from
8. to, for
9. from
10. for
11. on, of
12. of
13. on
14. to

Quiz 7, p. 202.

1. about
2. to
3. on
4. from
5. from
6. by, from
7. for
8. to, about
9. about/of, from
10. into
11. to

FINAL TEST, p. 203.

1. c
2. b
3. a
4. d
5. d
6. c
7. b
8. a
9. b
10. d
11. c
12. a
13. a
14. b
15. d
16. b
17. b
18. c
19. d
20. a